At the Lenin Shipyard

Other Books by Stan Persky

The House That Jack Built (*1980*)
Son of Socred (*1979*)

At the LENIN SHIPYARD

Poland and the Rise of the Solidarity Trade Union

STAN PERSKY

NEW STAR BOOKS

Vancouver

First printing December 1981
5 4 3 2 1
Second printing March 1982

Canadian Cataloguing in Publication Data

Persky, Stan, 1941-
  At the Lenin Shipyard

  Bibliography: p.
  ISBN 0-919888-46-1 (bound).—ISBN
0-919888-45-3 (pbk.)

  1. Strikes and lockouts—Ship-building—
Poland—Gdansk. 2. Solidarnosc (Trade-union)
3. Trade-unions—Poland. I. Title.
HD5397.7.S52 1980 G3   331.89'282382'094382
                         C81-091356-9

The publisher is grateful for
assistance provided by The Canada Council.

New Star Books Ltd.
2504 York Avenue
Vancouver, B.C.
Canada   V6K 1E3

"Workers of the world...my sincere apologies!"
     —*Karl Marx*
     —from Solidarity Strike Bulletin,
      No. 10, August 29, 1980

Contents

Preface

The idea of my going to Poland took shape one mid-February British Columbia morning as a bone-chilling rain sluiced down the foot of Mt. Benson. My friend Peggy Walker gamely trudged through the downpour. She was outfitted in a white plastic rain slicker and bore a "We're Out For Fair Pay" placard around her neck.

Peggy was the secretary and resident baseball expert of the social sciences department at Malaspina College, located at the base of Mt. Benson in Nanaimo, B.C. I was temporarily working there as a sociology teacher. Peggy was also a fledgling striker of the Canadian Union of Public Employees (CUPE) Local 1858. It was her first picket line.

I trudged alongside her in sympathy, under a rapidly deteriorating made-in-Taiwan umbrella. Meanwhile, my teaching colleagues "agonized" over whether or not to cross the picket lines of their fellow-and-sister trade unionists. The teachers belonged to an independent union of their own, and by the terms of their contract, it was left to their individual "consciences" to decide whether or not to respect the picket lines of CUPE, which represented the non-teaching staff. As it turned out, most of them crossed.

I was on loan to Malaspina from my regular teaching post at a college in the mountainous resource frontier of northwestern B.C. As our faculty happened to belong to the same union as Peggy, I was spared the minor agony of having to choose between my students' educations and a defence of the standard of living. For better or worse, I knew which side I was on.

This rain-soaked episode probably doesn't qualify as one of the great moments in working class history. It wasn't much different from the other days that Peggy and I paced in solidarity across the asphalt parking lots bordering the college's cluster of cedar buildings which overlooked the pulp-and-fishing town below. Yet somewhere along the way of this forced march (the strike dragged on for a rather bitter six weeks), I began, almost inadvertently, a 10,000-kilometre journey to Poland.

Like many others around the world, my imagination also had been set alight by the events of the previous August when Polish workers along the Baltic coast occupied their shipyards and factories. Led by a charismatic walrus-mustached electrician named Lech Walesa, they demanded from their communist government the unprecedented right to form "independent, self-governing" trade unions. The teaching season at Malaspina began in September, just days after the August 31, 1980 signing at the Lenin Shipyard of the historic compromise known as the Gdansk Agreement. I often found myself referring to it in the classroom.

For the first time, a "workers' state" had been forced to concede to its workers, among other things, the ironic right to form their own working class organization to defend themselves from the workers' state. In return, the workers pledged to observe most of the remaining rules of the game in Poland, including acceptance of the "socialist system...the leading role of the Polish United Workers Party [the name of Poland's communist party]* in the state...and the existing system of international alliances." As the conservative British magazine *The Economist* quipped: "Marx's irresistible force, the working class, has collided with Lenin's immovable object, the communist party." And had more than held its own.

I argued through the autumn with my students about the nature of social change. As usual, I was slightly appalled at these "products" of a self-centred educational system that rendered them apolitical, remarkably indifferent to foreign affairs, and rather despairing about their ability to shape the world around them. That fall, my last gasp on behalf of hope was a frequently sputtered, "But what about Poland?!" The students seemed to take my slight obsession with Poland in stride, displaying the same good humor with which they put up with my fulminations about life under our own capitalist

* References to "the party," "party members," "the Polish communist party," etc., are all intended to designate the Polish United Workers Party (PUWP). Another term the reader should be alerted to is the ubiquitous usage throughout Poland of "the authorities," a reference which uniformly designates all branches and levels of the regime.

system.

The day before the strike broke out at our college, I picked up a copy, again almost accidentally, of a standard history of modern Poland (I think it was M.K. Dziewanowski's *Poland in the 20th Century*). Soon I became increasingly involved with the strike. In addition to marching with Peggy, I gossiped with off-duty picketers at strike headquarters and wrote pro-union newspaper articles for the somewhat hostile local press. (The strikers often ironically wondered aloud why the media displayed so much enthusiasm for the striking Polish workers and so little for their own home-grown variety.) Nonetheless, I found myself using most of the unexpected time on my hands becoming immersed in Polish politics. I poured over old news clippings about the August events and watched the nightly minute-and-a-half television report from Poland with new avidity. Much of the reportage was competent enough, though perhaps it over-emphasized the threat of imminent Soviet invasion and dwelled too much on the personality of strike leader Walesa, who had now become the head of the Solidarity trade union. However, by its nature it was fragmentary, and I felt that the whole story of the strike, now set aside in the rush of new events, had yet to be told. When friends asked me what I planned to do (our strike had finally been settled) at the end of the teaching year, I said, only half-believing it, "Well, maybe I'll go over and take a look at Poland."

I arrived at the Lenin Shipyard on the international working class holiday, May 1, 1981, having come by train from Warsaw the night before. Gdansk is one of the Tri-Cities on the Baltic coast; the others are the resort town of Sopot and the port of Gdynia. Like so much else of Poland, Gdansk is a study in ironic contrasts. This industrial city of nearly 500,000 inhabitants contains, among other sights, the brick-by-brick renovated Old Town. Its tightly packed streets of Renaissance, Baroque and Roccoco houses are a veritable living monument to the sixteenth century Hanseatic League cradle of mercantile capitalism. At the same time, just across town, there are monumental, nearly anti-architectural housing projects such as in the Morena district. There, 50 or more look-alike five- and ten-story apartment buildings, constructed of concrete slabs hung on metal frames, dot the moonlike landscape in homage to the Soviet model of socialism.

In the morning I got my first glimpse of the giant industrial cranes behind the walls of the Lenin Shipyard as I rode out to the Solidarity trade union headquarters, located in the Hotel Morski in surburban and tongue-twisting Wrzeszcz. (It's pronounced, approximately, Ve-*zhesh*-ch.)*

Already, much had changed in Poland. The traditional militant May Day parade, in which the workers "spontaneously" marched before a reviewing stand of local dignitaries, was gone. As the Poles readily explained, the spontaneity had been created by obligatory participation enforced through checkoff lists at workplaces, and the march-past was regarded by workers as an act of forced homage to the party bosses.

The first May Day morning, I was whisked aboard a Solidarity-chartered bus and put under the maternal care of a middle-aged woman handing out decal-sticker patriotic calendars who attempted to explain the proceedings to me in a patient polyglot of English, French, German and Polish. We drove to Gdynia, where the busload of people disembarked and formed a solemn procession to lay a memorial wreath in the town square. Polish culture, I soon discovered, is reassuringly ritualistic and the Poles have an inordinate fondness for depositing heaps of flowers at ceremonial sites. One quickly becomes accustomed to the melange of nationalism, Catholicism and working class militancy that make up the current Polish scene.

Then we retraced our way along the coastal road, eventually arriving at the Lenin Shipyard, where the same wreath-laying procedure was repeated at the monument to the martyred 1970 strikers. Afterwards, we wandered with a milling holiday crowd into the shipyard, which was open to the public for the day. Thousands of families, kids in tow, ambled among the workshops, boarded the ocean-going vessels under construction, and visited the historic conference hall where eight months earlier the strikers and the government had hammered out an agreement.

If a Sunday-picnic atmosphere prevailed on May Day, the observance two days later—Sunday, May 3—of the 190th anniversary of the Polish constitution of 1791 presented a sombre contrast in mood.

---

* A guide to the pronunciation of the principal names and places that appear in this text can be found on page 239.

By five o'clock in the evening I was among the 20,000 people packed inside the basilica of the Holy Virgin Mary for mass. An hour later, the crowd, joined by thousands more, spilled out into nearby Jan Sobieski Square, surrounding the flower-bedecked equestrian statue of the seventeenth century Polish king. As the Constitution Day speakers from the Young Poland Movement (one of a burgeoning set of opposition groups active in the country) invoked the historic memories of democracy, the allusions to the present could hardly be lost on the crowd. Banners called for the release of political prisoners, and one succinctly but bluntly declared: "Today—them; tomorrow—us." "Them" obviously referred to the regime. The ceremonies concluded with the crowd singing the national anthem, "Poland Has Not Yet Perished."

That the Poles would respond with such evident emotion to what the casual observer might expect to be a perfunctory occasion helps to explain certain aspects of the contemporary situation. Though the parchment in question is at best a document expressing quasi-democratic sentiments in vogue during the era of the "rights of man," for Poles it is seen as the historic foundation of democratic ideology. Its flourishing was tragically brief. The country was finally partitioned among Russia, Austria and Prussia in 1795 and literally disappeared from the maps of Europe until the conclusion of World War I. The continued relevance of the 1791 constitution was apparent. Obviously, 25,000 people don't rush into the streets to praise democracy unless there's a shortage of it around.

Further, this year's legal observance of May 3 was the first such occurrence since World War II. For years, the date had been quietly suppressed by the regime. According to some Poles, that was to avoid "competition" with the officially favored May Day. Sometimes, the repression wasn't so quiet. In fact, a similar rally held illegally on the same spot the year before had resulted in the arrest of two speakers. They were sentenced to three months in prison on trumped-up charges—among them, the particularly ironic accusation of "displaying contempt for the nation." So much had the situation changed since last August, however, that this year's nation-wide observance was officially sanctioned by the regime.

Later that night, a group of us took an after-supper stroll through the now deserted but rather supernal Sobieski Square. The equestrian bronze was still draped in flags and banners.

Dozens of bouquets of red and white carnations lay heaped at the foot of the statue. Before it, the dregs of four or five candles cast flickering glimmers on the flanks of the horse as we passed under the square's about-to-bloom linden trees.

All in all, my first pageant-filled weekend in Gdansk had provided a striking introduction to the complexities of political and social life in Poland today, one that ought to induce all due caution in offering generalizations about the meaning of recent Polish events.

For the next three weeks, I was permitted to interview participants in the events of last August, both from the Lenin Shipyard and other factories and institutions. Equally important, I was allowed the pleasure of sharing some portion of the busy daily lives of my hosts. One can hardly exaggerate in reporting on their kindness and generosity, especially considering the difficult material conditions in which Poles presently find themselves. Even seemingly insignificant occasions—an evening of television viewing and conversation with Polish friends in which a lengthy filmed report on the doings of communist party First Secretary Stefan Kania was improbably juxtaposed with a dubbed version of *Charlie's Angels*—proved instructive. Let me hasten to add, however, especially in the light of some sensational (and even provocative) newspaper accounts that have appeared in the West, that I make no claims whatsoever to being privy to any privileged information or a confidant of any Polish public figures. (Like hundreds of others, though, I did get my picture taken with Solidarity leader Walesa while briefly conveying the greetings of my union local—just to show the folks back home.)

The modest intention of this account, then, is to tell the story of the events that led to the creation of Poland's ten-million-member Solidarity trade union, and more briefly, those that followed the signing of the Gdansk Agreement. Less modestly —though not through any special talents of mine, but rather by virtue of the magnitude of the process initiated by the Polish people—this is also, and perhaps inevitably, a book about freedom.

Though I am spared the author's traditional task of acknowledging spouse, neglected offspring, loyal spaniel, and dispensers of public funds, having acquired none of the foregoing, there are many people to thank for helping me with this project.

My carefully-laid linguistic plan was to acquire six or seven well-chosen Polish phrases and to repeat them as frequently as possible in order to give the impression of a complete mastery of the language. This succeeded in bringing me a more than adequate supply of translators' help. I'm grateful first of all to Maria Komorowska, head of the translation bureau of the Gdansk Solidarity offices, who not only led me to excellent translators, but also saw to it that I was properly housed, fed and advised. No one's sense of hospitality could be more complete.

Anna Maksymiuk, Kasia Kietlinska, Leslaw Ludwig, Zbigniew Jakowczyk, and Pawel Huelle provided consistently workable translations, a wealth of knowledgeable explanation and, equally important, friendship and camaraderie.

For granting me interviews, I wish to thank the following participants in the events described herein: Jerzy Borowczak, Bogdan Borusewicz, Andrzej Kolodziej, Bogdan Lis, Anna Walentynowicz, Jacek Kuron, Alina Pienkowska, Stanislaw Bury, Piotr Dyk, Mariusz Wilk, Lech Walesa, Robert Glebocki, Jan Rulewski, Henryk Lenarciak, Wojciech Gruszecki and Klemens Gniech.

My fellow traveller, photographer Vince Hemingson produced the principal photographs for this book and protected me from at least 99 per cent of Polish traffic. Others who graciously gave of their time and knowledge while I was in Poland and whom I do not wish to forget include Malgorzata Okraska, Wlodzimierz Rucewicz, Marek Podgorczyk, Alek and Irene Marchewicz, Hanna Jezioranska, Jadwiga Staniszkis, Lech Badkowski, Piotr Modrak, Einar Braathen, Leif Hallstan and Alan Lichter.

Back home, a remarkable number of altruists aided my endeavors. Lanny Beckman, my friend and editor, presents himself as a humble "sentence-cleaner," a kind of chimney-sweep of the editing world. I suspect most writers have one person in whose common-sense their trust reposes. I've been uncommonly lucky in the matter of whom the fates have allotted me.

University of British Columbia social sciences librarian Iza Laponce was also indispensable. She generously shared her expertise on the subject, introduced me to other knowledgeable people, did translations and guided me to useful references. Kathy Ford collected research materials for the book and I wish to join with her in thanking the ever-efficient UBC library government publications and microfilm department, and also add my own thanks to UBC head librarian Basil Stuart-Stubbs, who has rendered me numerous kindnesses.

Chris DeBresson, Henry Flam, Harry Lieber, Stu James, Bohdan Krawchenko and Berger Bergerson supplied research materials, introductions, and their insights, for which I'm most appreciative. I'm also grateful to Linda Gilbert, Ralph Maurer and Tom Hawthorn, who did a major share of the production work at New Star Books.

Although not immediately involved in the production of this book, nonetheless I'd like to thank the members of CUPE local 1858 Nanaimo (and especially Peggy Walker) for inspiring this adventure, and also record my pleasure in having had the opportunity of working with sympathetic colleagues at Malaspina College in the last year (particularly Dale Lovick, Chris McDonnell, Ken Baxter and Gary Bauslaugh). As well, I tender my thanks to Trevor Lautens, formerly of the Vancouver *Sun*, who saw to it that portions of this book first appeared in the pages of that paper.

The secondary sources used in this book are cited in the notes and bibliography. However, I would like to make appreciative mention of the journal, *Labour Focus on Eastern Europe*, Andrew Arato's essay "Civil Society Against the State" in the special Poland issue of *Telos*, and John Darnton's reportage for the New York *Times*. Hopefully, instances where I've inadvertently lifted sentences without acknowledgement will be regarded by their authors as signs of admiration rather than cause for suit.

Finally, my thanks to Richard M. Steele, Craig Naherniak, Rob Hovestad, Peter Weber, Tom Sandborn and Mirek for helping me to think.

Despite the appearance of comprehensiveness that the foregoing list suggests, no one knows better than I the gaps and omissions in the following account. Professional readers, I hope, will regard this version as it is intended: that is, as no more than a first draft of history. Given the constraints of time and resources, I have narrowed my project largely to events in the Gdansk region. As those familiar with the subject will know, equally significant events were simultaneously occurring in other parts of Poland—particularly in Szczecin and in the Silesian coal mining area—many of which had a political character importantly different from those in Gdansk. Even within the scope of my attention, there are omissions of the stories of relevant participants who, for one reason or another, I was unable to interview. I can only plead poverty, not of imagination, but of circumstance, and have proceeded in the belief that a popular account in English, despite evident inadequacies, might be useful to working people and intellectuals in augmenting their understanding of the present situation in Poland. I hope that this version is not marred by errors of fact or distortions of interpretation, and of course, I will be grateful for corrections and criticisms from readers.

Just before I left Gdansk, a veteran shipyard worker, Stanislaw Bury, offered some words of wisdom that bear repetition. "I know that abroad there's an interest in Poland," he said. "But I ask one thing: that people talk about Poland as it truly is. Because the people of Poland don't deserve to be talked about in a bad way. What we hear from abroad is that people think we Poles don't want to work, and that we want Saturdays off even though we're in debt. It's not true that we only want Saturdays off because we're lazy people," Bury insisted.

"From my viewpoint, as a shipyard worker, I'd like to say that we can go to work, not just for eight hours, but every day for twelve hours, even on Sundays and holidays. But we have to know for what, and for whom we're working. We have to be sure that our work won't be wasted. We want to work for ourselves.

"I ask once more: you have to write about Poland as it truly is in Poland. You have to talk to the people in Poland. In order to get to know us, you have to talk to the workers, to those who are close to the machines; to the peasants, who are working at the plough. . . because those people have in their bones, and their heads, and their hearts, the good of Poland." Then, as if to apologize for having worked himself up into a small rhetorical flourish, Bury made a slight self-dismissive gesture

with his hand, and with mock pomp concluded, "The very
simple words of a worker."

My hope is that I've remained faithful to his advice.

S.P.

Vancouver, B.C.
August, 1981

PART ONE

Eighteen Days That Shook
the Communist World

1 Strike

We are occupying the shipyard...and
I'll be the last one to leave.
—Lech Walesa, August 14, 1980

The purple neon sign of the downtown Gdansk train station glowed and hung in the mid-August night sky.

The clock tower attached to the red-brick railroad depot said it was time for Jerzy Borowczak, a 22-year-old ship's blacksmith employed at the Lenin Shipyard, to say goodbye to his girlfriend. She was about to catch the midnight express to Warsaw. Before she boarded, he broke the secret to her.

We're going to strike in the morning, Jerzy told her. He wanted her to spread the word in Warsaw.

She didn't believe him. She thought he was joking.

The midnight train pulled out, heading southeast toward the Polish capital, 325 km. away. For some of the sleepy passengers, it was the languorous end of summer holidays; for Borowczak, walking along the railway platform, it was the sleepness night on which history began.

The station faces onto Gorky Square. Light from the main hall filtered through an arch of greenish age-discolored glass above the station marquee, spilling into the Podwale Grodzkie, a main thoroughfare divided by streetcar tracks. Across the square, dance music came from the open windows of the second-floor restaurant in the squat three-story Hotel Monopol. A combo finished its last set for the slightly tipsy German and Scandinavian tourists. Soon they would go to bed, and as a breeze drifted in from the Baltic Sea, the last of the noisy downtown traffic would die away until the morning rush

3

hour began around 5 a.m.

The slight, but compactly-built young shipyard worker stood under the station marquee. It bore a faded, long-since-meaningless slogan—of the kind that adorned public buildings and factories throughout the country—exhorting the nation's workers to greater productivity. Jerzy wasn't sure they could pull the strike off. The small group of activists who had hatched the idea a week ago gave it only a fifty-fifty chance of success. The issue they were going with was the firing of a 50-year-old veteran crane operator, Anna Walentynowicz, something that, admittedly, didn't directly affect the shipyard crew. From the train station, Borowczak could look across the open square and see the silhouettes of the dinosaur-shaped shipyard cranes, visible even at night, a few blocks away.

The Lenin Shipyard of Gdansk, largest of the complex of shipbuilding and related enterprises that provides the major source of work in the Gdansk-Sopot-Gdynia Tri-Cities region, sprawls over 314 hectares and employs 17,000 workers. Its two dozen huge and grimy workshops are scattered on both sides of a canal-like appendage of the Wisla (or Vistula as it is also known), the great river that runs through the heart of Poland. The building of ships had been the main job of the local citizenry since the days of ancient Gdansk, as the information pamphlet handed out to new shipyard workers noted. The industry had especially flourished roughly between 1450 and 1650, in the heyday of mercantile capitalism, when the ships of the grain-exporting merchants of Gdansk were known throughout the Baltic and beyond. Jerzy had received his copy of the glossy brochure a year and a half before, having come to work at the yard after a tour in the Polish Army.

Devastated by the Nazis in World War II, the shipyard, like so much of war-ravaged Poland, had been rebuilt after liberation. They began by repairing deep-sea vessels and building steel-hulled fishing trawlers; soon the first of a series of 2,500-ton iron ore carriers was launched. Over the next three decades, the yards once again flourished. So did Gdansk itself, painfully renovating the Old Town along the banks of the Motlawa River (a tributary of the Wisla), recreating Renaissance, Baroque and Rococo dwellings, even as the Gdansk shipyard built sleek new factory fishing ships. Oil tankers and general cargo ships were followed by modern refrigerator and container vessels. By 1980, the Lenin Shipyard had produced over 800 ships, at the rate of more than 25 a year, and some of its now rather dilapidated shops housed high technology automated equipment.

That the yard, to which the name of the Russian revolutionary leader, V.I. Lenin, had been appended in 1967, was also the site of some of socialist Poland's bloodiest scenes of labor unrest was a fact that the shipyard brochure chose not to mention.

He had gone home, but he hadn't slept.

Now Jerzy Borowczak waited at a bus-stop, not far from the apartment building on Migowska Street, where he shared a room with another shipyard worker. At this time of night, the No. 184 bus that would take him to the shipyard came infrequently. Around him, the 50 or more five- and ten-story buildings of the Morena housing project, scattered across the rolling hills just west of Gdansk, stood like monoliths. The cheap Soviet-style concrete slab construction, built in the mid-1970s, was hidden in the chilly darkness. Yet, for Jerzy, it was an improvement over the room he had lived in with three others in Sopot when he first began work at the yards. The diesel-spewing No. 184 at last hove into sight, picked up Borowczak, and began the winding descent toward Gdansk, as the 10,000 inhabitants of the Morena slept in the early morning hours of Thursday, August 14, 1980.

Jerzy had arranged to meet fellow shipyard worker Ludwig Pradzynski at 4:15 in front of Gate No. 2, the main entrance to the Lenin Shipyard, but he had arrived far too early. It was still dark. Borowczak lit a cigarette as he paced outside the shipyard walls along the streetcar-track turnaround, which rimmed a grassy oval a hundred metres from the Second Gate. From there he could observe the iron-grill gate and the blockhouse of corrugated cement next to it where the shipyard security guards lazily checked the identification cards of entering workers. Pradzynski arrived. As the first light released the pale green motionless cranes from the gloom, the two of them entered the shipyard.

Bogdan Borusewicz woke at 4 a.m. For some nights now he had been staying at the home of a friend, avoiding the police stakeout at his own place. At age 30, Borusewicz was already a veteran political activist in Poland's "democratic opposition" to the ruling communist party regime.

His task that morning was to head one of two teams that would be distributing leaflets about Anna Walentynowicz to the workers streaming in by streetcar and commuter train to the Lenin Shipyard. Borusewicz's group was to cover the streetcars arriving from the districts and suburbs north of Gdansk, while another team would pick up workers travelling on the lines south of the shipyard.

As one of the strike's organizers, Borusewicz had been present a week earlier when the idea was born. It began at Piotr Dyk's apartment on Sienkiewicz Street, in the district of Wrzeszcz, just north of Gdansk proper. Dyk, a young doctor who in 1979 had helped to found a patriotic opposition group, the Young Poland Movement, was hosting a reception to celebrate the release of two political prisoners, one of whom, Darius Kobzdej, belonged to his group. The two had been arrested and sentenced to three months in prison for speaking at an illegal rally marking the anniversary of Poland's constitution of 1791, a document whose ringing praises of democracy echoed the eighteenth century revolutionary declarations of the United States, on which it was modelled. However, to celebrate its sentiments in Jan Sobieski Square in Gdansk in 1980 was apparently an act displaying "contempt for the nation," at least according to the judicial system of People's Poland.

Although the Young Poland Movement was primarily a group composed of students and intellectuals, it had made contact with some workers, especially those of the Baltic Free Trade Unions (a group founded in 1978). The two groups had been brought together through the May 3 demonstrations, which they had jointly organized. In fact, one of the Free Trade Unionists, Lech Walesa, had taken to the main streets of downtown Gdansk after the two men were arrested, flinging handfuls of leaflets into the air demanding their release. That accounted for the presence at Dyk's apartment that evening of Walesa and some of his colleagues—Andrzej Gwiazda, an engineer from the Elmor factory; Alina Pienkowska, a rather shy young nurse; Bogdan Felski, a 23-year-old Lenin Shipyard worker; Andrzej Kolodziej, a 21-year-old who had been fired from the Lenin yard; and of course, Borusewicz.

The soft-spoken Borusewicz was an early member of the older, rather more political Committee for the Defense of Workers (known by its Polish initials as KOR). The committee, a Warsaw-based national group, was founded in 1976 in response to government repression of workers who had participated in food price protests that summer. Borusewicz was soon in contact with the shipyard militants who would found the Free Trade Unions. Several of them joined the editorial board of the *Coastal Worker*, a clandestine newspaper organized by Borusewicz. It was one of several local papers around the country that had been spawned by the KOR-inspired illegal publication *The Worker* (in Polish, *Robotnik*). As was apparent from the composition of the gathering, whatever the shades of difference between the various opposition circles, their members intermingled easily and were united by their common resistance to the regime.

The spark that was to ignite that evening arrived with Anna Walentynowicz—Mrs. or *Pani* Anna, as everyone called her—the grandmotherly firebrand in a floral print dress, her hair tied back in a bun, who had worked at the Lenin Shipyard for nearly three decades. After months of harassment, threats and quasi-judicial proceedings, she had been fired that day. And there the idea of the strike was born—a very small, very silent, mild proposal to strike, as they described it afterwards. Someone said the word, "Strike..." and nothing else, and they all knew.

The group—fearing that Dyk's apartment was bugged—drifted into the courtyard outside. There, behind the unexceptional facades on Sienkiewicz Street, they settled things—who would print the leaflet, who would take care of distribution, who would prepare the posters, etc. To passers-by, they would appear to be an ordinary group of amiable young adults, drinking glasses of tea, smoking cigarettes and enjoying the evening air with Dr. Dyk and his wife.

The next day, Friday, August 8, Borusewicz visited Jerzy Borowczak. Borusewicz caught the bus just off Grunwald Avenue, the main store-lined street of Wrzeszcz, not far from where Anna Walentynowicz lived. Both sides of the wide avenue, divided by streetcar tracks, were filled with afternoon shoppers, just off work. Already there were lengthy now-familiar line-ups of people outside stores rumored to be selling some scarce commodity. Borusewicz squeezed aboard a hot, crowded bus that coughed and wheezed toward the hills of the Morena.

Borowczak quickly came to the same conclusion as the others

had. The only solution was to strike. That night at nine o'clock, Borusewicz, Borowczak, and Jerzy's friend Ludwig Pradzynski met at the home of Bogdan Felski, the Lenin Shipyard worker who had been at Piotr Dyk's the evening before. On each of the next few nights, the four young men met to map out strategy for organizing the strike. The other Free Trade Union members were generally informed, but the exact date was kept secret. In fact, they had to change the date at the last moment. Originally, they had picked Wednesday, August 13. But when they told Lech Walesa the night before—Walesa was older than them, everybody in the shipyard knew him from the years he had worked there, and they wanted his help—it turned out that Walesa had his new-born child to take care of that day, and so the strike was postponed to the 14th. Later, it would seem funny: a baby's cries had pushed history back a day.

At half-past four on the morning of August 14, Borusewicz was at the tram-stop where he was to meet two other members of the group that would distribute leaflets. About 6,500 sheets had been printed. The three shipyard workers had already taken 2,000 into the yard and stored them in their lockers. Borusewicz had a third of the leaflets and the rest were with the other group, led by Walesa, covering the south end of the line.

One of the members of Borusewicz's team didn't show. He had overslept. It was after 4:30 now, and beginning to get light. Borusewicz and his partner decided to start. After checking for police, they boarded the southbound car carrying the first of the workers headed toward the Lenin Shipyard, into whose hands they pressed the leaflets. Borusewicz was to cover the stretch of line running from the suburb of Oliwa toward the city. They handed out leaflets, rode to the next stop, got off, and waited to board the next car. Beginning just north of Oliwa, they travelled past the huge, bleak housing project at Zaspa where the workers poured out of the apartment buildings known as "ant hills," into just-awakening Wrzeszcz, stop-by-stop, until they arrived at Gdansk Shipyard terminal. At the same time, another group was working the system from the south.

By 5:30, as the streets filled with the usual rush hour complement of trucks, taxis and big transports, and crowds of people pushed on to the streetcars, the workers of the Lenin Shipyard, coming in for the shift that began at 6 a.m., were reading a remarkably detailed account of the case of Anna Walentynowicz.

"We appeal to you as the fellow-workers of Anna Walentynowicz," it began.

> She's been working in the shipyard since 1950, for 16 years as a welder, then as a crane-operator in the W-2 division. She's been decorated with the bronze, silver, and in 1979, gold cross of merit. She's always been an impeccable employee, and moreover, a person who always fought against injustice. This made her undertake activities aimed at creating trade unions independent of the employer. Since that time, she's been subject to all kinds of harassment—being sent off for a couple of months to a different plant, two official rebukes for distributing the *Worker*, a transfer to the stores division. Recently, the management isn't even trying to keep up the appearance of abiding by the law.

"This is what has happened," continued the leaflet, replete with names, dates and a level of detail that obviously contrasted with the usual vagaries of official language and the silences of the censored press. "On June 17, 1980, the District Labor Commission reinstated Anna Walentynowicz to her previous position as crane-operator of the W-2 division." An hour after she returned to work, the head of the prefabrication section of W-2 and her foreman switched off the power supply to the crane. They broke into her locker and officially assigned it to another worker. The next day she was stopped at the gate by security guards and detained for an hour and a half. The head of personnel threatened her with disciplinary action.

> Everyday she demanded that the lawful ruling of the Labor Commission be respected. On August 4, she met with the chief director. She offered to take a substitute job for the time being. During this meeting, the head of personnel, Szczypinski, told her that there was a new document at the District Labor Commission for her. It turned out to be a statement by the head of the Commission, Judge Gorecki, saying that the previous statement had been approved by mistake.

Three days later, while on doctor's leave, Walentynowicz received a disciplinary discharge, as of August 7, for "severe violation of employees' duties.''

The authors of the leaflet went on in measured but angry tones as the streetcars and commuter trains rattled toward the shipyard:

> We'd like to remind you that Anna Walentynowicz has five months left until retirement. The handling of her case shows that the shipyard's management takes into consideration neither public opinion nor the law, which it breaks or bends to fit its purpose. Anna Walentynowicz has become unacceptable because she influenced others. She's become unacceptable because she defended others and could organize her co-workers. This has been the unfaltering tactic of the authorities—to isolate those who could become leaders. After the 1976 strikes, the only ground for dismissal was often the fact of having authority. If we are not able to resist this, there won't be anybody who will speak out against raising work quotas, breaking safety regulations, or forcing people to work overtime.
>
> It is then in our own interest that such people be defended. That is why we are appealing to you: stand up for crane-operator Anna Walentynowicz. If you don't, many of you may find yourselves in a similar situation.

The appeal was signed by the founding committee of the Free Trade Unions and the editorial board of *Coastal Worker*, and bore the signatures of Borusewicz, Walesa and several others who had been present at Piotr Dyk's a week before.

Jerzy Borowczak worked in K-5, a small hull assembly shop employing 250 workers, located at the far side of the yard (see map). He and Ludwig took the main road through the centre of the shipyard, crossed the drawbridge over the river, and went to the K-5 locker room where they had stored the leaflets and posters calling for Walentynowicz's reinstatement.

After Borowczak and Pradzynski hung up several of the posters, Ludwig took the rest of the strike materials back to his own department, K-3, a large hull-making division with 1,300 workers near the Third Gate.

The men began arriving at K-5 to change into their blue overalls. As they entered, Jerzy gave a leaflet to each one. "Read it," he told them. "Today, the whole shipyard is

striking.'' To some whom he trusted, he gave handfuls of
leaflets and asked them to distribute them to the others.

By a quarter to six, a group of 20 or 30 workers had gathered
in the locker-room. Borowczak read out the demands. In
addition to calling for Walentynowicz's reinstatement, the
strike organizers had tacked on a demand for a pay hike and a
cost-of-living clause.

Some of the men seemed ready to join. Others were obviously
worried. It was easy for these young guys. But they had
families. What if the strike failed?

"Why doesn't a larger department begin the strike?"
someone asked.

K-1 and K-3 are already on strike, Jerzy replied confidently.

"We're not standing around here any longer," another man
grumbled. "Let's go back to the shop."

Borowczak couldn't stop them. He knew that if they got back
to the shop where the foreman and the local party
representative were waiting, everything could fail. A few
workers went to their machines and a familiar electric whirr
filled the air as they turned them on. Jerzy went up to them, a
small crowd of other workers tagging along. "Listen. Let's go
to K-3 and K-1. They've both stopped." He knew it was a shot
in the dark. He wasn't sure that anything had happened there
yet, but he wanted to get them to follow him.

For a long moment it hung in the balance. "Okay, let's go!"
one young machine operator shouted. The tension broke. The
machines stopped. Yet, they still hesitated.

Then the urge to get out won. Quickly, about 30 people came
together. The other workers milled around, waiting to see what
would happen, but not starting to work. The strikers, led by
Jerzy, moved out of K-5, into the morning light, marching into
the shipyard. It was 6:15 a.m. It had begun.

For many of the principals of Party, Church and State who
would soon be drawn into the drama, the morning of August 14
began uneventfully. Edward Gierek, the 67-year-old first
secretary of the Polish communist party, was at a Soviet holiday
retreat in the Crimea, far from the front lines on the Baltic. Ten
days earlier, he had met with Soviet president Leonid Brezhnev
to discuss Poland's deteriorating economic situation and the
"bubbling of unrest" (as it was officially described) that had
broken out six weeks before, on the heels of what were intended

to be quietly implemented meat price hikes.

Gierek, the son of a Silesian coal miner in southern Poland, and a miner himself before his ascent through party ranks, had every reason to be sensitive to worker discontent. He had come to power a decade ago, in the wake of bloody riots along the Baltic coast that ended the fourteen-year reign of his predecessor, party boss Wladyslaw Gomulka. The 1970 uprising had been precipitated by increased food prices, and when Gierek had attempted a similar move in 1976 to revive a flagging economy, he too had been forced to back off in the face of a wave of strikes. This time, the government sought a more subtle means of reaching its objective.

Already, the best cuts of meat were sold in special shops at higher, so-called "commercial" prices. Now the list of those cuts, whose prices went up by 40-80 per cent, was extended. However, rather than inviting a symbolic confrontation, the decree providing for the increase in meat prices was issued quietly. It was to be applied with regional variations, and local bureaucrats had been instructed to yield and adapt in case of resistance.

Nonetheless, by the end of July, workers in 68 enterprises had walked off the job. It had begun at the Ursus tractor factory near Warsaw and spread from there. The regime attempted to stave off worker discontent with pay increases. In fact, managers of major plants were flown to Warsaw on July 11 and told by the party's central committee to buy "social peace." The most dramatic protest had occurred in mid-month in Lublin, where railway and other transport workers brought the southeastern city of 300,000 to a standstill for three days. The army had to be called in to deliver milk and bread. The strike committees in Lublin formulated a variety of demands in addition to wage hikes. The Lublin strikers anticipated later events when they refused to accede to the formality of re-electing their old trade union officials, preferring instead to stand by their more militant strike committee.

What finally brought Lublin's workers back to their jobs was the wage offer and the regime's promise not to retaliate against strike leaders. Even as the Lublin walkout ended, other strikes were breaking out: at the Stalowa Wola steel mill 75 km. south of Lublin; among transport workers in Chelm 60 km. to the east; at an agricultural machinery plant in Wroclaw; and again in Warsaw.

Perhaps Gierek was still dreaming of those days ten years earlier when he had personally plunged in among the workers of the seething Baltic shipyards, asking them, "Will you help me?" and they had replied, "Yes, we'll help you!" In any case, the first secretary continued to bask under the Crimean sun.

Stefan Cardinal Wyszynski, the 78-year-old primate of Poland's 30-million-member Roman Catholic church, was in Czestochowa on August 14. More than a hundred thousand pilgrims had flocked to the shrine of the "Black Madonna," Our Lady of Czestochowa, for end-of-summer services. The tall, aged cardinal, a living symbol of moral authority in the country, and mentor to Karol Wojtyla (who had gone on to become Pope John Paul II), was busy preparing the sermon he would deliver the next day to mark the 60th anniversary of a major Polish military victory over Russian troops in 1920.

In Warsaw that morning, Polish Prime Minister Edward Babiuch, the 53-year-old close associate of Gierek, found himself beleaguered by the very economic crisis that put him in office six months before. For the past three days a flare-up in the public transportation sector had slowed the 1.5-million-person metropolis to a crawl. By the 12th, a bus drivers' strike had assumed serious proportions, and while the Warsaw party committee met, the authorities took the precaution of calling in foreign reporters for a briefing by information minister Jerzy Lukaszewicz on the regime's "restructuring" of food prices and wages. Late that night, a group of young people gathered near the main Warsaw tramway line and stopped streetcars that were still running. In less than an hour, the line of backed-up streetcars was a kilometre long. Police vans arrived as several hundred onlookers watched, but tempers remained even and the police quietly dispersed the crowd.

The next day, the situation appeared to cool. The Warsaw bus drivers, after obtaining a pay raise of 1,500 zlotys a month, said they would go back to work. The party newspaper, *Trybuna Ludu*, in its first reference to the local strikes, took a conciliatory line, conceding that the drivers faced unsatisfactory conditions. Even KOR, the opposition self-defence committee which had been monitoring and co-ordinating information on the six-week wave of sporadic strikes, issued an appeal to the public to avoid incidents. Perhaps the situation could be contained, party officials reasoned. After all, the incidents to date had been scattered, isolated. Nothing really major had occurred. That afternoon, half the city's drivers walked out, demanding higher fares.

When Prime Minister Babiuch awoke on the 14th, he looked out the window and saw a city at a standstill. The bus drivers had decided they weren't satisfied, and the streetcar drivers had joined them.

In Gdansk, director of the Lenin Shipyard Klemens Gniech was still at home. A stocky man of local Kaszubian peasant origin, he hadn't always occupied the huge corner office on the second floor of the administration building. Gniech had begun work in the Gdansk shipyard more than 22 years ago, as a young man of 20 in K-3, the department where now another young man, Ludwig Pradzynski, was hanging up strike posters. Gniech had expected something. There were rumors. Perhaps next week, he had thought. He had left instructions, just in case, for his office to call him immediately. Soon the phone would ring.

Up and down the coast, one could detect no hint of what was beginning in the Lenin Shipyard. Life was normal. More than anything, there were tourists. As in every other year, thousands of them had flocked to the coast, enjoying the last two weeks of the season. The hotels were full. The foreigners were sprawled along the famous beaches of Sopot. The local smart young set was at the lakes district, west of Gdansk, near Kartuzy. Others had gone further up the coast, camping out in tents. At the Grand Hotel in Sopot, a massive nineteenth century apparition that overlooked the Baltic, the guests, as in years past, crowded onto the long pier for an evening walk. They kindled romances and exchanged talk of having seen wild boars on the beaches, a legendary phenomenon that remained invisible to the local residents.

The group of marchers led by Jerzy Borowczak moved toward the bridge. Everywhere, workers in blue overalls and yellow plastic hardhats were coming out to see what was happening. "Leave your machines. Come with us," the strikers called to the men standing in the dark cavernous opening of C-5, near the approach to the bridge. A good number of them did. It was growing.

Meanwhile, in Department W-3, Bogdan Felski and two of his co-workers, who, like Jerzy and Ludwig, had arrived at work an hour early that morning, were putting up strike posters

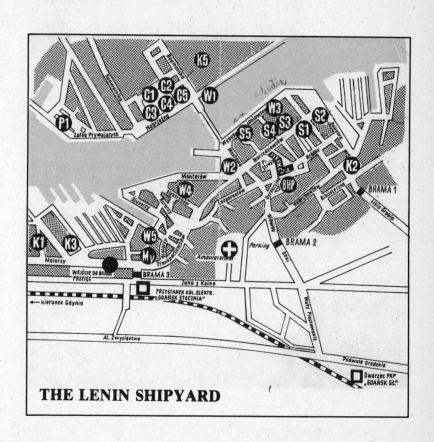

THE LENIN SHIPYARD

Old Gdansk

New Gdansk

Jan Sobieski Square, May 3, 1981

over the punch-clock. Leaving one of the strikers to make sure no one would tear them down, Felski went back to his own department. He pasted one of the posters onto the door of the first locker room, then he went into the other rooms and started hanging the signs.

Word of the strike had already gotten around, and people started coming up to Felski to congratulate him. Knots of people began to form, and Felski moved among them, saying that the strike had begun in the whole shipyard and that a meeting was being held in the square outside, opposite the conference hall.

By then, a group of 40 people had assembled and more were drifting in. Fearing that they might disperse, Felski began to explain the strike. He talked about the need for a pay increase and the case of Anna Walentynowicz, who had been thrown out of work unjustly. As he talked, Felski sensed that the crowd was gaining self-confidence. He urged them to move out to the square. They quickly made a banner and about 50 workers prepared to go outside.

At that moment, the division director, a man named Barc, shouldered his way into the crowded locker room. "What the hell's going on?" he demanded.

"We're on strike," Felski replied.

"Strike? Why strike? What's going on?" the director sputtered.

"Can't you read?" Felski asked, pointing to the poster. He left Barc arguing with the workers about Anna Walentynowicz while he went off to round up some others.

When Felski returned a few minutes later he saw that department party secretary Mazurkiewicz had arrived. Mazurkiewicz made a grab for the hastily lettered banner, but two or three of the younger workers quickly stepped in. "What's the meaning of this?" the party secretary shouted. "None of your business," replied someone. Somebody else shoved a swatch of leaflets into Mazurkiewicz's hand, and everyone started to laugh because it seemed the party secretary himself was handing out strike leaflets. Felski pushed into the crowd and shouted at the worker nearest Mazurkiewicz to take the leaflets away from him. They could save the clowning for later. The party secretary walked off in a huff. Felski moved in, picked up the strike banner, and led his group outside toward the square.

As Borowczak's growing band of strikers slowly crossed the

bridge, the men working on the ships berthed along the canal stopped what they were doing and crowded to the rail. A few clambered down the ladder onto the pier as the strikers passed. They hesitated. "We're not working," a ship's welder told Jerzy, "but we can't join you yet." Borowczak told him they were heading for K-3.

There were more than a hundred of them now. Jerzy stopped a passing tow-motor driver and told him to go ahead and tell the other departments that they were already marching toward them. As the procession continued its slow snake-dance along the perimeter of the south shore of the shipyard, the word rippled through the shops. As the march passed behind W-4, the electricians' shop, Stanislaw Bury and Henryk Lenarciak began organizing. The two men, both of whom had worked in the shipyard for over twenty years, were as different in appearance as could be imagined: Bury, a burly man with a handlebar mustache and a booming voice; Lenarciak, short, thin, a little stooped. Yet they had both been active in the strikes of 1970 and 1976, and had stayed in touch with fellow-electrician Lech Walesa after he'd been fired in '76. In every workshop, on each construction berth, there were people like that—veterans of previous struggles who had been shot at in the streets of Gdansk, as well as young men like Borowczak who hadn't known anything other than the system of People's Poland they had grown up in.

As the marchers (they had now linked up with Felski's group) reached K-3 they saw a crowd of people outside the hangar-sized shop. Excitement flickered through the procession. Suddenly, the first cheers broke from the ranks of the strikers. Across the road, the office workers in the drafting departments had come to the windows to watch. Jerzy began to feel the certainty of success. They passed through the waiting crowd into K-3.

Outside again, now nearly 2,000 strong as the workers from nearby K-1 joined in, Klemens Gniech, the shipyard director, was waiting for them. With him was the first secretary of the party organization in the shipyard and a half dozen other people from management. Jerzy didn't know any of them.

"What does this mean?" Gniech asked.

"It's a strike," Jerzy said.

"What's it all about?"

"The firing of Anna Walentynowicz."

"Anna Walentynowicz?" repeated the director.

"You know who she is?" Jerzy asked. "She was fired without notice." He began speaking rapidly. "Someone like her. She had three order of merit decorations, one in bronze, one in silver, and one in gold. She's got 30 years' work behind her, and only five months to go before she retires."

Gniech took a step backwards. He began to explain Walentynowicz's case. He was willing to offer evidence to prove that he had grounds to fire her. Bogdan Felski cut in. "We don't have anything to say to you right now. We can talk later." The march surged forward, leaving the director and his retinue behind, and moved across the shipyard again, gathering force as it went.

Anna Walentynowicz entered the Lenin Shipyard Health Service, a five-story building located outside the yard, about two blocks from Gate No. 2, at half-past six in the morning. She hadn't been feeling well lately. Even though she'd been fired from the shipyard itself, she was still officially on sick leave.

The veteran shipyard worker entered the elevator with two men and pressed the button for the fifth floor where she was slated to undergo a medical examination that morning. As they ascended, she overheard the men talking. One of them happened to be the director of the patient reception department on the fourth floor where Walentynowicz's friend, Alina Pienkowska, worked. He was explaining it to the other man. "I think it's in K-3... Yes, yes, they're on strike." Neither of them recognized their fellow-passenger as the immediate cause of the outbreak they were discussing. Walentynowicz gave up the idea of an examination. When the elevator doors opened on the fourth floor, she followed the men out, and headed straight for the nurses' station.

Alina Pienkowska, age 27, widowed mother of a three-year-old son, had known it was going to happen today. That morning, when she got off the streetcar at the Lenin Shipyard stop at ten to six, she saw her friends distributing the leaflets. She pretended to be an ordinary observer, passing Bogdan Borusewicz without offering any sign of recognition. Ever since the meeting at Piotr Dyk's place a week ago she had been fearful that the plan to strike might be discovered and that she would be one of those picked up by the authorities. Alina had gone straight from the meeting to her parents' house, taking her son Sebastian with her. She had stayed there for the last week.

Anna signalled to Alina. Together, the two women went to the bathroom, checking first to see if anyone was nearby, and locked the door behind them. In whispers, Walentynowicz repeated what she had overheard in the elevator. Pienkowska suggested that it would be best for Anna to go home and wait there. Then they separated.

As Walentynowicz walked along the health service corridor, she glanced out the window toward the shipyard. As if in a dream, the shipyard cranes were stilled. An eerie summer-morning peacefulness had settled over the yard. Before leaving the building, she went upstairs to the telephone exchange to call Warsaw and let them know. The operator looked a bit frightened.

"To where?" the young woman asked.

"To Warsaw." Anna Walentynowicz said her name. The switchboard operator became more obviously frightened. "I, well, I—I can't," she stumbled. They might dismiss her. Walentynowicz went downstairs and outside to look for a phone booth. When she saw the two men across the street, she gave up any hope of phoning Warsaw. They were police. Instead, she walked a block or two through the cobblestone-street residential neighborhood around the corner from the shipyard. When she came to the tram-stop, she got on the streetcar that would take her out to Grunwald Avenue in Wrzeszcz. From the window of the streetcar, as it rolled along the tracks in the middle of the broad avenue bordered by Kasprzaka Park, she could see the shipyard and the motionless cranes below.

Alina Pienkowska went to the emergency room. It was almost 7 a.m. She knew some of the drivers. They had come from the yard and gave her the details. Then Pienkowska phoned Warsaw.

Jacek Kuron was right by the orange plastic phone that sat on the desk of his book-lined study. It had been ringing all morning. One of KOR's founders, the moving spirit behind Poland's democratic opposition movement, Kuron was a man in his mid-forties with a balding boxer's head and a gravelly voice. He lived with his family in a long, grey block of older apartments surrounded by acacia trees on Mickiewicz Avenue (named after the nineteenth century Polish national poet) in a quiet section of Warsaw.

Andrzej Gwiazda had been the first to phone from Gdansk. Then Pienkowska. Kuron had been co-ordinating information on the strike wave since it began, passing on news to KOR representatives like Borusewicz in Gdansk and others around the country, while the official media maintained a chilly silence. He also stayed in touch with the foreign press. Kuron was excited. With Gdansk in the fray, the situation was immediately and qualitatively different. He phoned the Reuters correspondent. Reuters phoned back a few minutes later. Interpress, the Polish press service for foreign journalists, had denied Kuron's claims. You can believe me or you can believe them, Kuron snapped back. The phone kept ringing.

The official state news agency (known by its Polish initials, PAP) might be able to keep the rest of the country from knowing for a few hours yet. But throughout the enterprises of the Tri-Cities area the news would quickly reach waiting ears. Of the more than half-million workers scattered among 800 plants and factories along this stretch of the Bay of Gdansk, in each place, there were those ready to take the lead. As one of the workers whom Bogdan Felski talked to about the possibility of a strike had said the day before, "Just a touch and the avalanche will begin."

At the Paris Commune Shipyard in Gdynia, Andrzej Kolodziej began his first day of work on a new job. He had had to shave the truth in order to get taken on, since workers who had been fired from one shipyard, especially for political reasons, were seldom permitted to get work in another yard. He told the personnel manager that his firing had been the result of a personality conflict. If they hadn't been short of skilled shipyard workers in Gdynia, and if Kolodziej hadn't offered to take on one of the worst jobs—working outside on hulls—he might not have been at the Paris Commune yard that day.

At the Elmor factor, which produced ship's equipment, the news quickly reached Andrzej Gwiazda and the factory's improbable communist party secretary, 28-year-old Bogdan Lis. There were others: Florian Wisniewski, an electrician at Elektromontaz, the last plant the troublesome Walesa had been fired from; Henryka Krzywonos, a woman who drove a streetcar for the Gdansk municipal transportation system; Stefan Lewandowski, a crane driver at Gdansk Port; Lech

Sobieszek, a metal worker at the Siarkopol factory.

After he finished distributing the leaflets, Borusewicz, who hadn't been to bed for two nights, went straight home, and fell into a deep slumber. Not even the sirens from the shipyard woke him.

And somewhere outside the walls, a 37-year-old unemployed electrician, having shaken his police tail, clambered onto the outer perimeter of the Lenin shipyard. Then he leapt.

They had marched across the shipyard once again, passing through all the departments. Now everyone was joining them. Men from the shops had secured their machines and laid down their tools. The workers came off the ships. The strikers secured the bridge to make sure the road wasn't cut. It was the first step in the formation of a workers' militia. The huge procession, perhaps as many as 8,000 workers, slowly approached the Second Gate. It was after 9 a.m. Outside, in the city, they could hear the usual sounds of everyday life. Inside the gate, at the centre of the strike, there was an absolute stillness as the workers of the Lenin Shipyard observed a moment of silence in honor of the ones who had been killed in 1970. This was followed by the singing of the national anthem, at first hesitantly, and then with full voices.

The strike leaders moved the crowd back about a hundred metres, to the big square near the four-story hospital. In the adjacent lot, Jerzy and some of the others climbed onto a power shovel so they could be seen.

"We have to elect a strike committee," Borowczak declared. Someone passed him a bullhorn. He started again. "We need people we can trust, who have authority in the shops, in the work brigades. Let them come forward." Names began to be called out of the crowd. The young ones who had organized the strike were named. Groups from shops hastily met and picked someone to represent them. The electricians of W-4 chose Stanislaw Bury. Jerzy scrawled the names on a piece of paper.

After about 20 people had been elected to the strike committee, Director Gniech and his crew appeared again, at the side of the excavator. Gniech wanted to address the men. Borowczak gave the director a hand up onto the improvised platform.

At first Gniech tried to assert his authority, boldly demanding that the strike be stopped. The huge crowd of strikers spilling across the square was stolid in its refusal. A few of them began to shout up at Gniech that he should talk about the strikers' demands. It's impossible to talk about the issues here, the director protested. "I'll only talk with the elected strike committee." He wanted the others to disperse. Instead, they began whistling in derision. They wouldn't let Gniech finish.

In the excitement almost no one saw the man who had climbed onto the back of the excavator. He was several inches shorter than the director, from behind whose shoulder he suddenly appeared.

"Do you recognize me?" he shouted at the startled Gniech. The vast crowd surrounding the power-shovel immediately knew the elfin figure whose pale cheeks were almost hidden behind a walrus mustache, and whose whole person radiated an unmistakable air of authority.

"Tell them why I was fired from the shipyard," demanded a boiling-angry Lech Walesa. "Did I steal anything? Was I a thief?" Gniech opened his mouth, but no words came out. Walesa felt like a boxer who had dropped his opponent with one punch.

"I worked in the shipyard for more than ten years," Walesa went on, "and I still consider myself to be a real shipyard worker." They were cheering now. He was one of them and they shared his anger. "It's been four years already since I've had a regular job." Gniech stood aside. Jerzy, who had been writing down the names of the strike committee, added Walesa's name to the list.

Walesa, in his slightly raspy voice, formally declared the strike. "I have been given the trust of the workers," he confidently announced. "We are occupying the shipyard. The workers aren't going anywhere until we're sure we've gotten what we wanted. We're staying! This is a sit-in strike! And I'll be the last one to leave the shipyard." The last of his words were swallowed in the cheering.

Jerzy gave Walesa the strike committee list to read out for the workers' approval. He read out 20 names. Then Walesa read out the 21st name, his own. "Will you accept me?" he asked. "Even though I'm not a worker in the shipyard, do you want me on the strike committee?"

He had appeared like an apparition, a short man in a crumpled sports jacket and a pullover shirt, someone they all knew. It would stay in their memories, as though it had been sealed by one of those brilliant arc-welding torches they saw every day. They took him as their leader.

2   Long Memories

There are certain situations in which any honest person should consider himself Jewish.
—Jacek Kuron, 1968

It had begun long ago, almost a quarter-century before Lech Walesa leapt over the wall of the Lenin Shipyard into the forefront of history.

Just after 6 a.m., on Thursday morning, June 28, 1956, the 16,000 workers at ZISPO (initials of the Stalin railway car factory) filed out through the opening in the plant's towering red-brick walls and started marching up the narrow street that led to Poznan's Freedom Square. They had had enough.

One did not have to look far to discover the causes of their particular discontent. The national standard of living had dropped steadily since the late 1940s; the climb back in the last year or two was infinitesimal. It was not only a question of wages, which bought less each day. There were shortages of basic commodities, a chronic transportation crisis, and housing inadequacies to be added to the day's drudgery.

However, not everyone had to stand in line. For certain ranks of the army, militia and security, for party activists, ranking government bureaucrats and party big shots, special shops were opened. The yellow-curtained shops—named for the yellow screened doors and windows that hid their bulging shelves—were a visible refutation of the egalitarian slogans of the state. The system of privileges embraced special hospitals, housing complexes, pharmacies, holiday resorts and theatres. For ordinary workers, however, prices continued rising on everything except heavy machinery, and they bitterly joked that "the only bargain for a poor man in Poland is a locomotive."

ZISPO, where locomotives were manufactured, was the largest factory in this western Polish city of 300,000 inhabitants. The town was also the site of the annual Poznan industrial fair, which was then in progress. They marched through the run-down factory district, past their own dilapidated houses. For weeks, they had been demanding a pay raise. When no one in Poznan listened to them, they chose a delegation of 30 men to go to Warsaw and present their demands to the Minister of Machine Industry and to warn that they would strike on June 28. The minister was unimpressed. "If you take to the streets, you'll find tanks there." Now, in the streets, small groups dashed into the other factories and offices along the route to say that ZISPO was out and taking its demands to city hall. Those who heard poured into the streets to swell the procession and add their voices to the clamor for bread.

The moving crowd began to sing religious hymns and old patriotic songs that hadn't been heard since the Soviet-backed communist government took power in Poland a decade earlier, at the end of the war. Children ducked out of school to join the extraordinary parade. Office workers fled their dreary and cramped rooms. The working class joined the first truly spontaneous demonstration it had seen in years.

They heard something more than the chants that echoed throughout the square in front of city hall. Something had subtly changed in the fabric of life in post-war Poland, and that day, almost unwittingly, the workers would precisely define that change. It would be as understandable as the banners they held aloft above the gathering crowd, which read simply: "Bread and Freedom." Until that moment, all that had occurred since the death of Josef Stalin three years earlier were only signs, murmurs, barely legible indicators.

There was ferment among the usually obedient young, according to rumors from the international youth festival in Warsaw. There was the defection of Jozef Swiatlo, a high-ranking official of the secret police (known by its initials, U.B.). Millions of Poles listened nightly to the illicit Radio Free Europe broadcasts that carried Swiatlo's sensational revelations confirming the mechanism of terror.

Then the intellectuals. Adam Wazyk, a heretofore

unexceptional party poet who had dutifully penned the required odes to progress, suddenly, angrily, published *Poem for Adults*. "There are people overworked,/There are people in Nowa Huta who have never been inside a theatre.../There are people who wait for little documents,/There are people who wait for justice,/There are people who have waited very long." The unprecedented words were easy to comprehend, but what did they mean? And what was one to make of the new weekly paper, *Po Prostu* (a colloquial Polish phrase meaning, "Quite simply....")? Overnight, its circulation skyrocketed to 90,000 as its readers devoured exposes of corruption, bureaucratic stupidity, poverty.

Was it true that there had been special meetings of party cells throughout Poland, just that February, to hear recitations of the secret speech new Soviet party boss Nikita Khrushchev delivered to his party's 20th congress? That he had bluntly spoken of the revered Stalin's "intolerance, brutality and abuse of power"? But, were not the two men who symbolized Polish nationalism—former First Secretary Wladyslaw Gomulka and Stefan Cardinal Wyszynski—one a communist, one a priest, both in prison but lately?

There were signs, murmurs, but what was the text? Who could read it? Then the Poznan workers carried the banner of "Bread and Freedom," legible to all.

The thousands who had gathered in front of city hall wanted someone in authority to appear in person and at least listen to their demands. But no one would come out. In the crowd, someone asked where the delegation was that had been sent to Warsaw (they had been expected at the airport that morning). They at least might address the throng and tell how they were rebuffed. Suddenly the rumor raced through the crowd that the delegation had been arrested. Actually, they were on a train riding home, unaware of the events that lay before them.

"To the prison! We'll find them and free them ourselves!" No one knew who started the shouts, but in that confused moment an uprising was born. The crowd divided. Part veered off to the right toward the jail. The others turned left toward the grey stucco headquarters of the secret police.

The outraged workers who reached the prison quickly scaled its walls. The gates were opened and the crowd poured in, breaking open the cells, ransacking the offices, flinging armfuls of secret dossiers out of the window into the courtyard below where a bonfire was lit.

On the other side of town the protesters couldn't break into police headquarters. They massed in the street, shouting. Then someone threw a stone. The U.B. men turned on the fire hoses. Some of the children in the crowd found the water main and turned it off. Then firing began. People ran for cover in doorways and nearby houses. Word of the shooting spread. Soon bands of kids stormed militia stations to get their hands on guns.

The crowd overturned streetcars. The radio jamming station atop a four-story building two blocks from the U.B. head-quarters was attacked and huge pieces of its tower crashed into the street. At the railroad station, a man mistakenly identified as a U.B. member was beaten to death. At the fair-grounds protesters pushed past startled foreign businessmen attending the Poznan fair and climbed up on the flagpole to tear down the banner of the Soviet Union. On the spot where one man had been shot to death, a woman dipped Poland's red and white flag in the puddle of blood. The crowd sang the national anthem.

The local army garrison was called out. Some of the soldiers joined the rebels. A number turned over their arms and at least one tank crew crawled out and gave their tank to the workers. Most of the troops refused to shoot at all. All day Thursday Poznan was embattled.

By Friday the special security troops arrived from Warsaw. They rode into Poznan with tanks and heavy weapons, and they didn't hesitate to use them. The workers had no leaders, no organization, and no guns, except the few small arms they had been able to seize. It was over by Saturday. Fifty-four people were dead, including a dozen secret police and militiamen, a score of teenagers, and some workers from ZISPO. The prime minister of the day, Jozef Cyrankiewicz, arrived from Warsaw to deliver a stinging radio speech in which he told the very people who had been in the streets that the whole uprising was a capitalist plot launched by counter-revolutionaries. "Every provocateur or madman who dares to lift his hand against the power of People's Poland will have that hand chopped off," Cyrankiewicz proclaimed.

Propaganda notwithstanding, in the days that followed there was no real doubt as to the causes, nor that the people of Poznan had spoken for the nation. There had to be a change, or the appearance of one. The party tried to restore some confidence in the unions, the organization theoretically meant to defend workers' interests. Wiktor Klosiewicz, the new trade union minister, was dispatched to the factories. His raucous, bitter meeting with the workers lasted more than seven hours.

"The unions are a cancer on the body of the working class,". one older worker shouted. "The dues are deducted from our pay and no one asks us. And what do you do with our money?" he demanded of Klosiewicz. "It goes to provide the comforts for our bosses. They have their own cars, special country houses. Well, this is not socialism and not trade unions, not the way we workers see it." The minister blustered and squirmed and said, "The unions are not to blame." "Then who is?" came another voice from the floor. "If you ask, I'll tell you frankly," said Klosiewicz. "In my opinion, it is the government and the party who are responsible." Not even that startling admission could divert the torrent of contempt. "You're a member of the central committee," another worker shot back. "For once, you probably know what you're talking about."

If not the carrot, then the stick. In September, the trials of the Poznan rioters began. A stream of young people were brought forth (the regime didn't dare put the ZISPO workers in the dock), only to recant their confessions, and pour out the story of the years that had led to Poznan. Two weeks was all the government could stand. The accused were given light sentences. It was the regime that stood convicted.

The party recalled Wladyslaw Gomulka. He had been party first secretary at the end of the war, a position he held until 1948. Though a loyalist to Stalinism, Gomulka had mused about a "Polish road to socialism," he had opposed collectivization of agriculture as being unrealistic, he had fallen into occasional disputes with the Russians over policies that he felt harmed Polish national interests. When the wave of purges swept through the Soviet bloc Eastern European countries in the late forties, Gomulka was ousted for "nationalist and rightest deviations." They arrested him in 1951, but Gomulka's successor, Boleslaw Bierut, for reasons of his own, successfully stalled the demands that Gomulka be brought to trial to meet a fate similar to other deposed Eastern European heads.

Gomulka was to be brought back from oblivion. He had been released the year before, in 1955. Now, after the revelations about Stalin, after Poznan, they needed him. For the first time,

a Polish communist leader had a measure of popular appeal. He
had been imprisoned unjustly. His return would be taken as a
sign of justice. He had been disgraced for defending Polish
interests. His return was a signal of national revival.

The Russians balked. In the fall of 1956, Khrushchev himself
arrived to talk the Polish central committee down. The volatile
Russian leader had no sooner touched down at the airport one
Friday morning in mid-October than he took the opportunity of
greeting his honor guard in tones loud enough for the nearby
Polish leadership to hear. "We shed our blood for this country
and now they're trying to sell it out to the Americans and the
Zionists. But it won't work!"

A small bony man in a modest business suit shouted back,
"We shed more blood than you and we're not selling out to
anyone."

"Who are you?" Khrushchev demanded.

"I am Gomulka, whom you put in prison."

"What is he doing here?" the Russian leader asked the other
Poles.

"He is here because we decided to elect him first secretary,"
replied the leader of the Polish delegation.

For the next three days they argued while crowds milled in the
streets outside party headquarters. Khrushchev had come with
his generals. There were tanks moving toward Warsaw.
Gomulka didn't budge. In the end the disgruntled Russians
went home.

A wave of hope swept Poland. The tough, quiet man who
every morning at the stroke of eight could be seen on his way to
the swimming pool in Warsaw's 30-story Palace of Culture had
become, albeit briefly, a hero. It was called "spring in
October," or the "Polish October," a reference to the date of
the first socialist revolution, in Russia.

It was not to last. There were some changes, certainly.
Cardinal Wyszynski was released from the remote monastery
where he had been kept under house arrest for three years; new
accords between church and state were arranged. The forced
collectivization of farming was halted. Eastern Europe,
however, quickly sobered when Soviet tanks poured into
Budapest that same autumn to crush the Hungarian uprising.
Though Polish students marched in the streets carrying the
Hungarian colors alongside their own, the boundaries of revolt
had been drawn. In Poland, daily life continued to be grim. In

the euphoria, they had perhaps forgotten that Gomulka, despite his nationalistic inclinations, was a loyalist of the old school. He soon tired of all this thinking aloud. The status quo, Polish and Soviet, was firmly in place.

On the first anniversary of Poland's timorous revolt against Moscow, the young were in the streets of Warsaw, demonstrating againt Gomulka's authority. In a cold rain, they gathered in front of the university to protest the shutdown of *Po Prostu*, their militant magazine. Faceless defenders of the regime, in gas masks, and carrying rubber truncheons, moved in against them. There was bloodshed, and it smeared the text of any truth that might be spoken "quite simply." "It's not October any more," declared the party press.

Poland had existed for a thousand years. And before that, the tribe of the Polanie (meaning field dwellers) had established themselves in the fertile basins of the Vistula and Oder rivers. The history of the Polish nation begins with Mieszko I. When marauding tenth century Teuton bands, under the banners of the Holy Roman Empire, marched eastward to gain converts for Christ and land for themselves, the pagan ruler of Poland defended his realm by marrying a Christian princess and accepting the faith for himself and his nation in 966.

In the centuries that followed, the geographical boundaries of the realm shifted in accordance with the political realities of the day. Late in the fourteenth century, union with Lithuania, and religious conversion of that last pagan stronghold of Europe, made Poland a continental power. Class conflict in the feudal empire, which took the form of a struggle over succession to the throne, was temporarily resolved with the grant of a charter of liberties to Poland's nobles and occasional election of the monarch, which became customary after the union with Lithuania. Meanwhile, the politically silent classes—peasants and workers— continued to work the fields of grain. They hauled their harvest north to the Baltic, where the fishing villages of the Bay of Gdansk were gradually transformed into shipbuilding centres and prosperous ports under the rule of a Renaissance mercantile bourgeoisie.

In the seventeenth century, the Swedes, who dwelled across the Baltic Sea, threatened to extinguish the independent Polish nation. It was saved only by a sudden reversal in a battle fought on a field below the monastery at Czestochowa. The event was duly proclaimed a miracle and the site of the "Black Madonna" of Czestochowa was established as a shrine for pilgrimages.

In the ensuing century of European war and civil strife among the country's ruling strata, the national sorrow of Poland began, resulting in three partitions of the country in 1772, 1793, and 1795. Despite the quasi-democratic constitution of 1791 (the year the national mint struck a medal bearing the legend, "Poland, Free From Fear"), Russia, Prussia and Austria succeeded in erasing the nation from the maps of Europe by 1795.

When latter-day analysts seek to explain how the strands of Catholicism and nationalism have come to be inextricably woven into the contemporary conflicts between workers and the workers' state, it is to this hiatus of 123 years (1795-1918) that they must look. During this period of division and foreign occupation, the church, already deeply identified with the country's origins and periodic salvation, came to represent a sanctuary of nationalism. It continued to teach the catechism in Polish, as opposed to Russian and German which children were forced to learn in school. Similarly, all political projects, whether conceived as romantic revolutions or organized around class-based strategies, tended to take the form of a proposal for national restoration.

As the Western world was entering the modern era, Poland still was not to be found on twentieth century maps. Between the first and second World Wars, Poland came into existence again, briefly, as a troubled democracy. It disappeared once more under German tanks, as the most brutalized victim of World War II, suffering a higher proportion of deaths than any other country (22 per 100; among them, three million Jews). When the Nazi monster was destroyed, Poland, its boundaries shifted westward, found itself liberated by the Red Army and Polish resistance fighters. Its fate was settled among the great powers, and after the deals were concluded, Poland was governed by a communist party it had not asked for. After a thousand years, it was a country of Gomulka, 30 million Catholics, a large peasantry stubborn enough to resist the official ideology of collectivized farming, nationalists who fervently remembered the constitution of 1791, and an industrial working class that was gaining class consciousness—irrespective of the predictions of Marx and Lenin—in struggle with the Marxist-Leninist state.

In 1965, two young Communists unravelled the finery of propaganda in which the workers' state clothed itself to reveal the naked contradictions between the rulers and the ruled. The two, teachers at Warsaw University, did not cry out that the dictator had no clothes, but rather that he carried a bag of wool to pull over the workers' eyes. The authors of an *Open Letter to the Party* were Karol Modzelewski and Jacek Kuron. Kuron was the man who, fifteen years later, would receive a phone call at dawn saying that the workers of the Lenin Shipyard had risen against the state.

The party was not slow to appreciate the dangers posed by what began as the scholarly thesis of two young academics. When news of its existence reached the interior ministry, Kuron and Modzelewski were promptly arrested, but released after 48 hours. Two weeks later they were expelled from the party. Cut off from all contact, they appealed to the basic party organization of Warsaw University by means of open letter, on March 18, 1965.

"According to official doctrine, we are living in a socialist country," they began.

> This contention rests on the identification of state ownership of the means of production with their social ownership ...This sounds like Marxist logic. But in reality it introduces a fundamentally alien concept into Marxism, namely, the formalistic, legal notion of ownership. The concept of state property can conceal different social contents, depending on the class character of the state. The public sector of the national economies of capitalist countries has nothing in common with social ownership...because the workers in the state-owned factories have no real share in their ownership since they have no say in running the state and, therefore, no control over their own labor and its product.

The question then, as the two young Marxists posed it, was, "Who has the power in our state?" Their reply was blunt.

> One party has a monopoly, the Polish United Workers Party. All key decisions are made in the party first, and only afterwards in the official organs of state power... This is called the leading role of the party and, since the

monopolistic party considers that it represents the interests of the working class, its authority is supposed to insure workers' power.

The two ex-communist party members quickly stripped away any illusions about the power of the workers' voice in Poland. Outside the party, of course, they have none, Kuron and Modzelewski noted. Since the party enjoys a monopoly of power, the workers are not permitted to organize other parties to formulate different programs. Enforcing this ban was a massive state apparatus of administrative bodies, political police, courts and political organizations to "nip in the bud every attempt to question the party's leading role." Under the direction of the party, even the trade unions, the traditional organizations of workers' economic self-defence "have become passive and obedient tools of the bureaucracy...the working class has been deprived of its organization, its program and its means of self-defence." Democracy within the party, they argued, was a fiction. Its decisions were made by a "central political bureaucracy" which consulted neither workers nor the rest of society. Despite the official designation of Poland as a workers' state, the authors charged that in fact the country's workers were "exploited" by a sovereign elite, a ruling class.

The *Open Letter* was devastating, its arguments invested with more than historical curiosity. This was not a challenge mounted from outside the system, reiterating the capitalist West's familiar cries of totalitarianism. Rather, it was a critique produced from within, by those born and bred in a workers' state. Now they dared to turn the vocabulary and categories of the theory that had allegedly brought socialism into being against an actual instance of socialist society. Using the methods of Marxist sociology, the authors of the *Open Letter* offered, replete with statistics, a portrait of Polish workers in a workers' state. Further, they described with precision how "the bureaucracy uses the surplus product to maintain a vast army...which reinforces the social and productive relations on which bureaucratic rule is based."

Few were permitted to read the *Open Letter*. They did so under the supervision of two party members and without the right to take notes. It had taken a committee of the university senate, including Leszek Kolakowski, the nation's foremost philosopher, to authorize that much. Those who read it drew in their breath at the authors' programmatic vision. Kuron and Modzelewski called for a thoroughgoing workers' democracy, including genuine workers' councils in factories; a national council of workers' deputies; the right of workers to organize into a plurality of political parties; complete freedom of speech, press and assembly; the right to form "trade unions absolutely independent of the state and to organize economic and political strikes"; workers' education which ensures that the new democracy will not be turned into a "facade behind which all the old crap will reappear"; the end of the secret police and standing army. Finally, they called for an internationalist revolution to prevent, among other things, "the intervention of Soviet tanks." All this, in the name of socialism.

The letter was submitted on March 18. On the morning of March 19, Kuron and Modzelewski were arrested in their homes. Though they had addressed no gatherings, public or secret, distributed no inflammatory leaflets on streetcorners, nor formed any subversive group, they were imprisoned for advocating revolution. Kuron received a sentence of three years, Modzelewski three-and-a-half years, on the charge of calling for the "forcible overthrow of the political and socio-economic system of the People's Republic of Poland."

The silencing of Kuron and Modzelewski was not the end, but rather the beginning of a wave of intellectual discontent. As in many other countries throughout the world in the late 1960s, and for many similar reasons, Poland's "golden youth" (as the party press contemptuously termed them) demanded a society that lived up to the guarantees of freedom in the nation's constitution.

Ironically enough, it began with a fight over Mickiewicz, the Polish national poet, whose monument stands not far from the gates of the University of Warsaw. *Forefathers' Eve*, the epic drama portraying nineteenth century Russian despotism and the Polish struggle for freedom, was staged at the national theatre in late 1967 to mark the 50th anniversary of the Soviet revolution. "Am I to be free? Yes/ Where this news came from I do not know, but I am alive to what it means to be free under the hands of a Muscovite." Lines such as these brought the audience to its feet, cheering. The Polish censors decided to act. Mickiewicz was banned. At the end of the last performance on January 30, 1968, the audience cheered and applauded for half an hour, sang the national anthem, and then marched into the wintry Warsaw streets toward the monument of the poet. Brutality was soon added to philistinism as the police converged on the crowd and a scuffle broke out. In the days that followed, as the state built its case against the students it believed were responsible, particularly two young activists named Adam Michnik and Henryk Szlaifer, an ugly streak of anti-Semitism surfaced. This caused Jacek Kuron, recently released from prison, to warn the students against the dangers of "fascist provocation."

Meanwhile, at the Writers' Union, the outrage of banning Mickiewicz sparked a bitter debate in February. Kolakowski, the philosopher, was perhaps the most eloquent: "We have reached a shameful situation where the whole of dramaturgy, from Aeschylus through Brecht, has become a collection of allusions to People's Poland." He was furious, and his contempt ripped through the facade of what officially passed for cultural life. "Let us consider the appalling and miserable system of information in the press, let us consider the restrictions and harassment practiced in Poland in the humanities, in current history, sociology, political science and the law. Let us consider the poor, deplorable discussions in which no one ever dares say what is really the matter, for everything leads to the forbidden fruit." Kolakowski, who had himself been expelled from the party, declared: "I imagine a kind of socialist life in which this unbearable and destructive state of affairs, where cultural creativity and reflections on it are felt as permanently dangerous by the state, which uses suppressive countermeasures, shall be abolished. We want the abolition of such a situation in the name of socialism, not against it."

A week later, during the first days of March, student activists Michnik and Szlaifer were expelled. Two days later, several thousand students gathered to protest. Hundreds of plain-clothes police had entered the campus, forming a cordon around the students, and the inevitable happened. Outside the main gate of the University of Warsaw a massive squad of uniformed police, steel-helmeted and armed with clubs, rushed the campus and charged students indiscriminately. The scene was little different from those to be seen that year at campuses from Berkeley to the Sorbonne. As elsewhere, the administrators at Warsaw felt their sensibilities bruised at the unexpected ferocity of the watchdogs they had loosed.

The next day, the local press blatantly lied about the events that had occurred. In response, the students marched toward the newspaper offices to protest. In an hour's time, they were joined by 20,000 ordinary citizens who saw that the purpose of the demonstration went far beyond the mere rights of students. The police charged without warning, and mayhem broke out on the Marszalkowska and other main streets of Warsaw. That weekend Kuron and Modzelewski were rearrested.

On Monday, March 11, 1968, more than 3,000 students and teachers assembled at the university to draw up new protests in defence of democracy, against anti-Semitism, and to demand restoration of academic rights and punishment of the police riot. By that afternoon 700 more young people were under arrest, and the authorities attempted to seal off Warsaw. They failed. In the next three days, student uprisings occurred in Gdansk, Katowice, Krakow, Lodz, Poznan, Szczecin and Wroclaw.

The party responded to all this with acrimonious speeches from Gomulka, the ageing first secretary, and from regional leaders such as Edward Gierek, who denounced the "reactionary minority" and "revisionism." The main tactic of the party, apart from bluster, was to ensure that the workers did not ally themselves with the students. Those that attempted to do so were quickly and forcibly dissuaded. However, when the students held sit-ins at their universities, the public came and fed them, belying the myth in the party press that the students were isolated in Polish society. The church, in a letter signed by Cardinals Wyszynski and Wojtyla and the bishops of Poland, called for the students' release and an investigation into police brutality. The events of March, as they came to be known, ended with the firing of Kolakowski and several internationally known Polish scholars.

The end of March wasn't, however, the end. Throughout this springtime of protest, as students and intellectuals in Poland went to the barricades to defend the right of free speech for a nineteenth century poet, they frequently referred with approval to contemporary events taking place in neighboring Czechoslovakia. There, the ruling communist party, supported by intellectuals, was carrying out a series of liberal reforms from the top. On the night of August 20, 1968, the Czechoslovakian experiment in humanizing socialism was ended by invasion. While Polish students and intellectuals protested the tanks of the Warsaw Pact countries that rolled into Prague, they soon had even more immediate affairs to attend to.

Beginning in September and continuing well into spring of the following year, the Gomulka regime carried out a series of arrests and trials of Polish intellectuals. In Warsaw, Wroclaw, Krakow and Lodz, those who thought the impermissible were charged and tried in camera for the crime of "publicly degrading the Polish nation" and violating various other convenient articles of the criminal code. As if the proceedings weren't repulsive enough, the interrogations and other attempts to extract confessions were infested with anti-Semitism. As Jacek Kuron told the court, "The examining officers made a great effort to find a Jewish name among my ancestors. When they were not able, however, to make a Jew of me, they tried to make me at least a Ukrainian...There were days during the pretrial proceedings when I was ready to become a Jew. For there are certain situations in which any honest person should consider himself Jewish." Kuron was sentenced to three-and-a-half years, as was, again, Karol Modzelewski, in January 1969. The following month, Adam Michnik received a three year sentence.

Michnik, like his mentor, Kuron, was undaunted. Since it was impossible to address his judges, Michnik defended himself before history. "I wanted my country to have more freedom, more justice and more equality," he said from the dock. "I wanted the people of my country to live without fear, in other words—if I may put it this way—that the windows of our houses might look toward the sun."

Stanislaw Kociolek was worried. Having recently moved up the ladder from his previous post as party first secretary in the Gdansk region to become deputy premier, Kociolek was attempting to explain to his former colleagues the party's plan for drastic increases in the price of consumer goods, set to go into effect the next day, Sunday, December 13, 1970. The members of the Gdansk provincial committee, huddled together on a damp Saturday afternoon in their downtown party headquarters, were incredulous.

Was the party completely unaware that in this "people's democracy" of more than 30 million Catholic churchgoers, a major religious holiday season was about to begin? Did it think that raising the price of beef, pork, flour, jam and coffee at a time of year when consumers were about to splurge would go unnoticed? And weren't the simultaneous price reductions of televisions, car radios and tape recorders likely to merely emphasize the difference between haves and have-nots, despite the alleged ever-diminishing class differences in Polish society? The provincial committee called it "madness."

Kociolek nervously phoned first secretary Gomulka in Warsaw. There would be no going back, said the party leader. That evening, Radio Warsaw delivered the news.

It was still dark on Monday morning when a column of workers marched out the Second Gate of the Lenin Shipyard into the streets of downtown Gdansk. They massed in front of the headquarters of the Polish United Workers Party, tying up mid-morning traffic as they spilled into the street. A minor party official emerged from the building to order them back to work. "In our workers' democracy, there is a time and a place..." They shouted him down. Somewhere in the restive gathering a fight broke out. The shipyard workers seized a police car that had moved in on the scene. The crowd grew.

In Warsaw, First Secretary Gomulka, addressing a plenary session of the party's central committee, droned on about the crucial economic tasks facing the country in the coming year. By noon, news of the disturbances in Gdansk was being whispered about the hall. Delegates drifted into the lobby where a second, unofficial plenary session took place. Inside, Gomulka stubbornly continued to preside over the formalities.

The first clashes between demonstrators and the militia in the streets of Gdansk occurred around four in the afternoon. Two hours later the crowd—more than 3,000 people—attacked the party headquarters. Soon smoke was pouring out of the party's basement printing plant. Security police and militia moved in behind a cloud of tear gas. Instead of dispersing, the protesters surged across the street, toward the railroad station. By ten that night, scattered fires—burning buses, police cars, some shops— flickered angrily throughout the Baltic port.

Gomulka decided that it was counter-revolution. At midnight, he put his lieutenant, politburo member Zenon Kliszko, on a plane for Gdansk. Ignacy Loga-Sowinski, the politburo member responsible for trade unions, went with him. From Warsaw's squat, white party headquarters, whose lights remained on well into the night, the first messages were sent to Russian party boss Leonid Brezhnev in Moscow.

By the time the column of workers marched toward the Gdansk militia building the next morning, Tuesday, December 15, Kliszko had established an "operational command" in the provincial trade union headquarters. Soon a haze of tear gas and police helicopters hovered over downtown Gdansk as pitched battles between workers and security forces ebbed and flowed from the municipal council building to the railroad station. Columns of black smoke rose into the grey early morning sky.

As groups of workers left the Lenin Shipyard to join the demonstration, the first shots were fired. Over the loudspeakers in the shipyard, warnings were issued against venturing into the streets. In the uproar, no one listened. At the gates, they were hit by a hail of bullets from police and militia guns. The yards were surrounded. The workers backed off. In front of the gate, bodies lay on the pavement.

A few blocks away, the crowd of 10,000 soon knew. They retaliated with Molotov cocktails that smashed through the windows of the PUWP headquarters. The party building was quickly engulfed in flames.

At the end of the day, the results of the riots were grimly tallied: the headquarters of the provincial party committee, the municipal council building, and the railroad station were smoldering. Six people were dead, 300 injured, 120 arrested. At dinnertime, Deputy Premier Kociolek went on Gdansk television to claim that "the demonstrations and riots have been exploited by hooligans and social scum." That night, Kliszko hastily assembled the provincial party committee. Only half the members appeared (the rest were on strike). "Do you realize, comrades, what is happening?" an infuriated Kliszko asked. "The party building is on fire. This is counter-revolution." Kliszko phoned Gomulka to confirm the "correct" interpretation of what was occurring in the curfew-closed streets of the Tri-Cities.

Kliszko moved unhesitatingly. In Gdynia, where the municipal council had held amicable meetings with striking Paris Commune Shipyard workers throughout the day, the arrest of the council and the strike committee delegates was ordered. In the middle of the night, Kliszko called up the army. The tanks rolled into Gdansk at 4 a.m. on Wednesday morning.

In the Lenin Shipyard 5,000 workers gathered in front of the administration building, demanding that their grievances be

negotiated. In Gdynia, the workers took over the Paris
Commune Shipyard. Throughout the region, a sporadic general
strike spread as freshly elected strike committees, bypassing the
old union structures, drew up lists of demands at one enterprise
after another. From the school windows, kids watched the
tanks and troop carriers awkwardly grind through the streets.
On television, Kociolek appealed to the shipyard workers to
"resume your normal work."

When the commuter trains arrived at the Paris Commune
stop at 5:30 on Thursday morning, the workers emerging from
the packed cars were met by a cordon of militia, army, and
security police positioned between the railroad station and the
yards. A voice over the army loudspeaker called on the workers
to go back. In the pre-dawn, the crowd swelled with each
arriving train and pressed toward the tanks. Bullets suddenly
ricochetted off the paving stones under their feet. A bridge
above the train tracks was set ablaze. Helicopters swooped in,
dropping cannisters of tear gas. They battled into the early
afternoon. The dead were carried in the streets of Gdynia on
temporary biers made of railway carriage doors ripped from
their hinges.

Further west along the Baltic coast, in Szczecin, the militant
workers of the Adolf Warski Shipyard, like their counterparts
in Gdansk and Gdynia, were framed in the gunsights of the
state. By evening curfew, the party headquarters were gutted
and sixteen people were dead, according to official estimates. In
Gdynia, the death toll was placed at thirteen. In both places, it
was believed that the actual figures were more than twice those
of the official count.

That night in Warsaw, Gomulka didn't sleep. Reports of
strikes in other parts of the country began to filter in. In the
north, clashes had occurred in Elblag and Slupsk, as well as in
the larger cities. The Polish party boss asked his defence
minister, General Wojciech Jaruzelski, what the army would do
in case of an all-out uprising. When Jaruzelski replied
noncommittally, Gomulka made up his mind. He wired
Brezhnev in Moscow requesting Soviet military assistance in
putting down "the counter-revolution in the country." Then
he waited.

The answer came before dawn on Friday, December 18.
Brezhnev refused. Gomulka was finished. By morning, the
jockeying for power within the politburo was underway. As

streetfighting in Szczecin continued throughout the day, Gomulka, exhausted and weakening, resisted calls for a summoning of the politburo. On Saturday, the politburo met for a gruelling seven-hour session. Gomulka and his group held out as long as they could. Finally, the deadlock was broken and the decision taken to ask for the old party leader's resignation in favor of Edward Gierek. That night Gomulka suffered a minor stroke and was taken on a stretcher out of the party headquarters to hospital. A couple of hours later, on Sunday morning, he scrawled his signature on the official resignation statement. Throughout the day, planes brought central committee members to Warsaw where they met, in emergency session just outside the city, at the Natolin castle. At 7:45 p.m. the announcement was broadcast over Polish media. Fifteen minutes later Edward Gierek appeared on television.

The newly elected first secretary of the Polish communist party was conciliatory. Instead of talking about counter-revolution, Gierek acknowledged that workers had taken part in the uprising, that people had been killed, that the working class had been "provoked beyond endurance" and that the party must answer to the people. Although the price increases would not be revoked, there would be wage increases, promised the new leader.

The significance of the brutal events that had just occurred would not become clear for another two months, but as the smoke of burning buildings and tear gas dissipated, it was possible to glimpse a new outline of power relations in Poland. Notwithstanding the unceasing propaganda about the role of the working class, for the first time in a socialist regime, the actual working class—sans "vanguard" party, national organization or force of arms—had become a political factor. The workers, at significant physical cost to themselves (as many as 100 dead), had rejected, and to some degree were responsible for, changing the communist party leadership.

This assertiveness of the working class was all the more remarkable given the circumstances. It lacked an organizational structure (democratically chosen strike committees and civic inter-factory committees did, however, provide rudimentary organization). It was without a national leadership of its own (although local leaders such as Lech Walesa and Anna Walentynowicz appeared in Gdansk, as did similar figures elsewhere). It didn't have support from other social sectors (efforts to win over students and intellectuals had, in most cases, been rebuffed). Nonetheless, the Polish working class constituted a unique phenomenon in the communist world. That they were a force to be permanently reckoned with became apparent in the first two months of 1971. A fresh wave of strikes—although less known to the outside world than the headline-commanding outbreaks of December—required the personal intervention of Gierek, representing a humbled party, to defuse the situation.

The holiday period had no sooner ended than the workers along the Baltic demanded serious responses to their unanswered questions. They were not to be satisfied with conciliatory phrases. By the first week of January, the Lenin Shipyard workers were again on strike. A few days later, the Warski yards in Szczecin were on the verge of shutdown. The party saw to it that a few heads rolled (trade union boss Loga-Sowinski resigned; here and there a party provincial secretary got the boot), but mere personnel shuffles would not appease the shipbuilders. By mid-month, striking Gdansk workers had drawn up a comprehensive list of demands that called for everything from publication of a complete list of those killed and injured during December to free trade union elections. On January 23, the city of Szczecin went on strike.

Gierek and his prime minister, Piotr Jaroszewicz, stepped out of their limousine at the gates of the Warski shipyard the next evening and walked into a mass meeting with the shipyard workers. After strike committee chairman Edmund Baluka read out a list of demands that called for major changes in the decision-making process, the first secretary took the podium. Gierek was properly, even shrewdly, humble. "I say to you: help us, help me...When it was proposed that I take over the leadership of the party, at first I thought I would refuse...I am only a worker like you. But if I had done that, there would have been a bloodbath. You will tell me that a bloodbath took place anyway, that there were many deaths. That is true, and I pay homage to those who fell." However calculated, it was an impressive, moving performance as the former coal miner pleaded with the shipbuilders long after midnight. They did not let Gierek off easily. One worker after another rose and spoke, impressing on the new leader the exact nature of the outrages that had occurred.

"People were falling, bullets were whistling and those bullets were bought with money earned by our sweat," declared a delegate from the large hull department. "That's really too hard to bear. How is it possible that the working class can be turned against the working class?" Dozens of others spoke with equal frankness. Nine hours later, as morning broke and the meeting came to an end, Gierek asked them for their help and the workers said they would give it. Although the concessions actually offered by Gierek fell far short of the workers' demands, the confrontation was, by communist standards, a most unusual event. The next day the scene was repeated at the Lenin Shipyard. The denouement, however, occurred more than two weeks later in the textile mills of Lodz.

This time, Prime Minister Jaroszewicz went to the strike-bound textile city for a raucous all-night session with the plant workers, most of them women. "Do you support us?" shouted the prime minister in what by now had become a rote-like conclusion to these face-to-face encounters. "Yes!" answered the workers. "Are you going to help us?" asked Jaroszewicz, echoing Gierek's newly popular slogan.

"No!" answered the women of Lodz. "You have to help us first."

The next evening, the government capitulated to the Lodz strikers. Radio Warsaw announced that meat prices would be returned to the pre-December 13 levels. The workers' veto had been established.

Jacek Kuron, the resilient rebel, said it best. As though he were composing the collective epitaph of Poland's men in power, Kuron cried out in a voice rasping with contempt: "They have learned nothing and understood nothing."

Perhaps it was a moment of political amnesia. Or perhaps, as the official ideology had it, the forces of circumstance had accumulated to dictate an "inevitable" course of action. In any case, Edward Gierek attempted the very thing that had brought Gomulka's regime to grief and himself to power a half-decade earlier. On June 24, 1976, as the first secretary listened from his seat in the chamber of the Sejm, Prime Minister Jaroszewicz read "The Motion of the Council of Ministers on the subject of a proposal to make certain changes in the structure of retail prices and the principles on which the nation is to be compensated for the effects of these changes." Among the proposed staggering price increases: sausage up 90 per cent, cheaper meat cuts increased by 50 per cent, poultry 30 per cent, butter 50 per cent, sugar doubled, vegetables up a third. The proposal, made on a Thursday, provided for "consultation" with the nation on Friday, consideration by the parliament on Saturday, and implementation by Sunday.

As irrational as this plan would appear within 24 hours, it nonetheless had a rationale. In the respite provided by the workers after 1971, Gierek embarked upon a new, and ultimately reckless, economic course. He had inherited from his predecessors—despite five-year plans, exuberant slogans, production quotas and all the other paraphernalia of central planning—a chaotic agricultural system and an inefficient industrial base. The consequences were chronic shortages of foodstuffs and consumer goods. Whereas Gomulka had run the economy with deflationary and spartan caution, Gierek opted for all-out expansion, whatever the cost. His solution was a rapid modernization of industry intended to produce hard-currency-earning exports and to enable the government to import more food from the West. Borrowing from the East and West, and buoyed up by a short-term boom in coal, Poland's staple export, the new regime moved boldly.

The first years of Gierek's entrepreneurial strategy were apparently prosperous. Between 1970 and 1975, according to official figures, wages rose by 60 per cent, even more than the five-year plan called for. A good share of this new purchasing power was spent on food. Consumption of meat and meat products jumped from 118 to 156 pounds per person. To satisfy demand, Poland had to buy from abroad. From a net exporter of food, it became a net importer, as purchases of grain (primarily for fodder) climbed steadily. What also climbed steadily, since, for political reasons, prices were frozen, was the cost of food subsidies as a portion of the annual budget.

In the long run, the game plan failed. Poland borrowed heavily to import needed Western technology. The debts were supposed to be paid by re-exporting finished goods, but production was hampered by mismanagement, and foreign markets were reduced by the Western recession of the mid-1970s. Spiralling bills for imported oil, 80 per cent of which came from the Soviet Union, added to the difficulties. Moscow's preferential rates, though well below the prices of the Oil Producing and Exporting Countries (OPEC), nonetheless rose sharply. Instead of selling exports for hard Western currency, Warsaw had to divert more trade to the Soviet Union. Rather than returning hard currency, exports were used to service a mounting foreign debt. Hence, the prime minister's proposal to make "certain changes in the structure of retail prices."

The next morning the Polish proletariat "consulted" on the matter of the proposed price hikes. Although lacking the stately pace of parliamentary proceedings, their deliberations were not devoid of flair. The tractor workers of Ursus, outside Warsaw, stormed out first, occupying the nearby railway line, tearing up tracks and blocking trains, including the Paris-Moscow express. In Radom, an industrial city south of Warsaw, the employees walked out, stopping along the way to consult with workers in other factories. By the time they reached the provincial party headquarters, they had been joined by young people from the local technical and vocational schools, as well as by thousands of housewives.

The provincial first secretary's deputy was sent out to reason with these typical representatives of the nation. A woman member of the impromptu Radom strike committee, carrying her small child, said that she earned 2,200 zlotys a month and that it wasn't enough to feed her child. The deputy, outfitted in a rather elegant suit, attempted sarcasm. If the woman was so concerned for the child, she shouldn't have brought it to the demonstration, he said. She replied by hitting the startled bureaucrat with her shoe. A worker in worn overalls asked the price of the deputy's suit. Then, in a modern variation on the tale of the emperor's clothes, the party dignitary was quickly stripped to his underwear by the angry crowd, and sent fleeing into headquarters, a graphic illustration of the government's latest threadbare proposal to the workers.

The "consultations" spread like wildfire. In Plock, a once-sleepy town that was now a bustling petrochemical centre, the Friendship Pipeline that brought in Soviet oil was turned off. The women weavers of Lodz stopped their shuttles. The workers of Poznan summoned the ghosts of 20 summers past. At the Lenin Shipyard in Gdansk, the shipbuilders laid down their tools.

That same evening, June 25, Prime Minister Jaroszewicz was rushed into a television studio to inform the public that the government had decided to withdraw the proposed price increases. Dictated by the "highest interest in the nation," said the prime minister, the government thought it necessary to reanalyse the whole matter. It could have left it at that. It didn't.

Instead, the government embarked on a policy of reprisal against the working class. In Radom, where the party headquarters had been burned and two workers had died in the day's revolt, the security forces were spoiling for revenge. Given a free hand, they beat up and arrested anybody they could collar. The hasty in camera trials of Radom and Ursus workers, and the draconian sentences meted out to them (three to seven years), were merely the semi-visible face of a vast purge involving arrests, beatings and mass firings in factories throughout the country. Everywhere, the alleged ringleaders were fingered and dismissed, including a young electrician named Walesa at the Lenin Shipyard.

This time, however, the workers were no longer alone. As unprecedented as was the sight of the working class battling the "workers' state," equally novel was the appearance of the nation's intellectuals at the side of those to whom the cadences of the "Internationale" had promised "all."

The stirrings of the Polish intelligentsia predated the 1976 workers' revolt by six months. In late 1975 the government proposed changes to the Polish constitution, among them: that "the Polish United Workers' Party is the leading political force in the building of socialism"; a "civil-rights" threatening clause stating that "the rights of citizens are inseparably linked with the thorough and conscientious fulfilling of duties to the fatherland"; and finally a statement that Polish foreign policy would be "based on strengthening friendship and co-operation with the Soviet Union..." (Sardonic Polish optimists noted that this last was not quite as servile as the similar East German constitutional clause which declared the GDR to be "forever and irrevocably allied with the USSR...")

The first of several protests against the proposed amendments to the constitution was addressed to the Sejm by 59 Polish writers, lawyers, clerics and academicians. The signatories—including Kuron, Michnik and other luminaries—of what came to be known as the Memorandum of the 59, authorized the octogenerian doyen of Polish economists, Edward Lipinski, to present the protest to parliament. The document took up the issue of fundamental freedoms—of conscience, religion, work, expression, information and knowledge. "There is no freedom to work," said the 59, "when the state is the sole employer and when trade unions are subordinate to a party that virtually runs the state...workers should be allowed freely to elect their own representatives in the professional field, in order to make them independent of party and state. The right to strike should also be guaranteed." The 59 worked their way up to their main point: the fundamental freedoms they had cited "are not compatible with the prepared, official recognition of the leading role of only one party within the state." The logic was obvious. "Such recognition by the constitution would confer upon that party the character of a state agency, beyond control of public opinion. Under these circumstances, the Sejm cannot be regarded as the supreme body of power, the government as the highest executive arm, nor courts as independent." In short, a constitutional monstrosity had been produced; the constitution, which was to protect freedoms, authorized a body which could overrule them. If nothing else, such exercises put the intelligentsia in something of a state of readiness when summer 1976 came. If the intellectuals had held aloof from the workers in 1970 (as the workers had from them two years before), this time there was no standing on ceremony.

No sooner had the courts acted than the Polish novelist, Jerzy Andrzejewski, author of *Ashes and Diamonds*, responded with an unequivocal and moving open letter "to the persecuted participants of the workers' protest":

> Being deeply concerned and embittered by the wrongs and injustices which you are suffering and as each day brings fresh confirmation that many share my thoughts and feelings, I wish to extend to you in these your difficult days expressions of respect and solidarity and to send words of hope and encouragement.
>
> I realize that in the face of court verdicts sentencing you to many years of imprisonment, in the face of violence and physical oppression to which you were subjected and amidst feelings of helplessness which are your daily bread and which are the heaviest of defeats to suffer in all of human degradation, and in the face of your imperilled material existence resulting from the mass dismissals from work that fall to your lot each day, my words are just words and their gravity is incommensurably slight in comparison with your sufferings.

Although the intellectuals would soon discover weapons beyond their familiar arsenal of words, that they could see through, and stand up against, the system of misinformation was a start.

> I wish you to know that at a time when the authorities use the press, radio and television in an attempt to mislead public opinion and to turn its attention away from the real reasons for the crisis that has arisen, by making allegations against you of socially damaging activity, of destructive anarchy or even of hooliganism—there are people in Poland who are immune to deception and hypocrisy and have preserved the ability to discern truth from falsehood and who see in you, the persecuted workers, not only spokesmen for an immediate and specific cause, but, above all, fighters for true socialist democracy and for social liberty, without which all freedom perishes and deceitful cliches reign over public life.

Andrzejewski demanded amnesty, rehabilitation and reinstatement for the protesters. Kuron, Michnik, Lipinski and others immediately issued a statement:

> We declare our solidarity with the workers of Poland. A sense of responsibility for the fate of the nation and of the state requires us to recognize the gravity of the situation. The events of the last few days have proved that in the system of government presently prevailing the only form in which the real attitudes of people can find expression is outbursts of social discontent...

Already, the outlines of a strategy were taking shape. The authors noted that the government had promised a "penetrating examination" of price proposals, a dialogue with the nation. But how, they wondered, could a dialogue be held "in conditions of reprisal"?

> For authenticity of an all-national debate it is necessary to extend democratic freedoms in an essential way. On the agenda is the establishment of a real representation of the workers; without it nowadays it is not possible to study effectively the needs and aspirations of our society. In

their present form the trade unions do not fulfil this role. Recent events have once again confirmed how completely fictitious the unions are. It is also impossible to envisage any kind of serious and effective public discussion in the absence of an independent press. Public opinion cannot freely take shape and find expression unless freedom of association is guaranteed.

A month after the protests, the Polish intellectuals, through an open letter, took their case to "world public opinion."

We consider it our duty to oppose the description of a workers' protest against an unjust social policy and authoritarian methods of government, as "outbreaks of hooliganism."

They fought to restore meaning to ordinary language. To do so, they drew upon the ideological wellsprings of the regime responsible for the distortions. "The struggle of the Polish people for their rights...is a struggle for democratic socialism which, in accordance with the words of Karl Marx, we conceive to be the antithesis of 'any conditions in which man becomes a creature degraded, deprived of his freedom, abandoned and rendered worthy of contempt.'" Not content with appealing simply to other intellectuals, Kuron wrote directly to the general secretary of the Italian Communist Party, Enrico Berlinguer, as a spokesman of the more moderate and autonomous "Eurocommunism" then in vogue. Kuron argued that the workers could not be held "morally and legally" responsible for the demonstration, for had they had the means to express their opinions freedly, they would not have been provoked to cause damage. For this, the system was responsible. "It is a vendetta by men who, during their 30 years in power," said Kuron, "have learned nothing and understood nothing." Only a general amnesty for all participants in the June events "can arrest the terror against the workers. I know that your voice counts in Western Europe, as well as with the Polish authorities," he told Berlinguer. "I appeal to your conscience. Do not be indifferent to this cause." The Italian party was responsive. Kuron's letter appeared immediately in *L'Unita*, the party daily, and the central committee urged their Polish party counterparts to show "moderation and clemency."

In September 1976, there was a turning point in the relations between workers and intellectuals in Poland, though it would not be clear for some time that the intellectuals' solidarity would extend well beyond verbal declarations. It was recognized that the families of the convicted workers were in no position to hire adequate defence lawyers or to support themselves financially. On September 23, Jerzy Andrzejewski delivered to the Polish parliament the appeal that founded the Committee for the Defence of the Workers (KOR).

> The victims of the reprisals cannot count on any help or defence from the established institutions, such as the trade unions, which played a deplorable role. The society in whose interests the protesters were persecuted should now take up their cause. Society has no other method of defence against lawlessness except solidarity and mutual aid. That is why the undersigned formed the Committee for the Defence of the Workers to initiate versatile forms of such defence and aid.

The creation of KOR, seen in retrospect, was a brilliant tactical response to the totalitarian state. Several things were accomplished simultaneously. First, workers and their families were materially aided as hundreds of thousands of zlotys poured into the committee's coffers and were distributed. Second, the communiques issued by KOR disclosed precise details of the activities of the security agents, thus breaking the state's monopoly on information. At the same time, a Polish *samizdat* or underground press was created. Finally, a set of concepts was developed for organizing against the regime.

At first, party leader Gierek confined himself to ridiculing the committee members. "Depending on the situation and the group they wish to address, these people dress themselves in the garb of spokesmen of democracy, of defenders of national sovereignty and/or of the economic and social rights of the working people." By November, the party moved on to deeds, arresting KOR members. Others were fired from their jobs: Antoni Macierewicz, a Warsaw University lecturer, and Miroslaw Chojecki, a researcher at the Nuclear Research Institute. In December, the police raided the homes of Kuron, Lipinski and others.

As the trials continued and the crudely-printed communiques

circulated throughout Poland, Kuron and Michnik began to ponder the implications of what they had initiated. The obvious connection between current and later events makes it worth pausing briefly to follow their thinking. In an essay titled "Reflections on a Program of Action," written in November 1976 ("a hurried and brief attempt to reconstruct a previous version confiscated by the security men who searched my house on November 3," noted the author), Kuron attempted to make sense of "the depth of the current economic, political and social crisis in Poland which is now universally understood."

At the heart of the problem, as diagnosed by Kuron, was totalitarianism. "The present Polish socio-political system may be defined as a sum total of conditions most likely to give the party and government absolute control over the lives of individuals." In a totalitarian system such as this, "the power and the people are separated. All power—to initiate, to think, to decide—rests exclusively with the government. The people are destined to become an amorphous mass, with no personal rights of any kind." Worse, it was a system that hadn't been chosen by Poles.

> The totalitarian system was forced upon Poland over 30 years ago by the armed forces of the Soviet Union with the acquiescence of the Western powers, in particular the United States and Great Britain. The system's stability is guaranteed by the readiness of the Soviet Union...to reimpose it by force on any nation attempting to free itself. We should add that there are serious reasons for believing that the Polish government has to check all important decisions with the Soviet leadership. The Polish State is not sovereign and in the minds of our people this is the evil at the root of our political life.

It could not be put more plainly. Moving next to "the aims of the opposition," Kuron offered the goal—not as simplistic as it first appears—of parliamentary democracy as a substitute for totalitarianism. Although Kuron was quick to concede that parliamentary democracy "still leaves much to be desired," nonetheless, it "has been successful in providing conditions for individual aspirations to be fulfilled as far as leisure is concerned. It has failed to do so for individuals as workers. I am convinced that the solution of this remaining problem is crucial for humanity." Thus, while not harboring illusions about parliamentary democracy as a panacea, Kuron argued that it was a reasonable intermediate goal. The problem for the opposition and its campaigns of resistance to the regime, Kuron pointed out, was that the extent of its activities were determined "by the response of society on the one hand and on the other by the readiness on the part of the USSR to intervene militarily."

Finally, in sketching the rudiments of a program, Kuron argued that the principal need was "for an organized representation of industrial workers, particularly those employed in very large enterprises...Its demands should be backed by the professional advice of economists, engineers, lawyers and sociologists." Kuron foresaw the need for the creation of groups in every sector—among peasants, intellectuals, students, workers—linked by bonds of solidarity and communicating through an independent publishing movement. In short, society, unable to challenge the monopoly of "political power," should seek to carve out a territory—"civil society"—that might exist somewhat independently from the totalitarian state. It was an odd idea. But then, again, few had attempted to conceive the actual forms of resistance to a totalitarian political structure which claimed to exercise its authority in the name of the laboring masses. That its prognostications should bear some resemblance to the actual organization of social forces in Poland five years later is, at least, noteworthy.

About the same time, Kuron's younger colleague, Adam Michnik, published an essay called "The New Evolutionism." It too took account of the limitations that must be observed, and the centrality of the role of the workers. He held out no hope for "revisionism," the movement of the inner renovation of the party conceived during the mid-1950s. "A movement which would base itself on Marxism-Leninism or on some of its elements to produce a reform in the existing system is hardly conceivable: In Poland today the Marxist-Leninist doctrine is nothing but an empty shell, its gestures nothing but an official rite. It no longer provokes controversies, no longer excites emotions." Michnik's "new evolutionism," which might lead to Poland's transformation, realistically acknowledged that social, economic and political changes "have to be made, at least in their first stage, in line with the 'Brezhnev doctrine.'" Michnik elaborated his main thesis.

...the realization of the power of the workers who, by their firm and resolute attitude, have already wrested some spectacular concessions from the government. It is difficult to foresee the evolution of attitudes among the workers, but without any doubt it is of them that the government is really afraid; it is the pressure of this social class which is the *sine qua non* of the evolution of national life toward democratization. This will not be a simple process, nor one easy to foresee happening. It implies that every time one breaks down the barrier of fear, one formulates a new political consciousness. The fact that workers' institutions and unions have been destroyed threatens to slow down this process. But the first sign of the workers' new consciousness was revealed on the day that one saw the rebirth of the first independent organization for workers' defence, the day one saw strike committees formed in the shipyards at Szczecin and Gdansk. It is difficult to foretell when and how other—more durable—workers' institutions will see the light of day and what their shape will be: workers' commissions on the Spanish model, independent trade unions, solidarity funds? It is certain however that at the moment of their creation, "new evolutionism" will take shape and will cease to be a spiritual construction in search of hope.

By February 1977, Gierek began to use the word "clemency." It was too late to stem the unfolding of a "democratic opposition" whose semi-clandestine newspapers and completely open representatives now appeared in Poland's major cities. In March, the "Movement for the Defence of Human and Civil Rights" was founded in Warsaw. In May, in Krakow, a Student Solidarity Committee appeared, declaring, "There is a need for an independent student movement open to all without regard for political adherence and ideology. Such a movement would provide a platform in which everyone could take part. It would also genuinely represent student interests." The demands of the students were hardly revolutionary, but in Poland it was unheard of to make the demand that "there is a need for far-reaching changes leading to a more democratic structure of the universities and to a genuine participation of students in the planning of the curriculum." In the same month, the editor of the independent Catholic monthly *Wiez*, Tadeusz Mazowiecki, announced the existence of a hunger strike taking place in St. Martin's Church in Warsaw to protest "police terror," "tendentious trials" and "campaigns of lies."

After the killing of a dissident student by the militia in May 1977, the church weighed into the debate. Cardinal Wojtyla openly expressed his criticism of the Polish regime, first condemning all regimes which kill their political enemies, and second, offering a rather startling statement about economic systems: "We are still very far from the liberation of the workers, for which they themselves have fought for one-and-a-half centuries. Having liberated themselves from the capitalist pagan economy, they have fallen prey to the materialist pagan economy, and the people, just as they were slaves before, remain slaves today."

The protests did not abate. Fresh declarations opposed the treatment of workers, and the subsequent attacks on their KOR defenders. On July 22, the Polish government announced an amnesty, freeing the imprisoned KOR members and five workers who had been sentenced to lengthy terms.

Although this remarkable triumph was little known outside Poland, within the country it meant the continuing, even burgeoning, existence of a diversity of civil groups. In October 1977, a group of former members of the communist party central committee, the most prominent of whom was Edward Ochab, who had briefly served as interregnum first secretary of the party prior to Gomulka's reascension, issued a call for political and economic reforms within the PUWP. "At the root of our basic difficulties and misfortunes," said the veteran communists, "lie mainly political reasons. Nondemocratic forms of governing the country are one part of them, but it is mainly the lack of discussion and consultation in determining goals, and the lack of choice in selecting the means needed to solve the country's socio-economic problems that are at fault here." In the same month, 110 signers to the Declaration of the Democratic Movement, including Bogdan Borusewicz, who would pass out strike leaflets along the Gdansk tram lines three summers hence, counted up their gains.

In April 1978, the founding committee of the Free Trade Unions of the Baltic Coast issued a bold pronouncement on the existing workers' organizations: "The Polish trade union movement ceased to exist over 30 years ago." A succinct obituary.

What is necessary today is a process of widespread democratization. The population must continue to struggle for democratic control over its state. All social strata must regain their right to self-determination and be allowed to recreate social institutions which could truly realize society's rights. Only free unions and associations can save the state.

A charter of workers' rights was appended to the declaration. The publication of local editions of the *Worker* multiplied. Along the Baltic, the Young Poland Movement was born in 1979. There were local observances of the events of 1970, of the constitution of 1791—seeming disparate items, but, seen in the context of Polish affairs, clearly convergent matters. To all this was added the remarkable choice of the Polish cardinal, Wojtyla, to become Pope John Paul II, in October 1978. The Pope's visit to his homeland in the summer of the following year, an event which, despite conflicting views on the role of the church in Poland, functioned as a demonstration of the power of the Polish masses, who came out in the millions to greet him.

With declarations of protest multiplying, the state, of course, resisted the struggle over the control of information with all the considerable forces at its command. KOR continued to be harassed. Speakers at "illegal" rallies and ceremonials were arrested and jailed. As late as June 1980, Miroslav Chojecki, director of the independent publishing house Nowa, was before the Polish court demanding: "Why cannot George Orwell's classics be published in Poland? Why do the works of the Nobel laureates, Bertrand Russell, Isaac Bashevis Singer and Jacques Monod, have to be published in the unofficial press? Why is the publication of speeches by John Paul II censored and impeded? It is not we who are on trial in this courtroom: it is freedom of speech and thought, Polish culture and the honor of our society which are on trial."

Thus, from the Radom protests to the morning in August 1980 when Jerzy Borowczak distributed his leaflets, there had unfolded a popular and variegated democratic movement which claimed an ever-larger sphere of civil society in which to operate. The events in a shipyard on the Baltic coast of Poland would, within days, burst upon an astonished world. But Stanislaw Bury, an electrician at the Lenin Shipyard for over two decades, was not surprised: "Beginning in May, when I got out of bed in the morning, I expected a strike every day. I was prepared. I knew that each day could bring the strike."

3   Three Minutes at the Gate

> *In three minutes time, everybody will be able to leave, but I want to say a few words, and for three minutes you can wait.*
> —Alina Pienkowska, August 16, 1980

Klemens Gniech fought back.

Standing on the excavator in front of the massive crowd of workers while newly-acclaimed strike leader Lech Walesa chaired the impromptu meeting, the director of the Lenin Shipyard knew what he had to do. Ten years ago, Gniech had participated in the 1970 uprising. Then, he had been one of the veteran shipyard foremen, a prominent member of the party's factory branch, moving up into the ranks of management. Even after his appointment as director of the shipyard in 1976 at age 38, Gniech saw himself as a "progressive": he was sympathetic to the idea of effective trade unions rather than the moribund ones that now existed. He identified with the "radical" Gdansk provincial party branch, headed by First Secretary Tadeusz Fiszbach, which had been pressing for reforms of the party's disastrous economic course for some time. Gniech didn't feel that the walkout was directed against himself. But he knew that his job now was to end the strike.

Among the sea of faces before him, one striker suggested that the strike committee gather up the demands of the shipyard workers. Within minutes, slips of white paper were being passed among the crowd on their way to Walesa and the other committee members gathered around the power shovel. Where's *Pani* Anna? one of the strikers called out. Anna Walentynowicz's name was taken up. She should be added to the strike committee, another shouted. Yes, and brought to the shipyard in the director's car, someone added. Gniech didn't say anything. The crowd took up the cry. "In the director's car! In the director's car!" they chanted.

Walesa, picking up the cue, announced that the presence of Anna Walentynowicz was a precondition for beginning talks with management. He also demanded that the public address loudspeakers be turned on so that the forthcoming negotiations could be heard throughout the shipyard. The workers voiced their approval. We're going to arrange the demands, Walesa said as he climbed down from the excavator and led the 21-member strike committee off to the canteen at W-4, where he had once worked.

The committee worked through mid-morning, hammering out an initial package of demands. Seated around a big lunchroom table, they drank glasses of tea, and Walesa puffed on the pipe he never seemed to be without. There would have to be reinstatement of Walentynowicz, of course. And Walesa too. They argued for awhile about the size of the desired pay raise, as well as about a cost-of-living clause. An economic package began to take shape. The new meat prices would have to be rolled back. In fact, the whole system of selling meat at "commercial" prices should go. There oughtn't to be any special family allowances for the police or militia either. Or rather, the workers should get the same allowances as the security forces received.

There were non-economic demands also. What about the "free trade unions" that Walesa and others had been advocating for the last two years? That was added, too. Don't forget the ones who got killed in 1970. What happened to the monument to the martyred shipyard workers that had been promised years ago, and then conveniently forgotten by the management while the police harassed those who organized the annual memorial service on December 16? A demand for the monument was put on the list. And we'd better make sure the same thing doesn't happen after this strike as happened in 1976. There has to be a guarantee of no reprisals when it's over.

When the list was ready, they walked through the milling groups of strikers to the administration building. Gniech ushered them into a small conference room and asked the committee members to introduce themselves. They gave their names and the departments they were from. Gniech knew

Walesa and the long-time shipyard men, like Stanislaw Bury,
but the younger ones—Jerzy Borowczak, Bogdan Felski and
some of the others—were strangers to him. Have the preconditions been met? Walesa asked the director, referring to the
loudspeakers and Anna Walentynowicz. The public address
system isn't connected to this conference room, Gniech
explained. When they insisted, he gave ground, suggesting that
they could move to the L-shaped conference building next door.

What about Walentynowicz? Gniech tried to talk them out of
it. She's an old woman, the director said apologetically, and
she's not in good health. All of this will just get her excited. It
might affect her health. Someone from the committee sneered
at this sudden concern. Anyway, there's really no point to her
being here, Gniech went on, things can be settled without her.
Walesa chewed on his pipe, his chin pressed down into his chest,
and shook his head. The strike committee refused to begin talks
without her.

The old woman in the floral print dress got off the No. 12
streetcar at the corner of Grunwald and Hibernia. The security
men were still following her. Anna Walentynowicz went into
one of the stores, pretending to shop, but actually to look for a
phone. It was impossible. There were four plain-clothes men in
the store with her.

Outside again, she waited until a crush of mid-morning
pedestrians had gathered at the corner. When the light changed,
she plunged into the crowd and dashed across the streetcar
tracks that divided Grunwald Avenue, putting enough distance
between herself and the police to get around the corner and
disappear into the nearby residential sidestreets where she ran to
a friend's apartment.

She had run not because she was afraid of being arrested—
she'd been through that before—but because she was
determined to get to the shipyard. There had been an attempted
strike on her behalf the previous January, but it had fizzled,
partly because she had been kept out of the yard, unable to
communicate with her co-workers, while the director talked the
would-be strikers down. Young Andrzej Kolodziej had been
fired for organizing the abortive walkout. This time she wanted
to explain her side of it in person.

From behind the curtains, Walentynowicz could see the
befuddled police agents in the narrow, sunny street below. She

remembered that Lenin, in whose name these plain-clothes men were operating, had once said that if 5 per cent of what a worker says is true, then it should be taken into account. But she had told the whole truth, and they wanted to imprison her for it.

The truth had meant trouble, and it took courage to tell it. It started long ago. Walentynowicz was born in 1929 in the area east of the present Polish border (the boundaries had been shifted westward after World War II). Her father died when the war broke out, and the ten-year-old girl and her family were taken further east, to the Soviet Union. There, her mother died of heart trouble. In 1941, a German military transport took her back to Poland with a family that lived just outside Warsaw. They took care of her. In August 1945, when the war ended, the family moved to a small farm near Gdansk.

A short time later, Anna decided to leave the farm. She got a job in a privately-owned bakery in the city. Soon she decided to apply for a state job and was hired at a margarine factory. Some of the young women she met there were also attending technical school while getting practical training in the factory. Listening to them talk at lunch time, Anna got interested. She, too, wanted to become a skilled worker. A friend suggested that she might get on at the Gdansk shipyard. Once there, she heard that a welder's course was just beginning. She applied for admission and was accepted.

She was part of the new post-war Poland and she worked hard. She believed in all the slogans about patriotism and production and everything else. She wanted everyone to do well. They even sent her to a youth conference in Berlin in recognition of her work.

The trouble began when she realized that the slogans she believed in weren't being put into practice. At factory production meetings she began to criticize the bosses. In response, they claimed that she listened to the illegal Radio Free Europe broadcasts and attempted to punish her. She was made to report to the secret police.

Nonetheless, she continued at her job and continued speaking up. In 1966, she transferred to the W-2 shop where she learned to operate an inside crane. The truth continued to cause trouble. She revealed that union officers had spent dues money on the soccer pools. They responded to her exposure of the fraud by attempting to fire her, but other workers rallied around and prevented the sacking. In 1970, when the strikes broke out all along the Baltic, Walentynowicz, now 40 and still a crane operator at the Lenin Shipyard, was elected to the strike committee.

The real difficulties, though, came after 1976, with the formation of the "democratic opposition." She spoke to people on behalf of the newly-formed Free Trade Unions, distributed leaflets, and even wrote for the clandestine *Coastal Worker*. She had never written anything for publication before. Her first article was called "A Sincere Discussion over a Piece of Meat." It was about First Secretary Gierek's visit to the Lenin Shipyard in July 1978. For days, the shipyard had been a flurry of activity preparing for Gierek. There was new furniture, new carpets, they even tried to make the grass look green. A feast was given in Gierek's honor. The visit cost a million zlotys. Walentynowicz described it all in her article. Ever since then, the state had applied more pressure on her, sometimes attempting bribery, at other times intimidation.

Through the window she saw her next-door neighbor on Grunwald Avenue hurrying down the street toward the flat she was hiding in. It was 11 a.m. The woman was breathless. They're waiting for you, Anna. Yes, in front of your house. The director has sent his car! They want you at the shipyard.

At noon the director's grey Fiat-Lada carying Anna Walentynowicz inched its way into the agitated crowd of strikers waiting at the main gate. When she emerged, a roar of greeting went up, and a huge bouquet of flowers was pressed into her arms. As in a dream, she was carried forward, onto the quickly constructed rostrum. Everywhere she looked, she saw her fellow workers. They didn't trust the authorities, they wanted to see her in person. She took off her glasses, clutching the flowers with one hand and brushing the tears away with the other.

Bogdan Borusewicz woke up from a long sleep. It was 2:30 in the afternoon. He phoned Warsaw. Jacek Kuron told him the strike was going on in the Lenin Shipyard. He was happy. The leaflets he had handed out on the trams early that morning (it seemed like days ago already) had helped.

Now he got busy again. After checking security outside the shipyards to see how easy it would be to get in, Borusewicz went to the dock workers at nearby Nowy Port. They had already heard about the strike. He made arrangements with them to ensure the availability of printing equipment, and then continued his rounds, moving from factory to factory to pass the word.

Alina Pienkowska finished her nursing chores in mid-afternoon and went straight to the Lenin Shipyard. The square beyond the main gate was filled with strikers. Inside the grimy red-brick two-story conference building (the shipyard museum was housed on the second floor), the negotiations had already begun, and the building was bustling. Gniech was prepared to meet the demand for a monument and said he favored a revamping of the union structure. He first hedged on the reinstatement of Anna Walentynowicz, then gave in, but pleaded for more time to deal with the strictly economic issues.

Pienkowska, after greeting her father, a shipyard veteran of 33 years, took stock of the situation. She noticed that nothing had yet been done about food. She prepared a communique to be given to the local radio station appealing for food donations; then she organized a group of students who had gathered outside the main gate. They combed the nearby neighborhoods, collecting food and informing local residents about events in the yard.

In the midst of the chaos, one important decision seemed to have been made spontaneously. In marked contrast to events of the past, the workers had decided to occupy their enterprise and stay within its walls. Marching into the streets to confront the authorities, as in 1970 and 1976, had proved disastrous. This time they would stick to their own territory and turn it into a fortress.

By afternoon, the shipyard workers had taken control of their workplace. They made sure that there was plenty of drinking water, and established contact with the health services in case of medical emergency. Those who lived closest to the yard went home in the late afternoon and brought back mattresses, blankets and food.

In W-4, the electronics workers mounted antennas for the radio so that they could get the Radio Free Europe and BBC broadcasts. When the department manager came through, he asked what was going on. We're making an antenna to hear Radio Free Europe because they're jamming it, answered Stanislaw Bury boldly. The manager didn't say a word. Already, the atmosphere was changing. Before, no one would ever have thought of saying such a thing to the manager. Bury and a friend secured gas, acetylene and electrical equipment. They wanted to be sure that an "accidental" explosion didn't occur, thus giving the militia an excuse to enter the yard.

Here and there, people gathered pieces of canvas, and little tent cities began taking shape. By evening, a workers' militia had been formed to take complete charge of shipyard security. Bury and W-4 were given the job of guarding the main gate. The new militia's first act was to ban vodka from the shipyard.

That night few people slept. In thousands of homes throughout Gdansk, after the children were put to bed, the spouses of the striking shipyard workers stayed up, keeping watch and dozing only fitfully. Long after the combo at the Hotel Monopol put away its instruments and the tourists went to bed, the regional committee of the Polish United Workers Party met at party headquarters a few doors away. First Secretary Fiszbach, who had been kept informed by telephone all day, presided. Director Gniech was present. Some of the comrades were slightly hysterical. There was talk of "anarchy" and "antisocialist forces." Others kept a grip on themselves. A somewhat obscure member of the party's politburo, Stefan Kania, was also in attendance.

In an apartment across town, another kind of gathering was taking place. The militants of the Elmor factory were meeting. Bogdan Lis, Andrzej Gwiazda and a few others planned the details of what would happen at Elmor the next morning. The meeting didn't break up until 4 a.m. In an hour, it would be light out.

The Friday morning sky was just beginning to brighten when Andrzej Kolodziej left the Lenin Shipyard, where he had spent the night. He hitched a ride to Gdynia to the workers' hotel where he was living. He stopped long enough to pick up a pack of cigarettes and his workplace pass, and caught up with some friends at the bus stop who were also on their way to the Paris Commune Shipyard. On the bus, Kolodziej told them about the strike at the Lenin yard. We should also go on strike today, he urged.

Inside the yard, he continued encouraging his co-workers to strike. It was still early, before 6 a.m. Kolodziej approached small groups of workers in the locker room of K-2, the hull department to which he had been assigned the day before. As authoritatively as possible, he told them that the shipyard was definitely going on strike today, and that they shouldn't start work. After putting on his blue overalls, he went out to the square in front of K-2, looking for young people to talk to.

The work brigades were forming up in the square, where they received their daily instructions. Kolodziej went from brigade to brigade, starting with his own, trying to convince them not to start on the ships. The foremen and factory party officials moved in quickly to break up the groups and hustle the men off to work. Gradually, the shipyard workers succumbed to the pressure. Slowly, almost reluctantly, they moved toward the nearby workshops and ships. Kolodziej and two others his own age didn't give up. Instead of going to the job, they moved from group to group, trying to talk the men back to the square. It didn't work. People weren't convinced. They seemed tempted, but it was too dangerous.

Kolodziej and the other two climbed up the partially constructed ship overlooking the yard where they were supposed to be working. We'll wait until the morning break, Kolodziej proposed. I've got copies of the *Robotnik* bulletin we can distribute. I don't know my way around here, but all you've got to do is take me to the biggest canteen in the shipyard. He glanced away from them, looking across the roofs of the workshops and the squares below.

Although he was only 20, he felt as though he had always been part of the opposition. Born in a large family of eight children in Krosno province in southern Poland, near the Czechoslovakian border, he didn't have to look beyond his home to see the conditions in which workers lived. From the moment he began working in the Gdansk shipyard, in late 1977, he was interested in knowing what had happened in the famous Lenin yard. But when he asked his fellow workers in the W-3 department, where he was assembling ship's hatches, about the events of 1970 and 1976, he was surprised at how afraid they were to talk about those days. People simply tried to avoid the topic. You ought to keep your nose out of it, they told him, because there are a lot of people missing and nobody knows what happened to them.

But he couldn't keep his nose out of it, and the more evasive the answers, the more intense was his interest. In December, a month after he had begun work, he joined the workers who participated in the wreath-laying ceremonies at the graves of those who had been killed in 1970. He met activists like Bogdan Borusewicz and Walesa, and others who would organize the Free Trade Unions a few months later. Kolodziej began bringing illegal materials to the shipyard—copies of *Robotnik*, bulletins from KOR, announcements of demonstrations. The longer he worked in the shipyard, the better people got to know him; eventually they stopped suspecting he was a spy. Gradually, as the other workers came to trust him, he brought more and more clandestine literature. Still, they seemed almost afraid to read it, and a few even refused to take copies, fearful they might get caught with it in their possession. But one week when he hadn't brought any materials, some of the workers came up to him in the canteen. They were surprised. How come he hadn't brought anything? That's when he knew he was having an effect.

He also knew from the authorities. They began following him, they searched his house, they detained him for 48 hours. Instead of being intimidated, Kolodziej grew more determined. The management called him in for talks. First, it was once a week, and then, almost daily. They asked him to stop. Then they told him to stop, or else. Why don't you put the charges on paper, the young Kolodziej replied bluntly. The "talks" didn't bring any results. One day at morning break, the manager from Kolodziej's department in W-3, a man named Sztuba, came to the canteen and tried to take the opposition newspapers from the workers' hands. There was an uproar. The workers protested. Sztuba was nearly beaten up. After that, Sztuba was his enemy.

In the late summer of 1979, Kolodziej was working with Andrzej Butkewicz, a printer for the opposition movement. Butkewicz had an apartment in the Old City of Gdansk where the printing equipment was kept. They had just printed an issue of the *Coastal Worker*, and were about to start on the next one. Kolodziej climbed the two flights of stairs and was approaching Butkewicz's flat when, suddenly, the door was flung open and Kolodziej was pulled inside by two men. Butkewicz was sitting at the kitchen table along with another man, his next door neighbor, who was serving as a reluctant witness to the proceedings. The others were cops. After searching the place, they radioed the security people responsible for tailing Butkewicz, who quickly arrived and took the printer away.

Then they went to Kolodziej's and tore his place apart, too.

After that, Kolodziej worked more openly for the opposition. The repression was more open, too. On December 16, 1979, just before the memorial ceremony, he was arrested. When he returned to the shipyard the next day, they punished him for absenteeism. When he went home to Sanok for the Christmas holidays, he was detained. The police offered Kolodziej a statement to sign in which he would pledge to stop his oppositional activities. If you don't sign, we'll get your father fired, they said. When Andrzej got home, his father didn't say anything. Even though there was a large family to support, he knew that his father wouldn't say yes or no, that he'd have to decide for himself. He went back to the station, and refused to sign. He called their bluff.

Back in Gdansk at the beginning of 1980, he teamed up with Anna Walentynowicz. Together, the two of them—the 50-year-old crane-operator and the determined youth from the south—went through the yard, distributing leaflets and newspapers. At the end of January they attempted to organize a strike in the Lenin Shipyard. It failed and Kolodziej was fired. He remained unemployed, but politically active, until he talked his way into a job at the Paris Commune Shipyard.

Hey, what's going on? one of his mates asked, pointing down toward K-2, pulling Kolodziej from his revery. A group of 40 or 50 men were outside in the square. The department managers were there too. Other workers were drifting toward the crowd. Kolodziej clambered down the ship's ladder, his two friends on his heels, and dashed across the dock to the square.

In the crowd, he could feel the tension. It was everywhere. The ones they had first talked to *had* continued to think about it. People were just waiting. Someone cut the electricity. The machinery froze. The air was still. Then it broke. People left their tools, their workplaces. In five minutes, 2,000 workers had poured into the square. There were no leaders, no organizers, no plan, just a mass of people that slowly began walking, almost automatically, toward the Paris Commune administration building. The marchers seemed to be turning. Kolodziej moved to the edge of the crowd and then rushed along the flank to the front, glimpsing men in clean overalls and white hardhats—factory officials—at the head. One of the marchers told Kolodziej they were going to the big canteen to meet with management.

He hesitated for a second. If the bosses got control of the situation, they would talk the workers out of striking. On the spot, Kolodziej made his decision. He ran out in front of the crowd, stopping 20 metres ahead of them. "Hold it! Wait a minute," he cried. The slow-moving wave of blue-overalled men paused. Who was this? A young man, a kid really.

"Listen," he called. "My name is Andrzej Kolodziej. I'm a shipyard worker. I used to work in the Gdansk shipyard. I was just there last night, I know how they organized the strike there." Now they were listening to him. He seemed to know what he was talking about. "I suggest that we shouldn't go to any canteen. We shouldn't start talks with the management. Not yet. We have to get organized, we have to make things clear, and figure out what we want to gain." The words came in a rush. "It's better to go to the square in front of the main gate where we can prepare for the talks." There was applause and shouts of approval, and suddenly the crowd was moving again, with Kolodziej in the lead, toward the main gate.

If the situation at the Paris Commune Shipyard in Gdynia was chaotic and required a 20-year-old militant to give its 10,000 workers direction, at the Elmor factory, just two doors away from the Lenin Shipyard, it went like clockwork. Bogdan Lis and Andrzej Gwiazda went straight to the plant from the all-night meeting where they had planned the strike. At 6 a.m. the shutdown began in the machinery department, P-1, where Lis worked, which started production 45 minutes before the other divisions. They immediately elected an interim co-ordinating group which sent messengers to the various departments throughout the enterprise to announce that the strike had started in P-1 and that delegations should be sent to the factory strike committee.

The effectiveness of the strike mechanism at Elmor was no mystery. Thanks largely to the efforts of Gwiazda and Lis, Elmor had been a militant enterprise for a couple of years. Its 2,000 workers were highly conscious of themselves as a political force—they contributed money to ensure the existence of opposition publications, and the independent press was openly distributed and read in the factory.

Gwiazda, age 45, an electrical engineer and one of the founders of the Free Trade Union movement, was the older of the two strike leaders. Thickly bearded, with dark brown eyes

Jerzy Borowczak

Bogdan
Borusewicz

Photos: Hemingson

Jacek Kuron

Lech Walesa

Anna Walentynowicz

Bogdan Lis

Lenin Shipyard director
Klemens Gniech

Photos: Hemingson

Andrzej Kolodziej

and a heavily lined face, he was widely respected among workers in the region. If the older man presented an Old Testament demeanor, Lis, age 28, with a mop of curly brown hair, aquiline nose, and older-than-his-years blue eyes, was angelic by contrast. He was, however, a seraph with a party card.

Lis had joined the party in 1975, while he was in the army, stationed in Szczecin. He had done so for reasons that were as much practical as political. There was a detested captain in the unit, who had a habit of slapping his men across the face. The other soldiers asked Lis to write up their complaints about the captain. Lis soon realized that the reports of misconduct against the officer would be effective only if they came from someone in the army's party branch. So he joined. The captain was eventually dismissed.

Although many PUWP members were on strike in the nearby Lenin yard (where about a fifth of the 17,000-person work force were in the party), Lis was the sole party member among the strike leadership. However, upon finishing his military service in spring 1976, he had drifted from the PUWP and moved closer to men like Gwiazda. Within Elmor, the two men built a solid opposition organization.

In spring 1980, Lis was still a party member more or less in good standing. He, and other like-minded comrades in the party youth organization, decided to run for election to the party committee in the factory. Their "democratic opposition" slate swept 27 of the 29 seats on the Elmor party executive and soon became ensconced as the official party establishment at Elmor. The higher-ups in the provincial party organization were not amused. A stream of representatives from First Secretary Fiszbach began arriving at Elmor to explain in no uncertain terms that unless factory party chairman Lis resigned, he would find himself without a job. This ultimate irony was not lost on the men: a genuinely popular socialist worker, elected to office by his fellow-workers, was being threatened with dismissal by the workers' party of the socialist state. Lis, of course, refused to step down. When, on Friday, August 15, 1980, the strike began at Elmor, the PUWP factory branch chairman was at its head.

Within the hour 36 elected delegates had arrived from Elmor's various departments. After an initial discussion, they returned to their areas to develop each department's demands.

By nine o'clock in the morning, the Elmor strikers were ready to negotiate with management.

Nor were Elmor and the Paris Commune Shipyard the only ones to join the strike on Friday morning. When Alina Pienkowska went to work at the shipyard clinic that morning, she discovered that the other nurses were angry at her. You help the workers in the yard, they accused her, but you don't think about the health service. What about our demands? But I'm not entitled to represent you, Pienkowska replied; if you want to be represented, you have to elect a strike committee and write up the demands. They promptly did, electing Pienkowska the leader of their strike committee, thus becoming the first enterprise of another profession to join the shipyard workers.

By mid-morning the streetcars and buses had stopped. The 9,000 workers at the Remontow Shipyard across the canal from the Lenin workers were out. So was the 4,000-member crew of the Northern Shipyard next door. So, too, were the dockers at the Northern Harbor. The strike was rapidly spreading, the numbers increasing hourly by thousands of workers. By noon, more than 50,000 workers in the Tri-City ports had followed the lead of the Lenin Shipyard. The news had even reached the tourists at Sopot, who were clambering up from the beaches and packing their bags.

The news had also reached Warsaw. With Gdansk in the fray, the party leaders grasped that the trial of strength was on. For the fourth time in a quarter-century, the workers of Poland were confronting the workers' state. A grim-faced Edward Gierek, his iron-grey brush-cut bristling, arrived at Warsaw airport Friday morning, cutting short his holiday in the Crimea to attend to the crisis.

When Bogdan Borusewicz, on his way to Gdynia and the Paris Commune yard, paused long enough in his organizing trek to phone the capital, he heard nothing at the other end. He dialed again. The phone was dead. The authorities, it would be learned, had cut off communication between the Tri-Cities and the rest of the country.

At the Lenin Shipyard, the centre of the strike, the party also made its move. The strategy obviously had been worked out in the wee hours at provincial party headquarters. Klemens Gniech already had acceded to the two preconditions for talks—admission of Anna Walentynowicz to the yard and the broadcast of negotiations over the public address loudspeakers.

His instructions were to give in to the workers as much as possible and to conclude the strike quickly. Once the Lenin yard had settled, it would be relatively easy to come to terms with the other striking enterprises. When the workers outside the conference building heard Director Gniech suggesting over the loudspeakers that the strike committee should be enlarged to represent all the divisions of the Lenin Shipyard, it sounded only fair. The 22-person committee had been put together hastily and represented only a fraction of the shipyard's many departments. Wasn't it reasonable to ensure that everyone's views be heard at the negotiating table?

Walesa and the others on the strike committee inside the hall were in a bind. With thousands listening outside, could they very well deny that all the divisions should be represented? Reluctantly, they entered management's trap. It was agreed to recess the talks until afternoon in order to elect four representatives from each division. The move would prove almost fatal to the strikers.

When the enlarged strike committee trooped into the conference hall later that day, it numbered 150 delegates. Gniech and his superiors had calculated cleverly. Once the proceedings for selection became more formalized, they could count on the existing power structure coming into play; not only would the less militant departments send representatives who might be persuaded by management's arguments, but even the others would be influenced by those who already had authority in the factory—foremen, department party secretaries and various minor officials. All of this would tend to strengthen Gniech's hand.

The director was all the more conciliatory. There would be: reinstatement for those dismissed, a monument commemorating those killed in 1970, a wage hike (although the amount was yet to be fixed), significant changes in the activities of the trade union, and of course, a guarantee against reprisals for those who had taken part in the stoppage. It would be signed by Tadeusz Fiszbach himself. As for demands concerning better food supplies, rolling back meat prices, family benefits and strike pay, perhaps something could be done there, too. Of course, many of the demands, Gniech pointed out, were beyond the authority of the shipyard director to decide. Some of the original members of the strike committee, like Jerzy Borowczak, seeing that the new committee had been weakened politically, demanded that if the director was unable to settle the demands, then Prime Minister Babiuch should come to the shipyard himself. Nonetheless, when the day's session ended, the two sides were not far apart.

That evening, as delegations from the other factories began arriving at the Lenin Shipyard, the country's massive propaganda machine was moving into high gear. The local press hammered the strikers. "These stoppages fill one with concern," said the *Baltic Daily News*, "since they worsen the already difficult economic situation, and lower the production of goods and services, which are badly needed by all of us and which we keep looking for in the stores." The *Coastal Evening News* appealed to the workers' patriotism: "We know that there are big and painful problems, that there are shortcomings, weaknesses, strains. We cannot be silent about them, since we all want to eliminate them. But in the interests of every one of us, in the interest of society, in the interest of Poland, we should work when it is working time, and discuss at a time and place appropriate for talking. Methods other than those can bring only short-lived effects. And obviously, this is not what it is all about." The workers were unimpressed. "Obviously, *this* is not what it's all about," sneered one striking reader, pointing to the evening editorial.

If Premier Babiuch had no intention of appearing at the shipyard in person (as some of the strikers had demanded), he was, nevertheless, available on the evening television broadcast. The prime minister admitted that the strikes in Gdansk had assumed "large scale" proportions. He appealed for reason, wisdom and debate to save Poland from the "menace of sharp conflicts and tensions." Babiuch, Silesian-born like Gierek and considered to be the first secretary's right-hand man, asked that his government be given time to "put things in order." Poland, he said, owed so much money abroad that there was no possibility of borrowing any more. "Many changes will have to take place in the management of the economy," he pledged. But the increases in meat prices would not be rescinded. He called on the strikers to return to work to prevent an "interruption of the rhythm of production." At the end, the prime minister gravely warned that the situation was worrying Poland's friends. "Our allies believe that we shall be able to resolve our difficulties on our own," intoned Babiuch—shorthand for: If we Poles don't control the strikes, the Russians will.

Late that night, Bogdan Borusewicz was still on the go. He had gone to Gdynia that day where he found his friend Kolodziej in charge of the strike at the Paris Commune Shipyard. Kolodziej's lieutenants were the printer Butkewicz—whom he had sent for—and a group of young workers. They had set up a military-style regime. The meetings were held out in the open in the big square behind the main gate. Chalk lines had been drawn on the asphalt showing the numbers of the departments. Some of the workers had been joined by their families. Each department had its own kitchen, and there were common pots for soup. A strict discipline was enforced, with passes to get in and out of the main gate. The department managers had been thrown out of the yard and the director had been locked up in the administration building under guard.

Borusewicz stayed at the Paris Commune Shipyard until well past midnight, and then caught a ride to Gdansk. He arrived at the Lenin Shipyard in the middle of the night. Everyone was asleep. He woke up some of the leaders—Walesa, Walentynowicz and Gwiazda, who had climbed over the wall from Elmor—and they met briefly. They told Borusewicz that the director agreed to everything, even the question of free trade unions.

Borusewicz returned to Gdynia. It was just before dawn on Saturday, August 16. On the main square of the Paris Commune yard, sleeping on the ground, there were thousands of human bodies, masses of dreaming strikers, some still in their overalls. As he walked among the slumbering workers in the first hint of morning, Borusewicz felt as if he were in the seventeenth century, with a group of Cossacks, weary after some battle they had fought during the day.

On Saturday morning, Jerzy Borowczak made a tour of a half-dozen striking factories in Gdansk to report on the progress of negotiations at the Lenin Shipyard. The workers at these factories were worried. What will happen if your demands are met? they asked Borowczak. Will you go back to work then? He didn't know. But if you go back to work, they insisted, what'll happen to us? We'll be crushed because we're small factories.

When Borowczak arrived at the conference hall where the negotiations were in progress, he saw that the others had cause to worry. It was past noon now. They were close to a compromise. The one sticking point was the raise. Gniech was holding back. The committee had demanded 1,500 zlotys across the board. If I agree to a raise like that, Gniech pleaded, I'll get fired; this is a big raise, and it would set a precedent for the other enterprises.

Bogdan Borusewicz arrived in the middle of the debate. There was a small kafuffle. Gniech's assistant, seeing the new face, shouted, Who's this? What's he doing here? Borusewicz introduced himself, but already the management people were on their feet, telling him to get out. Walesa interrupted. This is our adviser. Borusewicz took a seat behind Walesa.

Suddenly, Gniech announced that he agreed to the raise. He would guarantee it in writing. The guarantee would be put in his safe. Borusewicz tugged on Walesa's jacket, trying to get him to stall. Others from the original strike committee put a motion on the floor urging the Lenin Shipyard workers to stay on strike in solidarity with the other factories until their demands were met too. They were outvoted. Then, all too quickly, the committee was voting on the question of ending the strike. They were tired, and wanted it over. Many of them were backers of management anyway. It was ending.

After the majority voted to end the strike, Gniech addressed Walesa. Why don't you announce the end of the strike? Walesa was trapped. There was nothing he could do. It was three in the afternoon. Walesa went to the microphone. His voice boomed through the shipyard loudspeakers. He tried to make the best of it. He told them that the management had agreed to everything and that the strike was over. "We have done a great thing," Walesa said, "but we shall do still bigger things for the good of the shipyards and our motherland." Even before he had finished speaking, the shouts of complaint could be heard from all directions.

There was confusion everywhere. Gniech and his team got up from their chairs and quickly marched out of the hall. Alina Pienkowska had just arrived from the health service. People were pushing and shoving. Delegates from the transport service and the nearby shipyards and factories were protesting. Walesa made his way outside. The representative from the Remontow yard yelled at him, "The Gdansk shipyard is betraying is!" Others demanded that they mustn't end the strike until the other factories settled. Some workers were leaving the yard.

Anna Walentynowicz was sitting and crying. Walesa had been outvoted, someone told Pienkowska.

Finally, in the huge crowd, Walesa calmed them down long enough to speak. He quickly sensed their mood. "I said that I would be the last person to leave the shipyard. And I meant it. If the workers who are gathered here want to continue the strike, then it'll be continued. Now: who wants to strike?" asked the chairman of the Lenin Shipyard strike committee.

"We do!" they roared, their voices echoing off the old red-brick buildings of the shipyard.

"Who does not want to strike?" Walesa said.

There was dead silence among the thousands.

"So we are striking!" Walesa shouted. "I'll be the last to leave the shipyard."

Walentynowicz and Pienkowska rushed back into the conference hall to get to the microphones and announce the continuation of the strike. The mikes were dead. Over the loudspeakers, they could hear Director Gniech's voice, coming from the administration building. "The strike is over. Everyone must leave the shipyard by four o'clock. Everyone must leave or the agreement will be cancelled."

"We have to do something!" Pienkowska said to Bogdan Borusewicz. Without thinking, she rushed outside. People were pouring out of the shipyard. The delegates from the other shipyards had left. Alina grabbed Anna Walentynowicz, and the two of them found a driver with an electric cart. They climbed in and told him to take them to the Remontow yard; their next stop was the North Shipyard. Alina tried to explain that the strike was still going on, that it hadn't ended, that a solidarity strike had been declared. The other strike committees were angry and wouldn't budge.

On the way to the conference hall, Pienkowska saw a crowd at Gate No. 3. They were going out, toward home. With Walentynowicz, she went up to the workers' guards. What's happening? Alina asked. Nothing, the guard replied, they don't believe us that the strike is still going on. Anna Walentynowicz tried to address the crowd of nearly a thousand workers. She told them the strike was still going on. In whose name are you declaring the strike? one of them shouted back; I have a family, I have children, and I have to go home. He was angry. Anna Walentynowicz couldn't stand it anymore, and burst into tears.

Suddenly, Alina Pienkowska took over. She was a quiet

person, and she had never done this in her life before, but she was excited, and at the same time, sure of herself. "Lock the gates!" she commanded the young men wearing the armbands of the workers' militia. The crowd pressed against the closed gate. "Now, you have to calm down and be quiet," she appealed. "In three minutes time, everybody will be able to leave, but I want to say a few words, and for three minutes you can wait." They gave her a barrel to stand on. There wasn't any loudspeaker and she had to shout.

She pulled out her workpass and showed it to them. "I'm a worker with the health service in the shipyard," Pienkowska began. "I'm a member of the Free Trade Unions. I want to tell you what's happening at the Second Gate because the communiques which you hear from the management over the loudspeakers are false." Her audience was quiet by now.

"The strike is still going on. Lech Walesa was outvoted in the conference hall, but the workers want the strike to go on, because there aren't any guarantees. And since there aren't any guarantees, there aren't any free trade unions. So the demands haven't been fulfilled," she explained. "That's why the meeting at the Second Gate didn't agree to end the strike. If you go out, the same thing will happen as in 1976; the people who are left will be surrounded by the militia and crushed. They will be fired from their jobs. Is that what you want?"

From the crowd, someone shouted, "She's right. They won't forgive us for this strike." She sensed that the crowd was with her. "The most important thing," Pienkowska continued, "is the solidarity of everyone, all the factories, all the workers. If you don't believe me, go to the Second Gate and find out for yourselves."

Alina Pienkowska stepped down. She didn't know where the words had come from—she, who had always thought of herself as shy, who as a schoolgirl had asked the boy in the next seat to raise the questions she wanted the teacher to answer. But they were applauding. More important, they weren't leaving. When the gate was opened, only four people out of nearly a thousand walked out. The women workers in the crowd were shaking their handbags and shouting at the deserters.

Seeing the effect of her words, the workers' guards rushed Pienkowska to the other gates to speak to more workers. Many people, feeling that the strike would end that day, had already put on their street clothes and left as soon as Walesa announced the settlement. When Borusewicz surveyed the yard sometime after five o'clock that afternoon, he counted up about 1,500 workers, mostly the younger, more militant members of the crew. The majority had gone home. The management strategy for buying social peace had come within a hair of succeeding. It still wasn't clear what the outcome would be. But it was significant that so many had stayed. Borusewicz was afraid that the militia would enter the shipyard, secure it for the weekend, and by Monday morning everything would be back to normal. But with the holdouts here, and the other striking enterprises in the Tri-Cities, maybe the situation could be saved.

The further one was from the epicentre of the strike, the greater the confusion. At Elmor, all they heard were the announcements over the Lenin Shipyard loudspeakers—Walesa declaring the end of the strike, and the shipyard director ordering people to clear the yard. Lis and Gwiazda were angry. They gathered the Elmor crew and delivered bitter speeches, designed to rouse their workmates' wrath. Elmor decided to continue the strike. The strike committee members jumped into a few cars and headed for the other striking factories, to bring their delegates back to Elmor, which would serve as a new centre for the confrontation. At the Paris Commune Shipyard in Gdynia there was chaos, but again the young chieftain, Andrzej Kolodziej, managed to hold things together. In Warsaw, Interpress, the Polish news agency for foreign journalists, announced the Lenin Shipyard settlement. The first dispatches trickling across the international wire services from United Press said that "tired but jubilant workers reported the settlement, saying they had won their three-day contest." But Associated Press, having talked to Jacek Kuron in Warsaw, had a different version. Interpress revised its release: now it said that "a certain number" of shipyard workers had initially agreed to return to their jobs and end the takeover, but that they later decided to continue their occupation of the shipyard.

As Saturday evening wore on, the situation in Gdansk began to come into focus. The workers who had arrived home from the Lenin yard heard that the strike was continuing, and a few of them went back to the yard after a hasty dinner. When the Elmor delegates drove back to their factory with representatives from other enterprises, they learned that the strike was still on next door. Everyone headed to the Lenin Shipyard. Inside the Lenin yard, the militants continuing the precarious occupation also had sent out messengers to dispell the confusion. By nine o'clock that night, delegations from 21 enterprises had assembled in the sweaty, smoke-filled conference hall of the Lenin Shipyard.

Late that night, a new working-class organization was formed. Realizing that the strike had a general character, the delegates began considering a formula which would encompass all the factories. The Inter-Factory Strike Committee (known by its Polish initials MKS) was born. An executive was elected, comprised mostly of people who knew each other, who had been in the illegal Free Trade Unions or had participated in demonstrations and ceremonies together over the years. As the night wore on, the workers' militia guarded the gates and walls of the shipyard with renewed vigilance. Inside, the MKS worked on a preliminary set of demands for all the factories.

At the head of the list was insistence on reopening communications with the rest of the country. The Inter-Factory Strike Committee also called for a guarantee of the right to strike, release of political prisoners in Poland, free speech and the end of censorship, respect for the conventions of the International Labor Organization, which included the right to establish free trade unions, access to the mass media by all religious groups, abolition of interference in trade union matters by the authorities, and a realistic economic program that would permit all classes and sections of society to discuss the reform proposals. There were also specific economic demands. Altogether, the initial set of MKS demands came to sixteen. Meanwhile, in the middle of the night, as delegates made their way back to their factories to report, someone was sent to visit the parish priest.

On Sunday morning, August 17, there was a stillness in the air as the sunshine poured over the great industrial cranes, swept across the grimy workshops and glittered in the canal of the Lenin Shipyard where the ocean-going vessels were berthed. For a moment the Gdansk yards lost some of the air of a besieged fortress. The calmness prevailed as the strike leaders, who had snatched a few hours of sleep before dawn, emerged from the conference hall into the morning.

Shortly after 8 a.m., the people began arriving from town. They came a few at a time, and then more and more of them. They bore armfuls of flowers, which they laid at the closed gates, as the 1,500 or so sleepy workers inside the yard began assembling. A portrait of the Polish pope, John Paul II, was affixed to the gate. The morning crowd of worshippers also brought flags and banners, the red and white colors of Poland and the blue ribbons that symbolized the Virgin Mary. The priest from St. Brigid's parish, Henryk Jankowski, arrived just before 9 a.m. The crowd outside exceeded 5,000, and the gate of the Lenin Shipyard had the appearance of a holy shrine. Inside, Lech Walesa, an emblem of Our Lady of Czestochowa on the lapel of his jacket, stood before the striking workers.

An altar was set up, and Father Jankowski, in his robes of office, faced the chalice glinting in the sun and began the field mass. The voices of those on both sides of the gates were joined in singing the traditional hymns. On both sides of the gate they kneeled on the pavement.

Apart from its spiritual functions, the mass had enormous political importance. It had brought thousands of people to the shipyard, many of them returning workers. The people brought encouragement to the strikers, urging them to continue the strike and showing by their very numbers the support the strike enjoyed throughout the city. Those who had come took the news back home with them, spreading a scarce commodity in the controlled and censored information channels of People's Poland. In Gdynia, where a similar ceremony occurred, the mass was particularly impressive because the priest, addressing the shipyard workers during the sermon, sharply criticized the authorities and supported the strikers' demands. His were the first words uttered by anyone in authority telling the workers that they were right. When the mass at the Lenin Shipyard ended, a small wooden cross was erected outside the gate to mark the place of those who had fallen in 1970.

In Warsaw, the confused story about events in the Baltic region had been straightened out. The communique proclaiming the end of the strike was now described by the international press as ''a premature announcement that turned out to be wishful thinking.'' They reported the formation of the MKS and said that the ''labor crisis in Poland had deepened.'' Jacek Kuron released a KOR bulletin saying that the new Inter-Factory Strike Committee was authorized to negotiate with the state in the name of all the strikers and it would carry on even after the work action was over. ''This committee creates an absolutely new situation,'' Kuron told the reporters assembled in his apartment. "It is a step toward a free trade union—a very important step." While the workers in Gdansk continued to meet throughout the day, the government announced, with some vagueness, the establishment of a special commission to investigate the workers' complaints.

The holdout strikers in the Lenin Shipyard had survived their first important test, just barely, but as the first weekend of the strike ended, there was a new question to face. What would happen tomorrow morning when the thousands of shipyard employees arrived at the gate? Would they go back to work or would they strike?

4   Sticking Together

*Our strike enjoys the support of the entire
country because our 21 demands are deeply
humanitarian. . . We have to oppose the
authorities' attempts to disrupt the unity
of our movement. We live up to the words:
man is born free.*
                —Inter-Factory Strike Committee
                  (MKS), August 20, 1980

The workers of the Lenin Shipyard gathered outside the
flower-bedecked gate in the first light of the late summer
morning.

At 5:40 a.m., Monday, August 18, 1980, the loudspeakers of
the public address system near Gate No. 2 began to carry the
voice of Klemens Gniech. "Attention! This is the director of the
shipyard speaking. I appeal to all the workers of our shipyard.
On Saturday we ended talks with the representatives of all
shipyard workers. We came to a full agreement. Let's
remember that we and we alone are responsible for the shipyard
and for everything that happens here. This is the director of the
shipyard speaking. . ." Gniech, broadcasting from the
administration building, repeated his prepared statement every
four minutes. The authorities had not yet given up the strategy
of breaking the strike along the Baltic by manoeuvring the
Lenin employees back to work. Throughout the weekend, the
party-controlled media had hammered home the same theme,
even accusing the holdouts of forcibly detaining workers within
the yard.

The crowd outside, facing their striking workmates through
the gate, was undecided. There was some hostility. People

shouted at the ones who wanted to return to work, calling them scabs and cowards. Walesa appeared. He climbed up where everyone could see him. The gate of the shipyard was opened. Inside, the strikers divided into two columns, on either side of the road leading into the yard.

In his raspy voice, the strike leader began the national anthem, "Poland Has Not Yet Perished." On both sides of the open gate, the workers of the Lenin Shipyard joined in the singing. When the patriotic hymn ended and silence fell upon the crowd, Walesa began. "The director says that the strike committee has broken the agreement. But what we agreed to was a raise of 1,500 zlotys per person. Now the director says that the average will be 1,500 slotys. Who'll get this average?" Walesa paused, then spoke of the other striking workers in the Tri-Cities area. The solidarity strike, he insisted, had been declared on behalf of all.

"Don't hesitate to come in," he appealed to the workers still outside the gate. "We have to fight for what is rightly ours. Come to us, shipyard workers. There's nothing to be afraid of." There was tension in the air as those outside made up their minds. Suddenly, one of the blue-overalled strikers standing on the wall, a young shipyard worker, called out to them: "If you don't feel that you're really shipyard workers, then go home. If you feel you *are* a shipyard worker, then come in!"

A group of younger workers outside—about 30 of them—broke from the crowd and started towards the gate. The others hung back for a moment. The first group entered, and the strikers on both sides of the road burst into applause as they passed into the yard. Then everybody rushed in amid a roar of cheering, and once again the workers of the Lenin Shipyard were united. The final efforts of Director Gniech had failed. The regime would have to devise a new strategy. And it would have to do so soon.

On a hill near the mouth of the Odra River, the weather-beaten hulk of St. Jacob's Cathedral stands with its back to the East German border. Its rough, rust-colored exterior, which resembles a capsized ship that has taken a pounding on the Baltic, greets those entering the northwestern Polish port city of Szczecin. Of its 400,000 inhabitants, more than 55,000 work in the shipbuilding industry—12,000 are employed in the famed Warski yards, and the others labor in the Parnica, Gryfia, Odra and Yacht shipyards, as well as in the other plants along the docks.

The workers of Szczecin, like those in Gdansk and Gdynia, also had fallen in the bloody repression of December 1970, and the bond forged with their fellow shipyard workers a decade earlier had remained intact. Before the Gdansk strike, the workers in the Warski yard knew of the sporadic strikes in various parts of the country following the price increases of July 1. On Friday, August 15, people from Gdansk arrived at the Warski yard with news of events at home. But the scope of the crisis became clear only the next day, Saturday, when an unprecedented event occurred: the entire shipyard work force was given a 10 per cent pay increase.

Over the weekend, as the Gdansk workers held out, those in Szczecin realized that something big was in the works. People remembered 1970 and said that the time had come to settle accounts over what had been going on in Poland. The time had come, some said, for great events.

Work began normally on Monday morning at the Warski Shipyard. But at the 10 a.m. morning break, a group of workers began to move through the yard, going from one canteen to another. "What shall we do?" they asked. "Gdansk is on strike. We must help." By noon, more than 2,000 Warski workers had gathered at the wrought-iron main gate, demanding that the shipyard director come out of the administration building and meet them.

Eventually the director arrived. He wasn't alone. With him was the first secretary of the Szczecin party branch, a man named Brych. Obviously, the party had expected trouble. A platform and loudspeakers were hastily set up. The shipyard director asked the crowd what it wanted. "What's the news from Gdansk?" one of the workers shouted.

The director hedged. He said that negotiations were in progress. "But what exactly are the demands of the Gdansk workers?" various people asked. Because the lines of communication between Gdansk and the rest of the country had been cut the Warski workers had no hard information, just the sure sense that something major was happening. The director wasn't dispensing hard information that morning. The workers soon turned to their own grievances. "Why is it so difficult to get a new apartment?" Someone else yelled, "What about the people thrown out in 1970?" Soon they were asking about political prisoners. First Secretary Brych intervened to say that there weren't any political prisoners in Poland. A few workers whistled derisively, and the heckling quickly spread. Brych, trying to get things back on track, proposed that one person should be delegated from each department to go to the administration building for discussions. The workers balked. The building was outside the shipyard gates and the delegates could easily be arrested. They remembered 1970.

The discussion was getting nowhere. One of the workers in the crowd took the platform. It's impossible to talk in this situation, he said, and suggested that each department ought to elect four or five delegates to get together among themselves to talk things over. It was agreed that the delegates would met at 4 p.m. in the hall on the first floor of the production management building—the same hall where the striking Szczecin workers had assembled in 1970-71. In the meantime, the Warski yard was on strike. Within the hour, word came from the Parnica Shipyard and the Gryfia repair yard. They, too, were out. Szczecin was joining the solidarity strike. The Tri-City workers were no longer on their own.

At the Lenin Shipyard, headquarters of the MKS, delegates from freshly-struck enterprises poured into the conference hall from early morning on. In Gdansk, Sopot and Gdynia, factory after factory shut down and their workers chose strike committees and sent representatives to the Lenin yard. By 9:30 a.m., the number of striking plants had reached 40. A message was sent to provincial governor Jerzy Kolodziejski informing him that the MKS was authorized to hold talks with government authorities. An hour later, the 55th delegation entered the yards.

On the stage of the great conference hall a larger-than-life-size statue of Lenin, with furrowed brow and one hand resting on an upended book, mutely watched the delegates file in. They took their places at tables that ran the length of the room. One after another, the representatives described the situation at their factories and pledged their solidarity to each other. Throughout the day, the delegations arrived; the strike grew. At noon, 82 enterprises were out; by day's end, the number would nearly double.

The continuing session of the MKS attended to a variety of tasks. Communiques were drafted and debated. Arrangements were made for the transport of necessary goods in the strike-bound city. Arguments with management continued over control of the broadcasting centre. Lunch was organized. Communications with workers' families were taken care of. The foreign press, now arriving in considerable numbers, had to be dealt with. They didn't speak Polish, and translators would have to be found. Soon accommodation would be needed for the reporters and television technicians. It was decided that daily plenary sessions of the MKS would be held at 10 a.m. and 8 p.m.

The most important event of the day, however, was ratification of the final list of demands, to which was appended the workers' precondition of re-establishing telephone service throughout the country. In the form presented to the MKS delegates on Monday the list read:

1. Acceptance of free trade unions independent of the the Polish United Workers Party in accordance with convention No. 87 of the International Labor Organization concerning the right to form free trade unions, which was ratified by the government of Poland.
2. A guarantee of the right to strike and of the security of strikers and those aiding them.
3. Compliance with the constitutional guarantee of freedom of speech, the press and publication, including freedom for independent publishers, and the availability of the mass media to representatives of all faiths.
4. (a) A return of former rights to: people dismissed from work after the 1970 and 1976 strikes; students expelled from school because of their views.
   (b) The release of all political prisoners, among them Edmund Zadrozynski, Jan Kozlowski and Marek Kozlowski.
   (c) A halt to repression of the individual because of personal conviction.
5. Availability to the mass media of information about the formation of the Inter-Factory Strike Committee and publication of its demands.
6. The undertaking of actions aimed at bringing the country out of its crisis situation by the following means:
   (a) Making public complete information about the social-economic situation.

(b) Enabling all sectors and social classes to take part in discussion of the reform program.

7. Compensation for all workers taking part in the strike for the period of the strike, with vacation pay from the Central Trade Union Council.

8. An increase in the base pay of each worker by 2,000 zlotys a month as compensation for the recent rise in prices.

9. Guaranteed automatic increases in pay on the basis of increases in prices and the decline of real income.

10. Full supply of food products for the domestic market, with exports limited to surpluses.

11. The abolition of "commercial" prices and of other sales for hard currency in special shops.

12. The selection of management personnel on the basis of qualifications, not party membership. Privileges of the secret police, regular police and party apparatus are to be eliminated by equalizing family subsidies, abolishing special stores, etc.

13. The introduction of food coupons for meat and meat products (during the period in which control of the market situation is regained).

14. Reduction in the age of retirement for women to 50 and for men to 55, or after 30 years' employment for women and 35 years for men, regardless of age.

15. Conformity of old-age pensions and annuities with what has actually been paid in.

16. Improvements in the working conditions of the health service to insure full medical care for workers.

17. Assurances of a reasonable number of places in day-care centres and kindergartens for the children of working mothers.

18. Paid maternity leave for three years.

19. A decrease in the waiting period for apartments.

20. An increase in the commuter's allowance to 100 zlotys from 40, with a supplemental benefit on separation.

21. A day of rest on Saturday. Workers in the brigade system or round-the-clock jobs are to be compensated for the loss of free Saturdays with increased leave or paid time off.

The list had been completed just after midnight on Sunday,

and although it constituted a thorough indictment of the present order, there were those who wanted to go even further, calling for such reforms as free elections in Poland and the abolition of censorship. It was Borusewicz of KOR who had pleaded with the MKS members to be reasonable and to soften the language so as not to be pointlessly provocative.

When they finally agreed, Walesa, a card player like all the rest, said, "It's 21!" Fatigued but exhilarated by how far they had come, they all laughed at his reference to blackjack, the game commonly played by the workers.

On Monday, during the MKS session, the demands were read out. One by one the delegations from the striking enterprises rose and announced their acceptance of the list. When unanimity had been formally reached, the workers rose and applauded their almost unbelievable progress. Now they were ready to negotiate.

Whether the regime was ready to do likewise was less clear. At eight o'clock that evening everyone in the Lenin Shipyard stopped what they were doing to listen—through the PA system or on car radios. In thousands of homes in the Tri-City area, and in millions throughout the country, television sets were turned on as Edward Gierek, first secretary of the communist party, addressed the nation.

The first secretary was suitably stern. He had postponed a trip to West Germany, where he was to seek economic aid, because of the crisis. An emergency meeting of the politburo of the central committee had lasted until moments before his speech, as the party leaders wrestled with strategy. Gierek conceded that the government had made mistakes in managing the economy. There was plenty of room for improvement, he admitted, and he promised that reforms would be speeded up and "reasonable" decentralization introduced to give individual firms increased decision-making power. He offered higher pay, but warned that it "must be spread out over a period of time" to avoid adding to the nation's economic ills. As well, there was a pledge of higher family allowances and better supplies in the shops.

But when it came to the workers' political demands, the first secretary put his foot down, flatly rejecting all of them. Allowing that the existing trade unions were not blameless, he made it clear that the regime nonetheless intended to rely on them. There already existed considerable scope in Poland for freedom to criticize and for tolerance, Gierek claimed. The workers in the Lenin Shipyard groaned in unison. The first secretary understood that people were tired of queues and shortages, but the strikes would not make things any better. "There are limits that must not be overstepped by anyone," Gierek declared. "These limits are marked by Poland's reason for being. Only a socialist Poland can be a free and independent state with inviolable frontiers." Then came the final rhetorical strophe: "Let this truth be present in the minds of every Polish woman and man. Actions that are aimed against the basic foundations of the socialist system will not be tolerated, and nobody can count on compromise on this issue."

The workers were unimpressed. The speech was no different from Babiuch's the previous Friday. "He acts as if he were talking to children," said Anna Walentynowicz. "The speech doesn't change anything. We will simply wait until somebody comes to us from Warsaw and talks to us seriously," the crane operator declared.

Somebody *was* coming from Warsaw. Despite Gierek's uncompromising posture, the politburo had chosen one of its alternate members, Deputy Premier Tadeusz Pyka, to go to the coast as the head of a commission examining workers' demands. He would start work the next day.

Gierek's speech hadn't gone over in Szczecin either. As planned, the Warski Shipyard delegates had met that afternoon. They had drawn up a list of 36 demands, elected a presidium, and chosen Marian Jurczyk (a member of the strike committee in 1970) to be their chairman.

It was the first evening of the strike in Szczecin. The summer night was warm and the feeling of unity in the shipyard was unforgettable. They weren't afraid. For years, the television had reminded them that they were living in a socialist society, that the shipyard was rightfully theirs, that they were the "owners." Now they had made the words a reality. That night, the workers felt that the Warski Shipyard really was theirs.

The delegation waited. Bogdan Lis, tram driver Henryka Krzywonos and Florian Wisniewski from the Elektromontaz factory had been chosen from the MKS executive to relay the strikers' demands, along with an appeal to begin talks, to provincial governor Jerzy Kolodziejski.

It was past noon, Tuesday, August 19. Kolodziejski's executive assistant finally emerged into the outer offices where the delegation waited. The governor didn't have time to see them, the assistant explained. Together with Deputy Premier Pyka, Kolodziejski was talking with delegations from individual factories. The assistant would receive their documents.

The regime had embarked on a new hard-line strategy. Its initial tactic had been to quickly reach agreement with the Lenin Shipyard workers, thus forcing the strikers at other factories to settle on the same terms. It had failed. Instead, strikers at various factories had joined with the Lenin Shipyard workers to form the Inter-Factory Strike Committee. Now the government, represented by Pyka, would try it the other way around. There were still enterprises that hadn't joined the MKS. Pyka would seek settlements with these individual factories. Once MKS members saw these agreements, they, too, would be inclined to settle, leaving the Lenin Shipyard workers isolated. Although this manoeuvre seemed unlikely to prove successful, the party strategists behind the move had some grounds for optimism.

A split existed between the main body of strikers and those from the Remontov, Northern Shipyard and Northern Harbor enterprises (three sizeable Gdansk work places accounting for 13,000 workers). The dispute had broken out on Saturday afternoon, in the midst of the confusion when the Lenin strike committee apparently settled, and then cancelled the settlement to proclaim a solidarity strike. The misunderstanding had persisted over the weekend.

If Pyka could offer one of these enterprises a package generous enough to reach an agreement, he might begin to chip away at MKS's solidarity. In addition, the regime had at its disposal a variety of support mechanisms. They included the existing trade unions, whose council was meeting in Gdansk that night, the full weight of the state's propaganda machine, and if necessary, even the police. The formal thrust of the government's strategy was to insist that the Inter-Factory Strike Committee was an illegal body and to refuse to deal with it.

The new situation was summed up in a concise jest produced by puns on the names of the leading adversaries. In Polish, the name Pyka is a form of the verb "to puff," and the name of the pipe-smoking Walesa is related to the verb "to wander." The word-play quickly made the rounds: Walesa puffs (Pyka) while Pyka wanders (Walesa). It neatly captured the stalemate, somewhat to the advantage of the MKS leader.

Back in the shipyard, the strikers lolled shirtless in the sun (the grassy area was promptly dubbed "nude beach"), played cards and ignored the rebroadcast of Gierek's speech from the previous night. At the Gdansk airport, party and government higher-ups flew in from Warsaw to bolster the state contingent; inside the conference hall, meanwhile, a stream of delegations arrived to join the strike. In mid-afternoon, a group from the Inter-Factory Strike Committee in Elblag, an industrial city east of Gdansk and 50 kilometres from the Soviet border, arrived to surrender their authority to the Gdansk MKS. A half-hour later, the first of the intellectual institutions, Gdansk Polytechnic, came to express solidarity with the striking workers.

It went on all day. In the midst of the hours of gruelling business, chaired by Walesa in his casual yet effective style, there were moments when the emotions of the delegates, each representing thousands of workers, were deeply stirred; it was as if they glimpsed for the first time the enormity of what they had accomplished. In the evening, still more delegates were joining in. A group of five from an electrical factory walked into the hall. A woman carrying a bouquet of carnations hesitantly approached the microphone. She pledged the solidarity of her co-workers. Spontaneously, the entire hall rose and sang the national anthem. Florian Wisniewski of the MKS presidium put into words the movement's unprecedented achievement: "We are the first full representatives of the workers in this district, free of the party, trade unions and the authorities. Until we have real trade unions, our only weapon is strikes. We want to restart work as soon as possible, but we must be the real masters of our factories." By nightfall, 263 enterprises belonged to the MKS.

The state had not been idle. During the day an unsigned statement was circulating in the shipyard, purportedly from representatives of other factories. "On August 19, strike committees from seventeen factories met with the government commission headed by Deputy Premier Tadeusz Pyka. During a joint meeting, the strikers' demands were considered. The chairman of the commission, Tadeusz Pyka, received and promised action within definite deadlines on over 20 demands raised by the delegates of the striking factories." Among the offers reported by the leaflet: a new formula for factory trade unions, improvement in meat and grocery supplies, better housing, better health care, three-year paid maternity leave, a 1,500-zloty raise, and Saturdays off as of January 1. The "remaining strike committees" were urged by the leaflet to "resume" talks with Pyka; the commission's telephone number was provided.

Meanwhile, the party central committee issued a letter to all levels of the organization to bolster morale and to spell out the political line adopted by the party. "The antisocialist elements amongst the Gdansk shipyard workers made political demands and hostile stipulations in order to seize control of the strike," it said. "Their demands threaten the essential security of the country. They put in danger our national survival, our common achievement and our unity built at such a high price and in such difficult conditions, at the cost of so many sacrifices." It went on in this high-flown language for paragraphs, conjuring up the demons of antisocialism and the familiar "enemies of the people" that the party trotted out whenever it was in trouble. "Those political enemies demand the establishment of free trade unions not for the sake of a better representation of the workers' interests, but in order to obtain a platform for activities aimed against our party and the people's democracy."

That evening, at the meeting of the official district trade union council, Jan Szydlak, politburo member and head of the country's trade unions, delivered the main report, inveighing against the strikers and the "antisocialist elements." "The authorities do not intend to give up their power or to share it with anyone else," Szydlak definitively declared.

The barrage continued well into the next day, Wednesday, August 20. The local communist party paper, the *Coastal Voice*, weighed in with its commentary: "The free will of citizens is limited and—not so infrequently—violated. People who want to leave idle factories are stopped by force. Employees wanting to fulfil their normal duties for the city's good have their equipment and tools broken. Vehicles carrying essential goods are being refused. The personnel of grocery stores are being threatened. The right to decide what is good and what is bad, what is necessary and what is not for the life of hundreds of thousands of people is being usurped."

In Warsaw that afternoon, the party unleashed the security forces. It had decided to stifle information about the strikes once and for all. In raids throughout the city, police swooped in and arrested KOR leader Jacek Kuron, Adam Michnik and a dozen other members of the democratic opposition.

Deputy Premier Pyka plodded on. A communique was broadcast over Gdansk radio in which Pyka claimed he had met with 47 delegations. He urged others to contact him. Provincial governor Kolodziejski helped out. A light aircraft buzzed the city scattering leaflets bearing the governor's signature, urging an end to the strikes.

The workers fought back. When the printers who had run off Governor Kolodziejski's airborne leaflet read it, they declared themselves on strike. Now other parts of the country began to take part. At the giant Nowa Huta steel mill near Cracow, a two-hour solidarity strike had taken place that morning. By afternoon, the Gdansk strikers learned that Szczecin was out. At 4 p.m. a delegation from distant Lower Silesia entered the hall. They promised to tell the coal miners back home the truth about what was happening in Gdansk. Again, the delegates stood up to sing the national anthem. They were moved. Some wept.

The MKS, now representing 304 enterprises, answered trade union boss Szydlak's blast of the night before. "The first of our demands is of crucial importance," the statement began. "Without independent trade unions all the other demands can be ruled out in the future, as has happened several times before in the short history of the Polish People's Republic. The official trade unions have not only failed to defend our interests; they have been more hostile to the justified strike action than the party and state organs." The MKS scorned Szydlak's insistence that he would represent the workers, with or without their consent. "The MKS and the workers on strike cannot be indifferent toward this official stand of the central trade union council. Our reaction is the decision of all the strikers within the MKS, taken this morning, to leave the party- and state-controlled trade unions."

The defiant statement ended eloquently: "Our strike enjoys the support and sympathy of the entire country and of other countries in the world, because our 21 demands are deeply humanitarian. The strikers and society at large are well aware of this and it is a source of our strength. The workers are not fighting for a mere pittance for themselves, but for justice for the whole nation. We have to oppose the local authorities' attempts to disrupt the unity of our strike movement. We live up to the words: Man is born free.''

Support from other sectors began to mount. In Rome, Pope John Paul II broke his delicate silence on the strike at his weekly public audience in St. Peter's Square, reading aloud two popular prayers in Polish. ''These prayers by themselves say how much we here in Rome are united with our fellow Poles,'' the Pope told the crowd of 20,000 below his balcony. His unmistakable message would soon percolate through the channels of the Polish church hierarchy.

Closer to home, 64 prominent Warsaw intellectuals, including Tadeusz Mazowiecki, editor of the Catholic weekly, the *Link*, issued an appeal on behalf of the strikers. ''As a result of years of ill-considered economic decisions and the authorities' assumption that they were infallible, the crisis arrived,'' said the writers. ''It was a result of broken promises, of all the attempts made to suppress the crisis, of disregard for civil rights. Once again it has become clear that it is impossible to rule the Polish nation without listening to its voice. With determination and maturity, Polish workers are fighting for the right to a better and more dignified life. The place of all the progressive intelligentsia in this fight is on the side of the workers,'' they declared.

To combat Pyka's efforts to split off the other shipyards, the MKS plenum decided to hold talks between themselves and the Remontow Shipyard. A delegation led by Walesa crossed the Lenin Shipyard and went to the gates of the adjoining Remontow yard. However, a rumor had circulated among the Remontow workers that the Lenin yard had decided that everyone who broke away from the MKS and held individual talks were traitors and should be beaten up. The government line that the strike was led by antisocialist elements had also taken its toll. The attempt to talk through the gate was unsuccessful.

By now, however, Pyka's strategy was coming apart. In the conference hall at the Lenin Shipyard that evening, workers from the factories which had participated in the talks with Pyka arrived. The delegate from Techmor explained that the discussions with the deputy premier had been conducted by a delegation that hadn't been authorized by the plant's workers. The Klimor representative told a similar story. Negotiations were undertaken in ''our name'' by the factory manager and party secretary, he said. A worker from the Northern Shipyard, which had yet to join the MKS, declared, "We're continuing our strike!"

Sometime in the middle of the night between Wednesday and Thursday, it became clear to the politburo that Gierek's gamble had failed. Pyka was dumped as head of the government commission.

The phase of party strategy spearheaded by Deputy Premier Pyka had been abandoned. The Polish working class had defeated the scheme. Representatives from hundreds of factories continued to gather at the Lenin Shipyard and declare their allegiance to the Inter-Factory Strike Committee. But it went beyond that. During the critical middle days of the strike, it had become something more than a matter of the MKS pitted against the state, more than leaflets, communiques, declarations.

Public opinion remained firmly on the side of the strikers despite the daily inconvenience. Notwithstanding the claims of local party newspapers about the alleged outrage of the citizenry, there was evidence of public support everywhere. Money for the strikers was collected, the red and white Polish flag flew from hundreds of dwellings in solidarity, farmers arrived from the countryside bringing food in trucks and wagons. Each day the crowds outside the gate of the Lenin Shipyard grew. In that abstraction of "public opinion" one could find countless individuals experiencing, and being transformed by, the strike.

The change in consciousness could be located in something as simple as the relationship between passersby and the strikers sitting atop the wall of the shipyard. Initially, Leslaw, a teaching assistant at the university, wasn't sure what to think. He was sympathetic to the workers, but he had no idea where the strike might lead or that it presaged anything special. As he passed by, he tentatively raised his arm toward the men overhead in blue overalls. But the eyes in the back of his head watched for the authorities and he worried about his fate should they see him. The next day, he waved, and the workers waved back. And the next day, he stopped and spoke. Soon he was at the shipyard gate every day, to hear the news, to listen to the proceedings over the loudspeakers, to speak with the others assembled there.

On Friday, the day after the strike broke out, Dr. Piotr Dyk took the morning train to Tczew, a town 50 km. south of Gdansk. Because of his political activities in the Young Poland Movement, he'd found it almost impossible to get a posting in town. Now he was on-call for the next 48 hours, and couldn't get back to Gdansk until Sunday. Even though the militants who planned the strike had held meetings in his apartment, it was only on his return from Tczew that he realized the magnitude of what was unfolding. He went straight to the shipyard.

Anna Maksymiuk and her friends had driven to the lakes district near Kartuzy for a mid-August holiday on the day the strike began. The slim, blonde woman of Russian ancestry had recently received her *magister* degree in English philology from the local university. She was a friend of Piotr Dyk and his wife, and was engaged to a medical student. Although many of those in the Young Poland Movement were part of her circle, she herself wasn't "political." At least not until the next day. The news was on the radio. She realized her friends would be at the shipyard. We have to turn back, she told her companions. When they arrived at the shipyard that first weekend, there was already a need for people with language skills. Anna stayed.

The universities were on holiday when the strike started. Although there were no students and only a few staff members available, Wojciech Gruszecki—a chemistry professor at Gdansk Polytechnic—called a meeting on Tuesday, August 19. Those present decided to throw their support behind the shipyard workers; they began by taking up a collection. The next day, a group from the polytechnic boarded the school bus and, carrying a Polish flag, drove to the Lenin Shipyard. The bus carefully inched through the crowd at the gate. When the strikers learned that these were the first representatives from the universities, they effusively waved the bus into the yard. Even the tall, pale Gruszecki, a man with a cool, somewhat Nordic demeanor, was excited. It was as if the strikers wanted to lift the bus onto their shoulders and carry it into the conference hall.

At the University of Gdansk in suburban Oliwa, Professor Robert Glebocki, an outspoken astrophysicist in his early forties, had just returned from summer holidays. Glebocki quickly organized a meeting on campus. It declared its solidarity with the strikers and sent the bearded scientist to the shipyard as its representative on Thursday, August 21. Although Polish intellectuals had supported embattled workers in various ways since 1976, Glebocki was somewhat shocked to find himself in the shipyard at the heart of the dispute. On the one hand, actual contact with masses of workers made real what had previously been only an abstract recognition of the practical and intellectual competence of the new generation of working class leaders. On the other hand, Glebocki became aware of his own inadequacies as the workers pressed around him, asking his opinion and expecting him to be able to elaborate on such things as the concept of free trade unions. The astrophysicist remained in the yard to learn the lessons of the strike. He would take them back to the campus.

For Mariusz Wilk, the road to the Lenin Shipyard was more roundabout. Wilk, a 27-year-old former student activist from the southern city of Wroclaw, was holidaying with friends on the Baltic coast near the town of Debek. A group of old political acquaintances from Warsaw, Cracow and Wroclaw had brought their families and tents to a seaside campsite for something of a reunion.

Wilk had been suspended from university in the late 1970s for political activities. One of the people who came forward to defend him was Karol Modzelewski—the former co-defendent of Jacek Kuron, and thus a link to an earlier student generation. Modzelewski had withdrawn from politics for a quieter, academic life in Wroclaw. Eventually, Wilk received his graduate degree, but it was impossible to get work, so the last year or so had been spent as a full-time activist in the ranks of the democratic opposition. Among the other campers was Miroslaw Chojecki, the head of the independent Nowa publishing house, who had been before the courts defending free speech as recently as June. In addition, there were various members of the Student Solidarity Committees, who, in the last years, had fought for university autonomy in opposition to the party-sponsored official student organizations.

When the group heard about the Gdansk strike, their first thought was that it was a transitory affair, like the other strikes that had occurred since July. But its scope soon became clear, and on the first weekend they drove to the shipyard and stayed the night. They came up with the idea of publishing a regular strike bulletin. On Monday morning, they were on the road back to the campsite to pick up their things when the police stopped them.

Wilk and the others were placed in separate cells in the main Gdansk police station. With a few calls, the police soon learned the identity of their captives. At eleven o'clock that night, Wilk was ordered out of his cell and told to put his shoelaces back in his shoes. He and another friend from Wroclaw were handcuffed and transferred to an unmarked police van. All night, the van headed south. In Wroclaw, Wilk served out the 48-hour detainment. On Wednesday night, he was released. They didn't even give him time to lace his shoes before he found himself on the street. It was an old trick activists knew well. As soon as the released prisoner crossed the street, he would be rearrested for an additional 48 hours, again without charges. Wilk pulled off his shoes and, barefoot, made a dash for it. As it turned out, he had guessed right. The friend who had been released at about the same time was nabbed again.

With his father's help, Wilk got out of Wroclaw and onto the northbound train to Slupsk, a town 95 km. west of Gdansk. By Friday, he was back in the shipyard, working on the first issue of the *Solidarity Strike Bulletin*.

From the most elaborate adventure to the simplest act of bringing bread to the shipyard gate for the striking workers, thousands of individuals had been touched. When the MKS declared itself the voice of the Polish nation, its claim was not merely rhetorical.

On Thursday morning, August 21, the government announced that it had replaced its chief labor negotiator, Pyka, with First Deputy Premier Mieczyslaw Jagielski. Simultaneously, Deputy Premier Kazimierz Barcikowski was dispatched to Szczecin. For the workers at the Lenin Shipyard, however, there remained two obstacles. The government had yet to recognize the Gdansk MKS as the legitimate representative of the strikers, and the split with the Remontow, Northern Shipyard and Northern Harbor workers was still to be healed.

While the new head of the government commission settled himself into a villa near Gdansk Polytechnic along embassy row, new delegations continued to arrive at the shipyard. The presidium was accordingly enlarged. A delegation of the Writers' Union was welcomed with a robust singing of *"Sto lat"* ("May He Live A Hundred Years"), and author Lech Badkowski was invited to join the MKS executive. When

Walesa proposed that Prof. Gruszecki of Gdansk Polytechnic be added to the presidium as an advisor, the delegates accepted unanimously. It was as if they sensed that the time was approaching when new intellectual skills would be needed. By early evening, just after the celebration of five o'clock mass at the Second Gate, the 350th delegation arrived in the conference hall to join the MKS.

Shortly after 6 p.m., strike committee representatives from the Remontow Shipyard and Northern Harbor made their appearance. In a room adjacent to the main conference chamber, talks began between an MKS committee and the dissident Remontow and Northern Harbor strikers in an effort to heal the rift. An hour later, the official delegation from the Northern Shipyard entered the main hall to announce that it had broken off separate talks with the government and wished to join the MKS. Later that night, the Remontow and Northern Harbor delegates appeared in the hall. It was almost midnight. The loudspeakers in the shipyard delivered the news to its thousands of residents: Remontow is with us! The split was ended. The cheering drifted into the summer night through sleepy, but worker-controlled Gdansk.

The government may have changed the faces and upgraded the status of the negotiating commission, but it had not yet changed its tactics. Deputy Premier Jagielski attempted to continue the branch-by-branch talks with individual factories. He went on Gdansk radio and said that his commission was prepared to go inside the closed plants and meet the workers on their own ground. Despite this small concession, which simply recognized the effectiveness of the occupation strategy adopted by the workers, it was common knowledge that Jagielski was only meeting the "troikas" of factory manager, party branch secretary, and official trade union chairman.

At the same time, the party stepped up its publicity campaign to sway public opinion. The controlled press, which had given only scant coverage to the unrest, was suddenly filled with long accounts of the strikes and laments over the shortages of bread, milk, butter, meat and flour resulting from the workers' disruption.

The MKS replied tartly: "The workers are not surprised by the vile methods of psychological warfare carried out by the authorities, aiming to provoke and mislead public opinion...

Everybody knows that the authorities are deliberately deferring negotiations. In this way, they have once again revealed themselves to the people. The working people have never failed and will never fail.'' As their confidence grew, so did the forthrightness, even blasphemy, of their public proclamations.

Again, the workers' presidium renewed its offer to begin negotiations. "Only by listening to the voice of the working people and by meeting their demands can normal life be resumed in our country," said the MKS. It denied that the striking workers were destroying national unity or harming the Polish state. "If the authorities want to find this out, let them come to the strikers and acquaint themselves with the resolutions of the MKS, which represents the workers. The truth is to be found here, not in government offices."

The truth began to sink in the next day, Friday, August 22. More than 200,000 workers were on strike along the Baltic coast. There were upwards of 350 enterprises in the Gdansk MKS, and over 60 in the Szczecin Inter-Factory Strike Committee. In addition, workers had idled plants in Elblag, Slupsk and countless smaller towns throughout the north. Deputy Premier Jagielski, meeting with the enterprises one by one, would not manoeuvre them back to work.

In Warsaw that morning, the Roman Catholic Church spoke out on the Polish labor crisis for the first time, expressing sympathy for the strikers' goals. After conferring with Stefan Cardinal Wyszynski, Bishop Lech Laczmarek of Gdansk released a statement. It was a typically careful document, diplomatically walking the line between the heavy-handedness of the party and the growing confidence of the stikers. The church voiced "understanding for the strikers, who seek to improve their lot, both in material well-being and matters concerning human rights," but it also warned that "prolonged stoppages, possible disturbances and fraternal bloodshedding are against the good of the society," and called on the workers to "act reasonably and prudently."

The intellectuals of Poznan, who also sent a message that day, were less restrained. "We support your just demands. They are of importance to each and every one of us. We are full of admiration for the dignity with which you have conducted the struggle for your rights, which are also ours."

That afternoon, the MKS sent a delegation to the government

commission to repeat the proposal that negotiations begin. Throughout the day, there were signs of movement. The big conference hall was cleaned, as if in anticipation. Walesa, as he had done each day, went into the crowds of workers outside the hall to report on the progress of the pre-negotiations.

In the evening, at 8 p.m., a three-member delegation from the MKS arrived at Jagielski's villa. At first there was a comic moment of misunderstanding. The delegation mistook the man who greeted them for Jagielski. He insisted that he was Jagielski's assistant, not the deputy premier. When the case of mistaken identity had been sorted out, the delegates were led into the room where Jagielski awaited them. The MKS representatives sipped mineral water and the government negotiator smoked nervously throughout the hour-long meeting at which they discussed the forthcoming negotiations.

It was only after they were back in the Fiat and speeding down the darkened boulevards of Gdansk toward the shipyard that they fully realized what had transpired. The government had at last recognized the indisputable authority of the Inter-Factory Strike Committee as the bargaining agent of the Tri-City workers. As they entered the gate of the Lenin Shipyard, they honked the horn continuously, leaning out of the car windows, shouting, "Victory! Victory!" At 10:30 p.m., Florian Wisniewski grabbed the microphone: "Tomorrow negotiations will begin—this is Wisniewski. Turn on the power to the PA system." He then delivered the long-awaited news. The government had agreed to meet. "We must maintain calm and behave with dignity," Wisniewski told the jubilant strikers outside.

Inside, the MKS presidium went into session once more. At midnight a press conference was held for the crowd of mostly foreign journalists. "On August 22, in the evening, a delegation of the MKS went to the chairman of the government commission and handed him the following statement," said the matter-of-fact press release that was read out. "The Inter-Factory Strike Committee once again informs the government commission headed by the deputy premier that it is ready to resume talks on the demands listed in our 21 points, which can terminate the strike." It was as if the strikers were determined to keep a lid on their emotions. "The deputy premier received the delegation and signed a receipt for the MKS statement." Thus the flat press release concluded. The press corps had no difficulty discerning that, indeed, a major victory had been achieved.

At one in the morning, two experts invited from Warsaw to aid the MKS—Tadeusz Mazowiecki and historian Bronislaw Geremek—wearily arrived at the conference hall. They stayed up late, talking with Walesa about the forthcoming negotiations.

Sometime the next day the unprecedented talks between the state and the self-organized workers would open. In previous crises, the leaders of the regime had occasionally plunged in among the workers to pledge that things would improve, to ask for their support. But never before had a communist state formally negotiated with the nation's working class, never before had the central issue been the very relationship between the state and the workers. But all that was for to-morrow.

Now, in the few hours before morning, the man at the centre of this vast social upheaval briefly slept. Lech Walesa was born during the last years of the Nazi occupation of Poland, in the village of Popow, between Warsaw and Gdansk. His father died shortly after release from a German camp, and Lech's mother married her brother-in-law Stanislaw Walesa; she was later killed in an auto accident while visiting the U.S., where Walesa's stepfather eventually settled.

Soon after completing an electrician's course at the vocational school near Lipno, he went to work in the W-4 shop of the Gdansk shipyard. Along with the other young electricians he met there—men like Bury and Henryk Lenarciak—he was part of the first generation raised under the new communist regime. His beliefs were a mixture typical of Poland's post-war years: the traditional faith in the church (he attended mass regularly) coupled with the increasing self-consciousness of workers. Added to this was his own strong personality. Walesa married a slim, brunette woman named Danuta. Living in a spartan two-room flat, the first of their six children was born.

In December 1970, when the Gdansk workers rebelled, Walesa had already been working at the Lenin Shipyard for several years, and he emerged as one of the leaders. After the strike, he remained at the shipyard. At first, life improved under the Gierek administration. When strikes broke out again in 1976, Walesa, then a delegate to the official trade union, drew up a list of workers' grievances. The shipyard management decided to get rid of a troublemaker.

During the next two years, the idea of independent trade unions took shape. Walesa was now working with the Zremb construction firm, but his free time was increasingly taken up with the fight over trade unions. In January 1979, he was laid off; again the reason was political. At the trade union elections, he was outraged to find the party secretary controlling the vote. "Why have I come here, to elect or to applaud?" he demanded. He found a job with the Elektromontaz engineering plant, where Wisniewski worked. As elsewhere, there were no complaints about his work; in fact, he received a small award for being the company's outstanding electrician. He had "golden hands," as the Polish phrase goes.

In December 1979 Walesa took part, as he had before, in the demonstration outside the Lenin Shipyard commemorating the workers killed in 1970. There was a crowd of about 5,000 and he addressed them on the need for free trade unions. A few weeks later, Elektromontaz fired him, allegedly for taking a day off without permission.

He had been arrested and detained by the police dozens of times. In jail, he had time to think. There wasn't any noisy machinery or crying children; he was alone. Even there, he sowed doubt in the mind of his jailers, singing the national anthem to their faces. They let him out after 48 hours. He stood at a bus stop and pretended to be penniless. He asked the others waiting there to buy his ticket, explaining that he had been arrested and why. People got interested, and during the bus ride, he continued to explain. It was a little rally. As recently as two weeks before the strike, while Walesa pushed the baby carriage in front of the family flat, the police had taken him away, leaving the baby for a neighbor to find.

Walesa saw himself as a man filled with anger, an anger that he had kept in his stomach since boyhood. This was perhaps part of the secret of his ability with crowds. One had to be very angry in order to know how to control the anger of the people. He could be alternately demagogic or good-humoredly humble with the crowd, but he knew them. He felt the situation and when the crowd was silent, he seemed to understand what it silently said. And he said it, with a voice, with the proper words.

There were some who said he was a man created by the strike. But that was too simple. Others, like Alina Pienkowska, who had worked with him politically, were surprised to find the moody Walesa emerge as the leader. Pienkowska had never thought it would be one of them who would lead, but then, she also surprised herself during the strike. Though there were some who mystified his undeniable power, there were others who claimed, perhaps more accurately, that his entire life had been shaped for the appearance of such a situation. When it burst forth, Lech Walesa was there, at the centre.

Yet he was an ordinary worker, an "uncouth man," as he himself insisted. He wore a baggy sports jacket and a turtleneck pullover or a checked flannel shirt. He smoked a pipe. He liked to laugh at Laurel and Hardy on television as he drank a glass of tea after work.

During the nine days of the strike, he had been everywhere. Time and again he had sensed the mood of the crowd before the gates of the Lenin Shipyard. He had chaired the gruelling sessions of the MKS, piloting it sometimes gruffly, but steadily, toward unity. His confidence had made it possible for the varied talents of the rest of the leadership to be activated. He had the trust of the workers, and they, in turn, were confident that they had made the right choice when they gave him their support that first afternoon.

Walesa's leadership abilities among his fellow-workers had been proven. His skills face-to-face with the state were yet to be tested. As the first light crept among the shipyard cranes, they soon would be.

5 A Dialogue
   Heard 'Round the World

*We consider our factories to be the
property of the Polish nation, but we
demand that we should be the real
masters in the factory and in the country.*
—Lech Walesa, August 26, 1980

The arrangements for Jagielski's arrival at the Lenin
Shipyard took almost all of Saturday, August 23. At two in the
afternoon, the top provincial administrator, Governor Jerzy
Kolodziejski, came to the yard to work out the details of the
meeting.

The government official appeared nervous as he approached
the thousand or so workers at the gate. "Look straight into the
eyes of the workers!" one of them shouted at him. "I will," the
governor replied. For two hours, Kolodziejski met with Lech
Badkowski (the elderly writer who had been added to the MKS),
Bogdan Lis, Andrzej Gwiazda and Zdzislaw Kobylinski, a
warehouseman. Walesa and shipyard director Gniech attended
as observers.

Meanwhile, the battle with the Polish media continued. That
afternoon, the first edition of the *Solidarity Strike Bulletin*—
30,000 copies—appeared from the presses of the Lenin
Shipyard, now occupied by the strikers. It contained the most
recent MKS statement complaining that "the news in the press,
radio and television is both distorted and incomplete. The
whole country awaits genuine and accurate news from the
strike-bound Baltic coast. The existence of the Inter-Factory
Strike Committee in Gdansk, Szczecin and Elblag is ignored.
Nothing has been said about the fact that the strike action is
co-ordinated and directed by the democratically elected

MKS... The full solidarity of the strikers with the MKS is being concealed from the public.''

There was myriad other "disinformation" to clear up. "A false impression is being created that the workers in public services have not joined the strike," the MKS pointed out. "In fact, they joined us very early, but continue to maintain essential services with the full consent of the MKS in order to provide for the basic needs of the community. We are accused of antisocialist tendencies, while in fact our demands are completely within the law and in no way in conflict with the existing system or the government's political alliances." That is, the MKS was challenging neither the formal supremacy of the party nor Poland's place in the Soviet-dominated Eastern European bloc. "We point out that the lies about the situation and the intentions of the strikers destroy all remnants of confidence in the official press, radio and television, and they do not lessen public disquiet." The MKS once more demanded that Poles be told the truth.

Along with the new factory delegations coming to join the MKS (membership now exceeded 375 plants), the rest of what would be a commission of MKS experts arrived. In addition to Mazowiecki, the group included another prominent Catholic intellectual, Andrzej Wielowiejski, and several academics who had participated in a KOR-related educational project known as the Flying University. Apart from historian Geremek, who arrived the night before, there were two economists, Waldemar Kuczynski and Tadeusz Kowalik, as well as Marxist sociologist Jadwiga Staniszkis.

At four o'clock the pre-negotiation meeting broke up and Walesa, accompanied by his wife, entered the conference hall to report that talks would commence that evening at eight.

The two teams faced each other over a long, narrow wooden table in a small meeting room off the main conference hall. Scores of Western newsmen looked on through a glass wall. The negotiating teams were as different as they could be. On one side sat the mustachioed Walesa, with Lis, Gwiazda and other MKS representatives around him. On the other was Deputy Premier Mieczyslaw Jagielski, age 56, whose greying hair and well-cut suit gave him the air of a distinguished Western banker. When the trouble first broke out in Lublin in July, it was Jagielski who had been sent to deal with the railway workers.

He had the reputation of being a shrewd and flexible mediator. Flanking the deputy premier on either side were provincial governor Kolodziejski and provincial party first secretary Tadeusz Fiszbach.

On the table between the two sides was a clutter of mineral water bottles, documents, and a tangle of electric cords attached to a battery of microphones. In an unprecedented arrangement, the voices of this dialogue were to be transmitted outside the enclave of negotiations. In the large conference hall 700 members of the MKS plenary were listening in, as were thousands more throughout the shipyard. Portions of the extraordinary meeting would be broadcast over Gdansk radio. It was to be a discussion held within earshot of the entire world.

"The first demand concerns the acceptance of trade unions which are independent of the party," Jagielski began, once the meeting got down to serious business. "I understand that the intention of this demand is to have trade unions which would be real and effective representatives of the interests of each worker.

"There is no doubt that the structure of the present law does not correspond with present requirements, the present situation, the present needs and aspirations of the working population," the deputy premier admitted. "I would like us to find a constructive solution. If I said that you can elect your own people to the trade unions, would they not be solid and effective?" he asked. "Why not elect the people who have your trust to the workers' councils or other bodies?" He went on to say that his proposed alternative to the free trade unions would permit the workers to do their own analyses of costs of living, on the basis of which pay increases could be calculated. "I think that this should be calmly discussed and thought over," Jagielski added in support of the government offer.

"This is not what we expected, but it can be discussed," Walesa cut in. "At the moment I propose that we move to another point."

The deputy premier seemed to welcome the chance to move on to the question of guarantees of safety for the strikers and their supporters, taking a leisurely fifteen minutes to offer a "positive" response. He then turned quickly to the question of political prisoners. "At present, according to the report I received before my departure, there are no political prisoners in Poland. That is, persons sentenced for their political convictions. This is a statement which I received from the minister of justice," Jagielski said.

"The thing is like this," replied one of the MKS negotiators. "These matters are known to us, to the community," he said, referring to prisoners specifically named in the MKS demand. "In the same way we know how these trials looked and that is why, if we are able to talk honestly, I suggest a review of these trials—but after these people have been released. This is the truth," he insisted. "We examined these trials. I was there. There were others there, and I can say it straight, because as a worker I do not have to mince words, that the trials were faked. Thank you." From outside the conference room the negotiators could hear thunderous applause from next door, and rumbling approval through the shipyard.

Florian Wisniewski spoke up. "I understand the premier presented things the way they were presented by the ministry of justice. But we are dealing with something completely different. A man who is undertaking actions because of his convictions should not be repressed or harassed—this is our point.

"I can give you an example," Wisniewski continued. "I'm staying in the shipyard. My home—I mean my apartment—was surrounded by the police because they knew I would enter the car park and they simply wanted to get me there. I have a difficult situation at home, as I have four children, and it is known that a man with such a big family would not risk too much." The electrician from Elektromontaz paused. "These are difficult matters and I understand that they are difficult and have to be seen against the social background. I am of the opinion that when the country was liberated we were fighting for the slogan 'Man is born and lives free.' I think, Mr. Premier, that you will understand this."

Another MKS representative jumped in. "Mr. Premier, up to now the press has said that everything was fine in our industry and economy. Until recently there was an official opinion that although there are difficulties, everything is going well. Now it turns out that there were numerous shortcomings which were hidden or glossed over. Does the premier think that a similar situation could exist in the justice ministry?" Jagielski was asked pointedly. "Why should things be better there?"

Another MKS speaker turned to a different aspect of the truth. "Tourists are arriving, people are returning from vacation. All are stating unanimously that they do not know what is happening in Gdansk. They are shocked when they find out. Can one in such a case speak of honest information?''

Someone else took up the issue of communications with a personal example. ''I sent my child to a holiday camp at Konstancin. He was supposed to return on the eighteenth. He didn't return. I tried to telephone to find out what is happening to the child, and I couldn't telephone. I believe this to be a purely social matter. I'm not the only one in such a situation. It cannot be like this. This should be considered, Mr. Premier.''

''Mr. Chairman,'' intervened Jagielski, addressing himself to Walesa, ''I can check on this matter, but not right now. I shall clarify this matter with the central authorities and let them have this information.''

Lech Sobieszek, a metal worker from the Siarkopol factory, wasn't satisfied. ''One of the first conditions—maybe I should read the conditions—one of the first conditions for the initiation of talks is the restoration of all telephone lines.'' He was angry, but restrained. ''I do not believe this has been fulfilled. I would simply propose that the talks should be interrupted. This is my opinion. . .'' A wave of applause was heard from outside the hall.

''This has been on our list,'' Jagielski said hastily, then quickly correcting himself, ''on *your* list of tabled demands, on the lists of subjects for the talks.'' The deputy premier attempted to steer the discussion back to safer waters. ''I would like to make the following proposal. Give me, gentlemen, a chance to clarify the matter. I came to the meeting and want to talk, to talk and to explain our viewpoint. I'm not in a position to clarify all matters.'' But they wouldn't let go. When would the deputy premier have the matter clarified? Tomorrow, Jagielski said. It wasn't enough. Jagielski hastened to offer an elaborate account of weather conditions in Warsaw—a gale the previous night that had knocked out much of the telephone exchange. Somebody reminded Jagielski that the links with Warsaw had been cut the previous Friday. Why hadn't the news about the alleged hurricane appeared in the media, someone else demanded. One of the skilled workers, his voice tinged with sarcasm, informed Jagielski that in modern telephone systems it wasn't necessary to reconnect the socket of every individual subscriber. ''It is a very simple matter. It just means the issuing of an order.'' Outside, they burst into laughter.

At last, Walesa stepped in to let Jagielski off the hook. ''I propose that, without discussion, we hear the views of the premier on the individual subjects," said the MKS leader. Jagielski resumed the government's presentation, but it was already clear what the state's initial position was on the critical first demand for independent unions.

The deputy minister agreed that workers ought to have information about the economic situation, but it was easy to agree to such a relatively abstract request. He went further, in fact, conceding that most of the economic demands put forward by the MKS were just, in principle, but it was out of the question to implement them in the present economic situation. Jagielski used the occasion to lecture on the complexities of economic calculations as he hedged on the questions of strike pay, raises, and cost-of-living adjustments. He was about to launch into a similarly detailed peroration on meat exports, but noticing the MKS negotiators getting restive, he moved on. He hinted that there might be some give on the matter of special family allowances for the police and militia, but remembered to throw in a good word for these particular forces of the state. Reminding the workers of the difficult hours put in by the police, and their frequent and disruptive changes of job location, Jagielski found himself surrounded by barely polite laughter. Overall, only partial economic changes could be considered at the moment, but, as the *Solidarity* bulletin sardonically reported the next day, "he omitted to specify what they were."

On the question of social and political issues, Jagielski didn't budge from the state's traditional position. He refused to publish the strikers' full list of demands in the media. Guarantees for the right to strike would require further discussion. The deputy premier feigned surprise at the news of harassment of strike supporters, despite the well-known fact that upwards of 20 KOR members were being held in Warsaw jails at that moment, and promised to investigate. In similar surrealistic fashion, Jagielski expressed his "sincere belief in the existence of freedom of speech and publication in Poland." The censorship, he remarked, "should be made to work more smoothly," but certainly there ought to be no let-up of repressive measures against publications which he described as "antisocialist and socially harmful."

The meeting had gone on for two hours before Jagielski summed up, insisting on his desire for honesty and to be able to "look straight in the eyes of everyone here in Gdansk." That's why he had spoken frankly. "If we made unrealistic pledges this would simply mean that we were dishonest. I want to thank you for your attention."

"Mr. Premier, we have listened to everything very carefully," replied Walesa. But he still wanted to know why there were these periodic crises in Poland and how one could avoid them. "But to avoid or draw conclusions, one must know the reasons," Walesa said, "and here we still have not discovered the reasons why—why we keep running in circles." The details of the joint communique were quickly wrapped up, the national anthem was sung, and Jagielski and his party were escorted to the gates of the Lenin Shipyard.

On the whole, it was disappointing. The excitement of being able to tell the representatives of the state exactly what one thought had quickly paled. The government's offer for revamped trade unions, according to the *Solidarity* bulletin issued the next afternoon, amounted to "no more than yet another sly attempt to avoid discussion on the establishment of free trade unions." Altogether, the government statement "was vague, filled with platitudes, at times inept, and devoid of any definite proposals." More talks had been agreed to, but it was clear that there was long, hard slogging ahead. Further, the precondition of restoring telephone links had yet to be met.

Late that night, the first delegation from the Szczecin MKS arrived. Their Inter-Factory Strike Committee now represented 134 enterprises, and at the main gate of the Warski Shipyard a large sign proclaimed: "We express our solidarity with the shipyard workers in Gdansk." Talks with government spokesman Barcikowski had begun two days before, the Szczecin delegates reported, and the demands in the western Baltic port closely resembled those of Gdansk, especially concerning the issue of independent trade unions.

At Sunday morning mass on August 24 at the Lenin Shipyard, twice as many people attended as had the week before. Father Jankowski, garbed in a pale green cassock, held up the symbolic wafer before more than 10,000 workers and their families.

To the south, in Warsaw, a somewhat different ritual was taking place on the eleventh day of the strike. The 140 members of the central committee of the Polish United Workers Party had been assembled for what First Secretary Gierek hoped would be a simple two-hour information session.

Instead, partially at the insistence of Defense Minister Wojciech Jaruzelski—the general whose reluctance to send in the troops against the Gdansk workers in 1970 had helped to topple Gomulka—the central committee session turned into a full-fledged six-hour debate over Gierek's handling of the present crisis. The deadlock-breaking speech came from Tadeusz Fiszbach, the slight, balding, mid-fiftyish first secretary of the Gdansk branch of the PUWP, the provincial organization most closely in touch with the events on the coast.

Fiszbach, who had flown to Warsaw with chief negotiator Jagielski following last night's talks, did not waste time reciting the usual self-justifying formulas of the party. "It would be a mistake to assume that the strike in the Gdansk shipyard and in several hundred other firms in the city is a result of the activities of a small group of antisocialist forces," said the Gdansk party chief. "It would be wrong to assume that the origin of the strike had its roots in groups isolated from the working class or hostile to People's Poland. During the strikes the workers haven't taken any actions directed against the authorities or against the bases on which the socialist system rests or against our alliances," Fiszbach assured the central committee.

He then offered a cold, empirical description of the situation as he saw it, unembroidered by wishful thinking. New strike committees were daily being formed in the enterprises; increasingly more institutions were declaring their solidarity with the MKS demands. MKS literature was being effectively distributed throughout the region. The population was unimpressed by government arguments about economic losses caused by the strike. The strategy of branch-by-branch talks had failed and a unanimous position had been adopted by all the strikers.

As for party efforts to reverse the tide, said Fiszbach, discussions initiated by party activists had totally failed to get people back to work. In fact, in many enterprises, party militants had gone over to the side of the MKS and were supporting its demands. At party meetings the day before, members had brought up the question of improving party work and complained that they were not properly informed. The attempt to sway opinion through the mechanism of the trade unions had only resulted in hundreds of workers turning in their union cards. The Gdansk branch, said its first secretary, was particularly critical of the recent speech made by trade union head Szydlak, and above all, of what he had said about the subject of sharing power.

Fiszbach noted that last night's talks, which were heard over the loudspeakers, had been greeted with shouts, whistling and worse. The strike committee criticized the government side for being unprepared. The striking workers considered that changes must take place in the party and in the government, he concluded, utilizing a familiar party circumlocution whose intent—a direct attack on Gierek—was unmistakable.

Edward Gierek, looking obviously drawn and tired after the debate, which he described as "sharp and painful," appeared on national television that evening to confess the party's, as well as his own, sins. The loudspeakers in the Lenin Shipyard carried his speech.

The party had made grave mistakes, Gierek admitted, and he promised "a basic shift in party and government policy." In a slight reversal of the notion of giving flesh to the spirit of the party's new policy, the first secretary announced the dismissal of Poland's prime minister, Edward Babiuch, and three other full members of the ruling politburo as well as several lesser figures. Babiuch, who had taken the reins of government only in February, was to be replaced by Jozef Pinkowski, the 51-year-old secretary of the central committee. Also ousted were trade union boss Jan Szydlak, would-be strike negotiator Tadeusz Pyka, and propaganda head Jerzy Lukaszewicz. A cabinet shuffle was also in the works. Former foreign minister Stefan Olszowski and economist Tadeusz Grabski—"comrades who had perceived earlier the growing irregularities and tried to counteract them and whose voices we had not heeded in time"—were reinstated to the central committee by the humble Gierek. Olszowski, aged 48, had been the chairman of a party group of experts that had drafted a widely disseminated paper on the need for economic change two years earlier. In February 1980, Gierek had bounced him from the politburo and sent him off to East Germany as ambassador. The burly 51-year-old Grabski was a provincial party chief whose speech the year before, lambasting government policies, had led to his removal from the politburo.

On the question of the strikers' central demand for independent unions, Gierek offered no more than a new fallback position. The party's central committee felt that the central trade union council should hold new elections in all factories, with secret ballots and an unlimited number of candidates (rather than the usual hand-picked few). If the "recently self-elected" representatives—meaning the strike committees—were lasting and popular, their members should "find themselves" in the new union executives, Gierek argued. "We are ready to talk to the workers' representatives, but we cannot make promises that cannot be fulfilled or agree to demands striking at the basis of the state's existence." He then repeated his words of the previous week, that "only socialist Poland can be a free country with inviolable frontiers"—an implicit reference to possible Soviet intervention.

In the shipyard, the sight of Gierek fighting for his political life was taken as a small victory, but the concessions were not impressive. "It's a patching up of holes," Lech Walesa told the waiting reporters. But wasn't he satisfied with the removal of figures whose policies had been the target of workers' criticisms? "I'm not interested in personnel matters," Walesa shot back. "I don't know these people. Our main problem is free trade unions, and it is not important for us who will meet with us."

It took all of Monday, August 25, to resolve the tussle over telephone communications. At three in the afternoon Bogdan Lis and Lech Badkowski negotiated by phone with provincial governor Kolodziejski on the issues of restoring communications and setting a date for the next negotiating session.

Kolodziejski called back at 6:30, saying that connections with Szczecin had been restored, and links with Warsaw would soon be operative. Communications with the rest of the country would open as talks progressed, he added. The MKS presidium met and decided to put the question of resuming negotiations to the Inter-Factory plenum. At 7:30 the 700 delegates in the conference hall unanimously rejected the idea of going ahead with talks, on the grounds that the government had yet to meet the strikers' preconditions. Badkowski phoned the governor after the meeting to inform him of the decision. An hour later it was possible to phone Warsaw. Kolodziejski arrived at the shipyard a little after 10 p.m. to meet with Lis and Badkowski. The agreement didn't come until after midnight. The government had given in. In addition to restored communications, Kolodziejski promised that the media would report on the talks nationally and that local television would broadcast a 20-minute report. It was agreed that negotiations would resume the next morning.

Throughout the day, an air of unhurried peacefulness pervaded the shipyard. It was almost as if the lull was welcomed. In the afternoon, Walesa napped in the glassed-in meeting room, stretched out on two armchairs. The decision by the MKS plenary to stand firm on the demand for restored telephone links was made easily. The MKS experts and a group of Polish journalists held meetings of their own. In the evening, in one of the big canteens, musicians from Gdansk arrived to perform a concert to express their solidarity with the strikers, and strains of Chopin floated through the shipyard.

Members of the striking workers' guards linked arms to form a corridor for the government commission on Tuesday morning, August 26. Jagielski and his team, followed by reporters, arrived just before eleven. They marched to the conference hall through a sea of silent blue-clad strikers. Inside, the two groups passed under the glare of television lights and took their places in the yellow-and-black-flecked easy chairs on either side of the table.

MKS chairman Walesa opened the session, his voice broadcast in all directions over the shipyard loudspeakers. "Three important days have passed since our previous meeting," he said, obliquely referring to the government shuffle. "The most important of our demands is the business of trade unions. We want free and independent—truly independent—trade unions. In the course of our talks, Mr. Premier, it has been possible for you to ascertain that we are not fighting against the socialist system. We do not want to disturb the principles of social ownership of the means of production. We consider our factories to be the property of the Polish nation, but we demand that we should be the real masters in the factory and in the country. We have been promised this many times; now we have decided to demand this through strikes." Concluding his opening remarks on a friendler note, Walesa added, "Our talks will be difficult. We all have to have lots of patience and goodwill."

The deputy minister, who had been squinting uncomfortably under the glare of television lights during Walesa's statement,

Alina Pienkowska

Photo: Hemingson

Andrzej Gwiazda

Photo: Hemingson

Mariusz Wilk

Piotr Dyk

*Jagielski and
Walesa sign the
Gdansk
Agreement*

*Walesa talks to
strikers*

began with a personal request. "Mr. Chairman, I've never had the pleasure of being filmed by television cameras all the time. Let's switch them off," Jagielski suggested. "I have bad eyes, ever since my stay in prison." (During World War II, he had been jailed by the Gestapo.) The spotlights were turned off. Jagielski reviewed the government's position, skipping the independent trade union demand to concentrate on those dealing with working conditions and economic matters. The government had clearly softened its line, and Jagielski now proposed that the two sides could set increases in wages and benefits, and could fix a date for bringing them into effect.

Walesa cut into Jagielski's recitation to say that the demands being addressed by the deputy premier, although important, were secondary, and that point one had to be tackled first. Without that, he insisted, the others meant nothing. At this point, room was made in the crowded conference chamber for the arrival of the government's team of experts, counterparts to the MKS's group of intellectual advisers. Jagielski, as requested, offered to talk about point one, "which you treat as the most important."

"Not me, but all of us," countered Walesa.

"I'll present my point of view once again. This problem was raised at the recent plenum of our party," Jagielski noted. He then reiterated the party position that Gierek had presented on television on Sunday night. Jagielski's only additional concession was one for which he himself took credit. "I said, under the influence of the atmosphere of our Saturday meeting, that a new trade union bill should be passed, and it would be beneficial to include in this new bill some regulations concerning procedures for work stoppages as a way of supporting workers' demands in those cases when more suitable and beneficial forms prove to be a failure." It was a roundabout way of saying that the government was officially prepared to recognize the right to strike—in certain cases.

The MKS responded to Jagielski by once more pressing home their basic stand. Andrzej Gwiazda, the bearded engineer from Elmor, took the lead. "We're meeting here during a social and economic crisis. What has led to this crisis?" he asked. "For years, local and branch authorities have given accounts of how much steel they produce, how much coal, how many metres of wire. But nobody gave an account of what it all meant for the life of the worker. The trade unions," he went on, "whose main aim was to protect the workers, did not defend their interests, but on the contrary, accommodated management, all the time ready to act hand in hand with management against the workers' interests.

"The only way to prevent the unions from degenerating," Gwiazda said, "is the right to form new ones. Sure, this may create some confusion; there might be unions made up of a couple of hundred people, there may be militant unions which will proclaim strikes every week. Still, we think agreement is possible. The people of this area have demonstrated their good judgment, calm and maturity. I think new unions should be formed.

"It is not a question of name," he insisted. Gwiazda argued that the old unions didn't have to be dissolved, simply that new ones must be permitted. For them to exist successfully, they also had to have their own publications. "It is necessary that these newspapers be able to write the truth, irrespective of whether or not this truth suits the current leadership. The press can be manipulated, that's true, but only for a limited time. Then indignation and ferment mount, and new unrest breaks out. Poles have had enough of hearing about 'errors and distortions,' repeated cyclically. We want to point out the errors before they grow so big that one has to make almost a revolution in this country." Outside, the crowd was electrified. Gwiazda was saying what hadn't been said aloud in years. "Workers have to have freedom of speech when they are right *and* when they are wrong. Discussion is possible only when there are opinions which are not considered in advance the 'correct' opinions."

The applause from outside had barely died down before Bogdan Lis took the floor. He couldn't understand why the government was trying so hard to reorganize the old unions. "The old unions are so discredited that even *our* presence in this institution would not change that fact. We don't want to replace old blood with young blood, we simply want a brand new organization." This point was made by several other MKS spokesmen. There was even the hint that the entire country might soon be facing a general strike if something wasn't done. A brief recess was taken after the MKS presentation. When the session reconvened, Jagielski immediately proposed that, rather than debating point one further, a subcommittee of representatives from both sides should be struck to study the issues raised by the first demand.

It wasn't clear whether the government was seeking a face-saving device by which they might give in or merely stalling for time; in any case, the MKS negotiators agreed to the subcommittee, and talks for the day were adjourned. The experts and a few members from each side stayed behind to work out an agenda for a subcommittee meeting later in the day. Walesa, meanwhile, went to the main conference hall to explain to the MKS plenum that the subcommittee would not be empowered to decide anything, but merely would record the points of view of the two sides. "These will be propositions only," he said. "We will all decide, all those gathered in the hall of delegates." At the main gate, the strike leader repeated to the crowd outside what he had said in the conference hall. "They won't cheat us," Walesa assured them. "We won't let them."

Polish television viewers were in for a surprise that evening. On millions of screens flickered the rare sight of Stefan Cardinal Wyszynski preaching in Czestochowa. It was clear that the unusual appearance on national media of the nearly 80-year-old primate of the Polish Roman Catholic Church was meant, among other things, to underscore the government's view of the seriousness of the crisis.

If the workers at the Lenin Shipyard were hoping for some words of encouragement in the cardinal's address, they would be disappointed. In his 45-minute sermon, Wyszynski counseled "peace, calm, reason, prudence and responsibility for the Polish nation." It was a medieval homily, laced with arcane turns of speech as formulaic in their own way as the pat phrases of party bosses, but its meaning was unmistakable.

The primate harped on the themes of order, duty and responsibility. The state was duly chided for its atheism, a rebuke that the authorities were apparently prepared to accept meekly in return for the sermon's overall stress on moderation. The defence of religious and moral order was linked to the order of the family. Even in this paean to the family and its children—"shaped with divine powers under the hearts of their mothers"—there were allusions to the present turmoil. "If there is the priority of the family in society," intoned the cardinal, "in this case the national economy must be in a way a family affair."

Wyszynski wrapped the heart of his message in a passage on

the "vocational order." "Although man has the right to rest, although sometimes—when he has no other means—he has the right to make his stand by refraining from work, we know, however, that the argument is very costly. The cost of this argument runs into billions, which burdens the whole national economy," said Wyszynski, sounding more like the minister of finance than the nation's chief spiritual adviser. "Work and not idleness is man's ally in his personal life, in family and home well-being, as well as in national well-being. The more conscientiously we work, the less we shall borrow." The cardinal seemed willing to abandon much of the workers' program, "as long as order is restored in Poland. Even though the demands may be well-founded—and they usually are—it never happens that they can be satisfied immediately, today. Their implementation must be gradual."

In the Lenin Shipyard, the cardinal's speech was received in disappointed silence. The workers mulled over his words as his image gave way to that of political commentator and central committee member Ryszard Wojna. Wojna read passages from tomorrow's editorial in the main party newspaper, *Trybuna Ludu*, warning that Poland was approaching the "brink of catastrophe that recalls the events of the eighteenth century," when the country was partitioned out of existence. Wyszynski had also made a reference to "the difficulty with which we regained our freedom."

It had been a letdown. If the head of the church was willing to recognize the right to strike, his insinuation that the present shutdown could be seen as "idleness" seemed singularly inappropriate. In the conference hall, the devout Walesa attempted to shrug it off. "We don't want Poland swamped because of us. We want Poland to be rich and smiling," he joked, avoiding direct reference to the sermon.

That Wyszynski had blundered was made clear the following day when local priests arrived at the shipyard to claim that the cardinal's intentions had been misrepresented through censorship. Believers were quick to believe these charges, but publication of Wyszynski's sermon in *Trybuna Ludu* that day —an unusual event in itself—proved beyond doubt that the prelate had been unusually pressing in his efforts to restrain the strikers. It was a miscalculation which the church, mindful of its efforts to serve as a loyal opposition to a communist regime, would seek to repair.

While the workers watched Wyszynski, the focus of events in the shipyard quietly shifted out of the spotlight to a nearby building where the experts were meeting. Representing the strikers were Lis, Gwiazda, Zdzislaw Kobylinski, and three advisers—Mazowiecki, Tadeusz Kowalik, and sociologist Jadwiga Staniszkis. The government side consisted of Governor Kolodziejski, the minister and deputy minister of the engineering industry, and three professors.

The first meeting was technical and abstract. The subcommittee discussed the possibility of independent trade unions in hypothetical terms: *If* independent unions were created, then such-and-such legislation should be changed. Other topics included: when and how to introduce legal changes to regulate access of the new unions to funds and property; the new functions of labor courts; control of work safety and other related matters. The MKS workers, impatient with the legalistic theorizing, warned that if such new regulations were not introduced, the new unions would simply "exist and strike."

The question of how to register the new unions posed a legal problem. One of the government experts argued that the only legal possibility was registration in the existing monopoly central union organization. The MKS rejected that proposal. By the end of the meeting a concession was gained—the government would find a way of registering the new unions independently from the central trade union council.

Another controversy centred on the MKS demand that a guarantee be written into the agreement giving all Polish workers, not just themselves, the right to organize independent unions. The government side balked. It would look as though the government were promoting new unions, they argued, remembering that the Czechoslovakian regime overthrown by Russian tanks in 1968 had been criticized for having "encouraged from above." The MKS presidium members were puzzled by this refusal. "It will cost a lot of money," they said, meaning that if the right to form independent unions wasn't clearly nation-wide, costly strikes would inevitably break out in other parts of the country to achieve the same goal.

On the whole, however, the first meeting of the working group had gone well. Sociologist Staniszkis, who later produced an account of the session, noted its relaxed atmosphere and the untruculent tones that prevailed. One of the reasons for this, she thought, was that the intellectuals on both sides were more or less members of the same Warsaw social circles. The government advisers could be viewed as somewhat critical but still loyal party supporters, the MKS advisers as more openly critical but nonetheless acceptable participants in the pattern of liberalization permitted by the Gierek regime. This atmosphere made the negotiations of the working group easier. Elements of mutual trust already existed among the advisers and "leaks" from both sides allowed the work to proceed more smoothly. From Staniszkis' point of view this "internal loyalty" among the intellectuals posed dangers for the workers. In any case, the first meeting ended in an optimistic mood.

When the subcommittee met again on the following day, Wednesday, August 27, much had already changed. For one thing, it had become clear why the regime fought so hard to cut off communications between the Baltic coast and the rest of the country. With telephones restored and news of the strikes in the media, workers throughout the country were joining the protest. In addition to the nearly 500 enterprises on strike in the Gdansk area, there were shutdowns in Bydgoszcz and Torun, two important industrial centres 175 km. south of the Tri-Cities. In southern Poland, an auto plant in Bielsko-Biala was out, the buses in Cracow had stopped, the workers at the Nowa Huta steel mill were drawing up a list of grievances. In Wroclaw, 30 factories employing over 60,000 workers were on strike and an MKS had been formed. All of these developments had occurred in a matter of two days.

In between the first and second sessions of the subcommittee, Jagielski had shuttled back to Warsaw once more. He met with politburo officials to discuss the rough draft of the text being prepared by the advisers. The party editorial in *Trybuna Ludu*, underlining the fact that Poland lay "in the direct security zone" of the Soviet Union, hinted that the spreading strikes were raising the "danger of anarchy" and "could bring about results fatal to Poland." In the shipyard, rumors circulated about a state of emergency being declared if the strike didn't end by September 1.

In the subcommittee meeting, a stony-faced government side declared, "Your demand for indendent unions has become an ideological precedent." The MKS advisers sensed what was coming. The government negotiators asked the MKS to produce a political formula, defining its position on the "leading role" of the communist party and related matters. Kobylinski, the warehouseman in the MKS contingent, was surprised. "Why? We thought that such problems would be elaborated in practice, step by step. We do not want to play the role of a political party," he assured the government side. He was taken aback by the sudden change from yesterday's relaxed atmosphere to the deadly serious tone that had replaced it.

The MKS advisers were not surprised. They understood exactly what sort of precedent the MKS represented and how crucial it was for the government to secure in the text of an agreement some sort of formula that would clearly mark the limits of possible reform. They also understood that they were expected by the government to act as a bridge between the regime and the workers. Staniszkis felt that the situation should be explained to the MKS presidium, leaving the decision to them. They could either accept the political formula, or reject it and bargain for a different one. But the other MKS advisers tried to convince their side that such a political formula "didn't mean anything," so "let's use their double-talk." Later, there would be considerable debate about the performance of the MKS advisers and the importance of the political preamble.

In the end, an "editorial" group was formed to draft the exact wording of the formula. Staniszkis decided not to participate in it. She believed that the best guarantee for the long-term survival of the workers' movement was to create strong links with progressive, antibureaucratic groups in the communist party rather than to emphasize connections with clerics and nationalists. In the days that followed, as she sat in the large conference hall, she remained haunted by the sight of workers' faces pressed to the windows, trying to catch a glimpse of the country's future.

The main topic of the brief talks that took place between the government and the strikers on Thursday morning, August 28, was freedom. As Jagielski and his team listened, MKS presidium members Lech Badkowski and Andrzej Gwiazda made the main presentations.

Badkowski, a writer in his fifties, outlined the workers' case for compliance with the already existing constitutional guarantees of free speech, press, and religion, the third demand on the MKS list. Citing the repeated interference of censorship into political, social and cultural life over the years, the white-haired author expressed the fear that agreement on point No. 3 might be only temporary. While the MKS wasn't seeking the abolition of censorship, it was calling for legal guarantees that would allow freedom of expression for people of different opinions and a full and truthful flow of information.

Deputy Premier Jagielski replied that the position of the government commission coincided, in principle, with that of the MKS. Only questions of detail were left to be resolved, he said, implying that the editorial subcommittee could readily come up with a draft that would prove acceptable.

Andrzej Gwiazda presented the next item on the agenda, MKS demand No. 4, concerning political prisoners, repression, and the matter of workers and students who had been fired or expelled. He quickly summed up the facts about a series of faked trials that had led to the conviction of political opponents of the regime. The engineer reminded the government about those students expelled from the universities in 1968 and the workers fired from their jobs as a result of the strikes of 1970 and 1976.

Although Gwiazda was as exhausted as the other strike leaders who, for two weeks now, had lived on short sleep and under immense pressure, the memories were still fresh. He presented Jagielski with a list of those currently under detention. "Mr. Premier, this is the key issue: Are we going to live in a democratic system or a police state?" Gwiazda asked. Outside the shipyard gate, among the thousands who listened over the loudspeakers, his words struck a spark of passion. While Walesa had a magnetism of personality that he communicated to the crowd, it was Gwiazda who more often seemed to cut through to the heart of the issue. "What are the guarantees that these things won't happen again?" he asked. "People are afraid, afraid even to speak out. And this has to be done away with."

There were a few sharp exchanges between the two sides on the question of the administration of justice, but at the end of the flurry, Jagielski soothingly announced that the intentions which inspired point No. 4 coincided, in principle, with those of the government commission, and that the matter could be turned over to the working group.

The talks broke up at 1 p.m. Although many in the shipyard wouldn't believe it until they saw the signatures, it seemed that the two sides were moving toward a formal agreement.

Now it was in the hands of the teams of experts, who were responsible for drafting the language of the agreement. They retreated into almost continual session, hammering out details on the remaining points. It was a matter of time now.

Walesa was prepared to give the government some room. At the shipyard gate after the bargaining session, he issued an appeal to workers in the rest of Poland to refrain from further walkouts. "It is not good to have the whole country paralysed," the strike leader said. "Let Poland work. We'll settle everything, just like we said the first day." He added that if the talks hadn't brought results in three or four days, "then let the strikes spread."

Afterwards, Walesa even prepared the text of a brief appeal that asked workers not to start new strikes. The statement was handed over to government officials, who were left to decide whether to make it public. They apparently concluded that the appeal would make Walesa into too much of a national figure and therefore dropped the plan.

Although the government commission under Jagielski appeared inclined to reach a settlement with the strikers, it wasn't as clear that the regime itself was prepared to do likewise. Ever since the crisis began on August 14, the party leadership had vacillated between concessions and threats. No public address system broadcast the debates within the inner sanctum of the politburo, but the actions of the party apparatus and the line enunciated in the party press provided good clues to the regime's main position.

On the very day that Jagielski seemed to be heading toward agreement on certain demands, the party was still fighting a rearguard action. A document from the ideological department of the party's central committee had gone out to all party branches that afternoon. It pointed out the hazards inherent in the creation of free trade unions. "It would lead to a split in the trade union movement," argued ideologues. "At least two central bodies, representing different fractions of the working class, would come into play." More importantly, "the existence of a socio-political structure independent of the ruling party and the state power would be a bridgehead for anticommunist forces in our country." The idea of "antisocialist elements" orchestrating the strike movement apparently died hard in certain crannies of the party. "Such unions would have the practical function of an opposition party...They would give birth to a situation of dual power." The last of these fears was less far-fetched than the threat of antisocialist conspirators at the helm of the new trade union movement. The ideological department's text concluded by underlining "the need for the party to play a leading role in relation to the trade union movement."

At ten o'clock on Thursday night, foreign correspondents in Warsaw were summoned to the offices of the Interpress agency, located on the rim of Victory Square, the site of Poland's Tomb of the Unknown Soldier. The occasion was an opportunity to hear agency head Miroslaw Wojciechowski deliver one of the most direct warnings yet to the Baltic strikers. "The situation in Poland is very difficult, with the number of strikes rising every day like an avalanche. This cannot go on much longer," said the news agency chief. He, too, accused "certain antisocial elements and extremists who are escalating their activities" of "threatening workers who don't want to join the strike. The situation is very, very serious. It can provoke an abnormal situation in our country," Wojciechowski hinted darkly. His refusal to answer questions and his abrupt departure from the press conference heightened the impression that this was a message direct from the politburo.

The barrage continued the next day, Friday, August 29, as the party press hacked away at "antisocialist elements" among the strikers and underscored the country's link to "that great power, the Soviet Union." Further arrests of dissidents in Warsaw were reported. An official at the Ministry of Information said the workers did "not realize how serious the situation has become," adding that there were "limits where there must be a reaction by the state." No formal negotiations were held at the Lenin Shipyard that day, although the subcommittee working on the text of an agreement remained in session well past midnight. Life in the MKS headquarters was enlivened, however, by the arrival of Polish film director Andrzej Wajda, who talked about making a sequel to his 1977 hit *Man of Marble*, based on the events taking place in the shipyard. "Let's hope it will have a happy ending," said the director.

As for the debates taking place within the inner recesses of the party, one could only continue to speculate. For days, there had been rumors that First Secretary Gierek was on his way out.

Perhaps the beleaguered party head was thrashing about in a last-ditch effort to retain power. According to some sources, Gierek proposed taking military action against the Lenin Shipyard strikers. It was even claimed that the first secretary's plan had a slight majority in the politburo, but that it fell apart when Defense Minister Jaruzelski and security chief Stefan Kania refused to sanction such action, saying that they could not vouch for the loyalty of their forces.

If the party had any serious thoughts of dispersing the strikers by means of force, the practicality of such a risky scheme was brought into further question by major new walkouts. On Friday, 20,000 Silesian copper miners joined the Baltic strikers. The official Polish press agency confirmed that it was the first significant action to occur close to the 81 coal mines centred near Katowice. It was the area that produced the country's chief export and provided the political base for party leader Gierek. A delegate from southern Silesia arrived at the Lenin Shipyard to report on the walkout and to wish the workers luck in their debate with the government commission. Though some in the party may have been dreaming of a lightning-quick assault on the strike headquarters, with the appearance of the Silesian miners on the scene, the country in fact was on the verge of a general strike.

Deputy Premier Jagielski returned to the Lenin Shipyard on Saturday morning, August 31, his usual placid exterior betraying nothing of whatever stormy debates had taken place within the party. It was as if the heated rhetoric of the past two days had passed like a late summer squall, leaving clear blue skies.

In the glassed-in conference room, Walesa opened the new round of talks. His words could be heard throughout the shipyard. "I greet the government commission for the fourth time," he said. "The text of the agreed version of point one is still in the typewriter. It'll be ready in five minutes."

The document which the typist was hastily preparing began: "On Point No. 1, which reads: 'To accept trade unions as free and independent of the party, as laid down in Convention No. 87 of the ILO and ratified by Poland, which refers to the matter of trade union rights,' the following decision has been reached." There were seven subsections. "The activity of the trade unions of People's Poland has not lived up to the hopes and aspirations of the workers," said the first subsection. "We thus consider that it will be beneficial to create new union organizations, which will run themselves, and which will be authentic expressions of the working class." The old trade unions would continue to exist, the document added.

In return for the concession above, the crucial second subsection gave the party what it was seeking: "The MKS declares that it will respect the principles laid down in the Polish constitution while creating the new independent and self-governing unions. These new unions are intended to defend the social and material interests of the workers, and not to play the role of a political party. They will be established on the basis of the socialization of the means of production of the socialist system which exists in Poland today." The formulization continued: "They will recognize the leading role of the PUWP in the state, and will not oppose the existing system of international alliances." The government, for its part, guaranteed respect for the independent, self-governing character of the new unions, and promised that they would have the means of carrying out their functions.

In the remaining subsections, practical matters of implementation were addressed. The government pledged to make the necessary legal changes now that there was to be more than one union organization in the country, and it was stated that the new unions would not join the existing central council. The unions' right to print and distribute their own publications was recognized, as was the right of participating with government in decisions affecting the conditions of workers, including such matters as the allocation of national assets to consumption and accumulation.

Inside the conference room Jagielski said, "The time has come to finish this. Negotiations were difficult because they concerned fundamental matters. The first point is a cornerstone of the agreement, but economic problems cannot be treated as marginal...I'm glad to say that the MKS took an explicit stand saying that the new unions will recognize social ownership of the means of production and the leading role of the PUWP as well as the system of our alliances. This means that they base themselves on the Polish constitution."

The discussion moved on to the text of point No. 2. The proposed clause briefly promised to guarantee the right to strike in a new trade union law, and committed the government not to undertake reprisals against the strikers or those supporting them. Jagielski momentarily balked at the reference to those supporting the strikers. "It should be as it is," said Walesa. "These people were doing good things." Andrzej Gwiazda and others echoed Walesa's point. The deputy premier nodded, and then the two parties initialed the first and second points of agreement.

Jagielski said that he would now go to Warsaw to secure approval of the central committee and return to Gdansk later in the day for formal signing of the complete agreement. He suggested that the strikers could return to work almost immediately.

"We'll return to work on Monday," Walesa replied. "There are still many loose ends."

"But the agreement will be ready today." Jagielski said.

"One more thing," Walesa added. "We are coming to an agreement, so arresting KOR members should be stopped. They were helping us although they weren't with us. If they start doing something wrong, we'll stop them ourselves." Gwiazda said that the MKS had information about new arrests in Warsaw.

Jagielski promised to look into the matter. "I'll be leaving now," he said. The two sides stood up and sang the national anthem. Throughout the shipyard, thousands joined them.

When Walesa emerged from the conference room into the crowded corridor, he was lifted onto the shoulders of the shipyard workers and carried outside. The Lenin Shipyard was in an uproar. For the first time, the communist government of a "workers' state" had tentatively conceded to its workers the right to form their own organization, independent of party and state. Clambering to the top of the high iron gate, the electrician with the drooping mustache stretched out his arms, waving down the combined cheers of the workers behind him and the massed crowd of sympathizers outside the gate. He lifted a microphone to his mouth.

"You've heard what we've been talking about," he said. "Essentially, we've got things the way we want them. We've got the right to strike and independent unions. We have only one step to go to full success."

But it wasn't over yet. That afternoon the shipyard was a scene of jubilation, exhaustion and confusion. The group of advisers continued to work on the final points of the agreement.

The huge press corps, numbering over 300, demanded interviews. Among the MKS delegates, the idea began to sink in of what had and hadn't been achieved. Jagielski's reference to the leading role of the party was a reaffirmation of the status quo, despite the victory of having achieved independent trade unions.

In the packed conference hall that afternoon, a furious debate burst out over the agreement on point No. 1. Some called the phrase about the leading role of the party "a betrayal of the interests of the working class." Mazowiecki, the chairman of the MKS advisory group, attempted to mollify those who were dissatisfied. Every new organization, he said, has to be in agreement with the constitution. Walesa, characteristically, was more down-to-earth about the compromise. "It would be better without it," he said, referring to the political formula, "but it was necessary and we must all understand that."

The strike leader attempted to emphasize the gains. "We will have a building of our own, with a large sign: Independent Unions." Nonetheless, other delegates complained that the agreement wasn't precise about whether the new unions would be national in scope or limited to the coastal region. Walesa replied that the new trade union law would apply throughout Poland once the independent unions had a firm foothold in the Gdansk area. He then proposed that the MKS deliver an ultimatum to the government, demanding the relase of KOR members and others who had been arrested. The entire hall shouted, "Yes, yes." Once again, the delegates were with him.

The meeting had gone on well into the evening, punctuated by the arrival of new delegations, telegrams of congratulations, and bouquets of flowers. The evening news announced that the central committee had approved the terms of the agreement on independent trade unions. It also reported the conclusion of a similar agreement in Szczecin. Although Jagielski, as promised, had already returned to Gdansk, it was decided to put off further talks until the next day.

Outside the gate on Sunday morning, August 31, the crowd was enormous by the time Father Jankowski began 9 a.m. mass at the Lenin Shipyard.

The final round of talks began at 11:30. "We begin this meeting with hope," Walesa said. He asked Jagielski for an account of the arrestees in Warsaw and promised that the end of the strike would be proclaimed within a few hours of the settlement of outstanding matters.

"I'd also like to express my satisfaction and hope that we'll successfully complete our talks today," Jagielski said. Ignoring the request for a report on the fate of arrested opponents of the regime, Jagielski turned to procedural matters concerning final statements and communiques. "Who's going to read the points?" the deputy premier asked.

"We can read them," Walesa answered.

Bogdan Lis read out the third point about freedom of speech and press. The government promised to bring in a new, more liberal censorship law, ensured that Sunday mass would be regularly transmited, and agreed that the mass media would be open to different points of view.

"I accept this point," said Jagielski. In the shipyard, there was applause.

Lis read out the next passage of the proposed agreement. In it, the government pledged to investigate firings and expulsions that had occurred in the past. It also promised to re-examine the cases of those who had been sentenced for political reasons and release them pending new decisions on their cases. As though responding to the catechism, Jagielski said, "In the spirit of understanding the problem, I agree and I'm signing it."

Gwiazda broke into the ritual to ask Jagielski what had happened to the list of recent detainees he had provided. The deputy premier said he would present his point of view at the end of the proceedings. Walesa insisted. "We'd like to know something about those arrested. People demand it." Again, the deputy premier hedged. "I'm a representative of the government and these matters are within the jurisdiction of the prosecutor general. I can commit myself and sign the agreement. Then I'm going to Warsaw and I will clear it up," Jagielski said.

Anna Walentynowicz, the crane operator in whose name the strike had been launched more than seventeen days ago, pressed for further assurances. "Mr. Premier has guaranteed safety for the strikers and those supporting the strike," Walentynowicz noted. She then named Miroslaw Chojecki, the head of the independent Nowa publishing house. "He's in jail now," she said accusingly.

"I assure you that I will present the matter in the light in

which it has been presented here," Jagielski promised.
"Anything more is outside my authority."

Walesa ended the scuffle. "Since we have the right to strike
and a headquarters at 13 Marchlewskiego Street"—the address
of the newly secured union offices—"then if they are not
released, we'll proclaim a strike once again," said the striker's
spokesman.

The reading of the agreement and initialling of the clauses
was resumed. On each of the remaining points, which concerned economics and social services, the government made
important, if occasionally vague, concessions. The clauses
took up issues ranging from an improved program for the
allocation of housing to a promise of instituting the principle of
non-working Saturdays by the end of the year. (See Appendix
1 for the complete text of the Gdansk Agreement.)

It was almost over. "I suggest we take a break to prepare a
communique, and Mr. Premier will call Warsaw about those
people," Walesa proposed. "After the break, we'll sign
everything in the conference hall in front of everybody."

At 4:30 the two sides reconvened in their familiar places.

"I suggest that Mr. Premier present a statement about the
arrestees," Walesa said.

"Firstly, I'd like to state once again that participation in
the strike and aid in organizing it will not be penalized," said
Jagielski. "Secondly, I think that there is a lot of misunderstanding. Therefore I'd like to state that the prosecutor's office
will make a decision about the release of those detained by noon
tomorrow, that is, September 1. I can say that the work on these
matters has already been undertaken in the proper agencies.
Therefore, I'd like to ask you, Mr. Chairman, to make a
statement that after signing the document the strike will be
ended."

"Yes, Mr. Premier, I have such a statement ready and I'll
make it," Walesa replied. He then proceeded to sum up the
negotiations. "Our talks, difficult at the beginning, were
conducted later in the spirit of better and better understanding.
I can say with pleasure that we ended our conflict without the
use of force, through negotiations and argumentation. We have
shown that Poles can come to an understanding if they want to.
So this is a success for both sides." The strike leader paused for

a second. "And now I'd like to address all those who followed me.

"Dear friends. We go back to work on September 1. We all know what this day reminds us of," Walesa said, recalling the date on which Poland had been invaded by the Nazis. "About our motherland, about the national cause, about the common interests of the family whose name is Poland. We have been thinking a lot about this during the strike. That's what we are thinking about as we end this strike.

"Have we achieved everything we wanted?" Walesa asked. "I always say frankly and openly what I think. So now I will say frankly: no, not everything, but we all know that we've achieved a lot. We have achieved all that we could in the present situation. We'll achieve the rest too, because we have the most important thing: our independent, self-governing trade unions. This is our guarantee for the future.

"I proclaim the strike to be over."

In the conference hall, in the shipyard, and beyond the shipyard gate, they began to sing the national anthem. At the end, Walesa said, "Everything is ready. Let's go to the conference hall."

As the members of the government commission and the MKS presidium entered the jammed main conference hall to formally sign the agreement, the television lights came on. Millions of Poles looked on from their living rooms while the two delegations filed to the head of the long room and mounted the stage. Walesa spoke first, basically repeating the spirit of his earlier address. The deputy premier echoed Walesa's sentiments, noting that the resolution of the strike had produced "no losers or winners."

It was almost five o'clock in the evening. Their brief speeches over, the two protagonists signed the 21-point protocol contained in a blue plastic binder. Jagielski quickly flipped through the pages, and signed with an ordinary ballpoint. When his turn came, Walesa ceremoniously produced a foot-long red-and-white sausage of a pen, a souvenir of the pope's visit to Poland the previous summer. With it, he penned his signature to history.

PART TWO

Solidarity

6   The Road from Gdansk

*We cannot surrender, for those who will
follow us will say, "They were so close,
and they failed." History would not
absolve us then.*
—Lech Walesa, October 1980

Before dawn on Monday, September 1, city trams and buses
began their rounds through the chilly, rain-swept streets of
Gdansk. At the Lenin Shipyard workers streamed through the
open gate under a steady downpour. Garlands of flowers still
tied to the grillwork had begun to wilt, and the portrait of Pope
John Paul II which adorned the gate during the strike had been
discreetly removed. Within minutes, the gangly overhead cranes
arced through the air hauling heavy metal parts as seagulls
wheeled and cried above the shipyard. Carts piled with material
crossed the yard and sparks flew from welders' torches. Along
the docks, longshoremen started to unload the dozens of ships
stacked up in the harbor.

Across town, in the district of Wrzeszcz, Lech Walesa arrived
at 10 a.m. at a nondescript apartment building a couple of
blocks from Grunwald Avenue. His arms full, he climbed two
flights of stairs, passed the office of a nose-and-throat specialist
and approached the door of his new place. Encumbered by a set
of pennants from a bicycle-racing club, a handful of gladioluses
and a wooden crucifix about the length of a tennis racquet that
was hooked over his shoulder, he looked in vain for the door
key. As a small group of friends and reporters looked on, he
fished one from his pocket. It wouldn't fit. Someone offered
another. It was no good either. Waiting for the right key to

appear, Walesa talked awhile with his friends and joked with reporters that he wasn't going to worry much about what Moscow wrote about him and his cohorts. They waited. After ten minutes or so, a janitor pushed through the crowd. He turned the key and the temporary offices of the Independent Trade Union were officially open.

Inside, there was next to nothing, barely a stick of furniture. A telephone sat on the floor. Walesa looked around. He stretched out his arms, gazed skyward, and quietly proclaimed: "I am in an empty room, but one full of hope."

In Warsaw, a small knot of members from the Committee of Social Self-Defence (KOR) waited in the drizzle outside Rakowiecka Prison. The detainees, who had been shuffled from one police station to another for the last ten days, emerged in groups of two and three. They were greeted with shouts and hugs.

That evening, Jacek Kuron was back in his familiar book-lined study on Mickiewicz Street chain-smoking Gauloises. He wore a white T-shirt that bore the distinctive red legend *Solidarnosc*. Its exuberant lettering had been designed during the strike—the last stroke in the "n" rose into a mast that bore a small Polish flag—and was becoming familiar throughout the country, as it soon would be around the world. Friends and reporters filed into the room. His release, he said, had come about only because the workers demanded it. Kuron called the Gdansk Agreement "a victory for the workers, but also for the government, which showed a sense of realism." Then, as though the work of KOR had not been interrupted, he reported on the striking coal miners in Jastrzebie.

The Silesian coal field strikers had been almost overlooked in the drama of the weekend accord reached in Gdansk. As the Gdansk MKS had predicted, the government's ambiguity about whether the right to form independent trade unions applied nationally would prove costly. On the day that the workers on the Baltic coast and most other regions returned to their jobs, a runaway coal car killed eight men in the Halemba Mine near Katowice, and the strikes in Silesia mushroomed into a potential new crisis.

By noon the next day, September 2, 200,000 workers were out, and the MKS headquarters established at the Manifest

Lipcowy Mine at Jastrzebie near the Czechoslovakian border was hung with banners, posters and other signs of the coal miners' rebellion. The miners refused to deal with Mines Minister Wlodzimierz Lejczak, and a nervous Warsaw government promptly dispatched a top-level delegation headed by Deputy Premier Aleksander Kopec to Jastrzebie. Negotiations continued through the night in a stuffy conference room whose walls were draped with black cloth as a sign of mourning for the eight dead miners. Just after midnight on September 3, the negotiators emerged with an agreement.

The Manifest Lipcowy Agreement began with the recognition that the miners "fully support the 21 demands advanced by the striking crews of the coast, and in particular, the point concerning trade unions." The miners' major specific grievance concerned a recently introduced new shift shedule—the "four-brigade" system—that kept the coal mines functioning 24 hours a day, seven days a week. Though workers in each shift got two days off after six working days, on the average they ended up with only one free Sunday a month—an arrangement bitterly resented for both family and religious reasons. The settlement included abandonment of the four-shift system and work-free Saturdays and Sundays effective January 1, 1981. As well, there were new safety and health measures, including recognition of anthracosis as an occupational disease.

By the next morning, the coal and lignite that provided 85 per cent of Poland's energy and 15 per cent of its hard-currency export earnings were again being mined. As one party member in Warsaw had predicted, "Whatever is demanded by the miners, the government will accept." As a bulwark of the Polish economy, the coal miners were clearly the last people in Poland that the party wanted trouble with.

The party had enough problems of its own. There had been rumors all week long that Edward Gierek's tenure as first secretary of the PUWP was in serious jeopardy. Foreshadowing the imminent party showdown was the sudden eruption of a bizarre, high-level scandal.

The gossip centred on Gierek's associate and close friend, Maciej Szczepanski, the former chairman of the country's radio and television commission. Szczepanski was one of the lesser officials who had been dismissed during the mid-strike government shakeup that saw the fall of Premier Babiuch and politburo members Pyka and Szydlak. Now, according to leaks emanating from both party and parliamentary investigative bodies, a list of 21 charges of embezzlement, personal enrichment and moral depravity had been drawn up against the former television head. The high-living official was said to have amassed a vast fortune by siphoning off government funds intended for the media industry. Among Szczepanski's alleged indulgences were a 40-acre sheep farm, a villa with a glass-bottomed swimming pool, four prostitutes in residence, a luxuriously appointed yacht, and a palace with a staff of servants and over 900 pornographic videotapes in the viewing room.

Various Poland-watchers noted that there might be something more to the affair than the exposure of Szczepanski's exotic tastes. "There are only two explanations: either the party wants to heap all the public indignation upon Szczepanski and make him a scapegoat, or the organized discussions against him are a campaign against Gierek, who is a close friend and protected him." While the fate of the deposed television executive remained uncertain—a final lurid note suggested that he had retired to a sanitorium after an intensive bout of drinking—one didn't have to wait long to learn about the fortunes of First Secretary Gierek.

The news came the next day, September 5, during a session of the Polish parliament which was to ratify the recently concluded labor agreements. The normally placid Sejm (or parliament) had whipped itself up into several hours of unprecedented criticism of the government and the party when parliamentary speaker Andrzej Werblan interrupted with a brief announcement: "PUWP First Secretary Edward Gierek developed serious disturbances in the action of the heart this morning. A medical council found hospitalization indispensable. The patient is in the hospital under the solicitous care of specialists." Few members of parliament appeared surprised by the news of Gierek's heart attack. The proceedings continued, and in a two-hour televised address, Premier Jozef Pinkowski outlined an ambitious government program to right the economic ills of the country and "rebuild the confidence of the nation."

A few blocks away, a late-night session of the PUWP central committee had been suddenly convened. Cars of the politburo and central committee members converged on the Party House, the PUWP's white sandstone-faced headquarters. At 1:30 a.m. Saturday, the official announcement was made that the ailing Gierek had been replaced. The new communist party boss was Stanislaw Kania, aged 53, a heavy-set dour-faced organization man in charge of security forces. Gierek had paid the traditional price exacted of Polish leaders who had lost control of the nation's workers.

For the next several weeks, the new first secretary would be preoccupied with the behind-the-scenes protocol and rituals necessary to consolidate his hold on power.

In his first speech to the central committee, Kania adopted a moderately progressive, appropriately humble stance designed to satisfy the country's de facto power triumvirate: the workers, the party machine and the neighboring Soviets. He affirmed that the party would honor the agreements it had made with striking workers, but he also warned "antisocialist elements" against seeking to turn the country's troubles "to their own purposes." He legitimized the series of strikes that brought down his predecessor as "a protest not against the principles of socialism but against the mistakes of the party." For party members, he served up a declaration of personal modesty: "I am not so sure that our party needs that which is usually termed a 'leader.' I am deeply convinced that my obligation should consist above all in ensuring that the collective wisdom of people should function." And bowing to the Soviet shadow, Kania pulled from his back pocket a message of congratulations from Soviet leader Brezhnev and pledged that Poland would "strengthen our position in the Warsaw Treaty." In all, it was a carefully balanced opening performance.

By mid-week, as government officials calculated the cost of the recent agreements, Kania went on tour. On the Baltic coast, he met with party officials in Gdansk, visited a shipyard in Gdynia, and nodded approvingly as regional party secretary Tadeusz Fiszbach reiterated pledges to honor the Gdansk Agreement. Kania told a party gathering that the PUWP must work hard to restore its links with the working class and hinted at an unscheduled party congress to be held in the near future. The next day in southern Katowice he urged party comrades to help restore production levels. With an eye on continuing strikes that ranged from Koszalin in the northwest to Bialystok in the northeast to the textile mills of Lodz, Kania warned, "If we fail to restore the normal rhythm of work, we shall not be able to fulfil the welfare part of our promises given to workers. So the community must be made fully aware."

While Kania continued his morale-bolstering pilgrimage, similar to the one Gierek had made a decade before upon taking office, Deputy Premier Jagielski was sent to Moscow to personally reaffirm Poland's allegiance to the Soviet Union and to discuss his country's economic plight. Jagielski, after ritualistically hugging Leonid Brezhnev at the Moscow airport, returned to Warsaw bearing promises of increased Soviet aid in food and other goods to tide Poland over its present crisis. Other party officials were charged with the task of spelling out the economic dilemma and underscoring the need for change.

Deputy Premier Henryk Kisiel, the new economic planning chief, announced at a press conference that the 10 per cent wage increase for the twelve million workers employed in the socialized sector would cost 90 billion zlotys. He acknowledged that the outlays would cause problems in the already skewed relationship between purchasing power and the availability of goods. "The entire skill of the new government will try to balance the increase of salaries with an increase in goods." Kisiel waxed philosophic. "Will we succeed? That remains to be seen. It's almost like Hamlet's question, 'To be or not to be.'"

This reflective mood was echoed in the remarks of Mieczyslaw Rakowski, editor of the party weekly *Polityka*. In a mid-September interview, Rakowski conceded that the party had been shocked by the August events. "There is now a deeply rooted knowledge that we must change the structure of power," said the editor, considered to be one of the party's liberals. "That includes the whole concept of management, self-government by the workers and other areas of society—the elimination of censorship, a lot of things." In his office, Rakowski gesticulated with a cigarette as he paced between his desk and an easy chair. "All that stretches ahead of us is darkness," he said in one of the lugubrious moments that alternated with bouts of optimism.

As sporadic strikes continued into the latter part of September—tram drivers in Katowice had most recently walked out—internal pressure mounted for changes within the party. The official organ, *Trybuna Ludu*, editorialized against party careerists and called for more open debate. Gdansk party secretary Fiszbach, in an interview with Western journalists, admitted that the party had lost its credibility. He reported that 300 members in the Gdansk region had resigned in disillusionment. Decentralization must not stop at the economy and the administration, he said; regional party organizations demand a real voice in creating policy. "We need a new party," Fiszbach declared flatly.

Beyond the spotlight designed to turn First Secretary Kania into a recognizable public figure, another process was unfolding in Poland. With less fanfare, but perhaps more efficiency, a trade union was being built. Although it received little coverage from the Polish media busily documenting First Secretary Kania's whereabouts, it was, nonetheless, an epic activity.

At the Lenin Shipyard, in the first days after the strike, men and women in blue overalls trooped up a rickety set of stairs to a grimy foreman's office to sign up for membership in the new union. Outside union headquarters in Gdansk, there were long queues of factory representatives eager to know how they and their fellow workers could join.

On Copernicus Street in Warsaw, across from the ashen facade of the official trade union headquarters, a small office opened. Factory delegates arrived throughout the day to consult with experts on how to bring independent unions to places like the Warsaw archaeological museum or the city's largest pump-making factory. Within the first ten days of September, representatives from over 150 Warsaw-area factories and offices received an array of practical information—how to announce the formation of a union to management, establish an organizing committee, request that union dues be deducted from salaries, and then how to deposit the money in a union bank account.

The information was organized by the Catholic intellectuals who had advised the Gdansk shipyard workers during the strike. Their expertise was, admittedly, rather instant. "The truth is," said Krzysztof Silwinski, who along with Tadeusz Mazowiecki was running the counselling effort, "at first we had no idea of what to do when people started to ask us questions." Within days, however, there were photocopied kits that included organizing forms and even sample letters informing the plant manager and the local government of the union's formation. The volunteer counsellors, seated at long wooden tables, also dispensed advice about dealing with recalcitrant plant managers.

A variety of local officials offered more than sporadic resistance. At the Mielec aircraft factory in southeastern Poland, the first secretary of the party committee for the Rzeszow region, Alojzy Kotarba, told Mielec workers that there was "no need for independent trade unions" and asked them to sign petitions declaring they would not organize unions free of party and government control. The workers responded by drawing up a list of demands that included the dismissal of Kotarba. Despite the fact that top party officials repeatedly pledged to honor the Gdansk Agreement, the situation at Mielec was more typical than not. In hundreds of factories there was foot-dragging by management and subtle and not-so-subtle intimidation. Often, unfounded rumors flew, sometimes landing on factory notice boards, claiming that workers would lose existing social benefits if they left the party-controlled unions.

Yet the organizing went on. In Lublin, where the first major strikes had broken out in July, a founding committee appeal was issued. Signed by elected representatives from firms as diverse as the locomotive works and the Enterprise for the Conservation of Historical Buildings, the appeal demanded that the "provincial authorities make available to the committee an appropriate office in Lublin, without delay, as well as all essential means to conduct its business in a normal way." If the local government failed to comply with the Gdansk Agreement, said the no-nonsense appeal, the Lublin Committee "reserves the right to take a decision on the declaration of a strike by the enterprises and groups of employees that it represents."

In Szczecin, the local union election at the small Odra Shipyard was typical of the situation in literally thousands of factories throughout the country that autumn. Some 98 per cent of Odra's 400 workers had joined the new union and a mandate commission was set up to organize the first election meeting. The factory intercom was used to make announcements about the election, posters were put up, and leaflets urging participation were distributed. Management agreed to let workers knock off a half-hour early on election day. A meeting hall at the nearby Economic Secondary School had been acquired for the occasion.

At three in the afternoon, the meeting in the crowded

assembly hall began with a singing of the national anthem. The agenda was read out and a factory delegate from the neighboring Warski Shipyard was proposed as chairman of the meeting. He offered a few words of greeting and invited a representative from the Parnica Shipyard and the Odra director onto the podium. The electoral rules were read out and accepted by voice vote. At 3:45 the election began. From the hall came the names of the first candidates. It was hard to hear. Someone proposed that the nominators should go up to the microphone. By 4:30, more than 20 candidates had been nominated and introduced themselves. While the typists entered the names on the ballots, a scrutineers' committee was chosen.

At five o'clock the ballots were handed out. There was a moment of concentration as the workers weighed considerations for and against various candidates. Slowly, the ballot box filled up. After casting their votes the workers went out into the corridor for a smoke and a chance to stretch their legs. While the votes were being counted, there were a few speeches. The representative from Parnica described an exchange of letters with Lech Walesa and answered questions about trade unions. The shipyard director talked about production.

At 7 p.m., the chairman of the scrutineers' committee entered the hall and silence fell as he read out the names of the 13 successful candidates, who were to become members of the local executive of the Independent Self-Governing Trade Union (NSZZ are the Polish initials). The election for chairman was quickly carried out by the whole assembly. Forty minutes later, it was announced that Jan Szylar had been elected chairman of the Odra presidium. People slowly left the hall, leaving only the executive behind to discuss the start of its work.

It had been an ordinary election, like ones held perfunctorily or enthusiastically in countless workers' organizations around the world. Yet in the Baltic port of Szczecin, it was a first for the Odra workers. It had been marked by solemnity, thoughtfulness and surprisingly deep emotions. Never before had the Odra workers chosen their representatives openly, with unlimited candiddates, irrespective of party affiliation, and by secret ballot. The Odra executive sat in a school assembly hall that evening, debating various current questions facing the union. How would the dues check-off be arranged? What would happen over registration of the union statutes? There were a hundred other questions. In one Polish workplace, something had changed.

When representatives from 35 inter-factory committees and 150 large individual factories gathered in Gdansk on September 17, 1980, for the first national delegates meeting of the NSZZ, they too were asking about the process of registering the union with the courts in Warsaw. The review of organizational matters revealed that over three million workers from approximately 3,500 factories had joined or were about to join the NSZZ. In a little over two weeks, more than a quarter of the non-agricultural work force had signed up with the new unions, dispelling any lingering notions that the solidarity displayed during the Gdansk strike was a fluke or the product of momentary emotion. The accomplishment was, by anyone's standards, remarkable.

There were, naturally, countless problems, and during a sometimes stormy five-hour session, delegates recited difficulties, argued proposals and speculated on the immediate future. Oganization was progressing in the face of constant obstacles. In weaker or less numerous centres, emergence of the new unions was accompanied by hints of victimization and reprisals. Access to the mass media remained closed in most places. In workplaces with a majority of women workers, the threatening hand of management was particularly heavy. The old unions from the Central Trade Union Council (in Polish, CRZZ) conducted fraudulent propaganda campaigns about the alleged losses awaiting those crossing over to the new unions.

There would even be a small problem about the name of the union. As the old unions pulled out of the CRZZ (eventually this body would fold) and registered with the courts, they too claimed to be "independent, self-governing trade unions" (NSZZs). That difficulty would be resolved in a couple of days by the expedient of appending the word "Solidarity" to the genuinely independent unions, the term by which the new body would be ultimately known.

Within the sprawling new unions, there was a debate about the structure of the organization. Walesa was inclined to favor loose, relatively unstructured relations between the various NSZZs. But the majority of those at the national delegate meeting argued for a national confederation, both to keep the weaker unions from being picked off by the state and to coordinate country-wide activities. In the end, it was agreed to form a confederation of regional bodies, with a national co-ordinating commission (known by its Polish initials KKP), and a national headquarters in Gdansk. Walesa, elected chairman of the commission, gave in gracefully. "We had different views," he admitted to reporters afterwards, "but I have to follow the will of the people."

One of the worrisome aspects of the immediate future concerned registration of the new unions. The Council of State (a cabinet level body of the Polish parliament) had just passed a vaguely worded resolution on registering the unions. "Until such time as the principles and method of their registration has been regulated by law" the new unions would register with the Warsaw provincial court, which would render its decision on registration "after ascertaining that the statutes voted by the founding committee are not contrary to the constitution or other regulations of law." There was uneasiness among the delegates as to whether this amounted to full or merely temporary legal status, and uncertainty about how long the court would take to make its decisions. Mistrust of the authorities had only increased in the last weeks, and Solidarity's advisers asked who would decide what conformed to the law. Part of the mistrust could be seen in the delegates' adoption of a resolution accusing the government of creating "obstacles" to the formation of independent unions, in contravention of the recent labor agreements.

A week after the national delegates meeting, Walesa went to Warsaw to register Solidarity. After depositing the union's documents with the provincial court, the Solidarity chairman led a celebratory procession through the main streets of the capital. Walesa and 50 Solidarity delegates then proceeded to government offices for a meeting with Deputy Premier Jagielski.

The delegates complained that their organizing efforts were being blocked by local authorities and representatives of the old trade unions. They also said that their activities were receiving no coverage from the media and that the government was pursuing a campaign against the democratic opposition. The evening before, the television news had carried an explicit attack on Jacek Kuron, presenting him as a radical calling for a violent uprising and the hanging of the communists. At the meeting with Jagielski, the delegates asked that Walesa be allowed to make a national television address assuring workers of their right to join the new unions. When the meeting ended, it was clear the two sides were far apart.

That afternoon, before a roaring crowd of 5,000 workers in a soccer stadium at the huge Ursus tractor factory, Walesa warned, "If there are difficult problems we can all strike together. If things get bad we stand together as a united Poland." The same day, Solidarity's national office issued a statement refuting the attack on Kuron as "a slanderous attempt" to discredit activists and people assisting the unions. The propaganda campaign, it said, was tantamount to breaking the Gdansk Agreement.

Three days after filing with the court, on September 28, Solidarity announced that it would call for a nation-wide, one-hour "warning strike" at noon on Friday, October 3. The union would protest the government's failure to pay promised wage increases, obstructions to organizing, and refusal to provide access to the media. Intentionally or not, the fledgling organization had thrust itself into its first test of strength barely a fortnight after its formation.

Instead of seeking accommodation with the union, the government put Deputy Premier Kazimierz Barcikowski, the Szczecin negotiator, on national television Tuesday evening to warn that the authorities would regard the threatened strike as disruptive and provocative. "We should consider whether the authors of the idea are really concerned with normal work or whether they're more interested in pushing us into chaos," said Barcikowski. The next day the government took a more conciliatory tack, flying Deputy Premier Jagielski to Gdansk to meet with Solidarity in an effort to avert the warning strike. The union was unimpressed by his warning that the action could lead to cancellation of the Gdansk accords. By Thursday, almost every shop in Gdansk was plastered with strike posters.

At noon on Friday, as factory sirens blared out a signal of work stoppage, Saweryn Jaworski, the 49-year-old furnace supervisor and chairman of the Solidarity branch at the Warsaw steelworks, stood by the factory gate carrying a neatly printed placard reading "Freedom of Speech." Accompanied by members of the plant's strike committee, Jaworski marched through each department leading the chants of "No more lies...No decisions about us without us..." His clenched fist greeting to groups of the factory's 11,000 workers was answered with smiles, cheers and clenched fists. The first nationally organized labor protest in 36 years of party rule was on.

In Warsaw, four major factories shut down, and bus and streetcar drivers turned on their headlights to express sympathy with the action. At the Lenin Shipyard and thousands of other selected enterprises throughout the country, hundreds of thousands of Solidarity unionists put on an impressive display of restrained force. "It was a complete success," pronounced Walesa at the end of the operation, clutching a fistful of telexes from various regional union headquarters. "We showed that we know how to start a strike and how to end a strike," he said, noting that workers had promptly resumed work at the conclusion of the one-hour break. "That is what we needed to achieve." If the regime intended to footdrag on the agreement, they were at least forewarned as to what they could expect in response.

While Solidarity flexed its muscle and the party attempted to refurbish its image with a new leader, the country's other major institution, the church, had some pew-mending of its own to do.

One of the most frequently heard observations immediately after the Gdansk strike was that the church had misjudged the mood of the workers and the threat of Soviet intervention. Cardinal Wyszynski's statement midway through the strike, which appeared to urge workers back to the job before obtaining independent trade unions, was considered a blunder. "It was clearly a mistake," said Jacek Wejroch, political affairs commentator for Tadeusz Mazowiecki's Catholic monthly, *Wiez*. "Reaction to it was very bad among workers. The aim appeared to be getting people back to work, but it was not the right moment."

The church hastened to make amends. A week after the Gdansk accords were signed, Cardinal Wyszynski invited Lech Walesa to visit him. The strike leader and the Roman Catholic primate met in the cardinal's palace in Warsaw. Walesa attended mass in Wyszynski's private chapel and was then received in the cardinal's apartments with a group of workers who had accompanied Walesa from Gdansk. Although no public statements were issued, the cardinal's embrace carried clear symbolic significance. The move was seen as an attempt by the church to bring itself closer to the workers and to repair some of the damage done by the cautious stance it had taken during the strike. Walesa, known as a devout Catholic, was obviously willing to lend his presence to this show of reconciliation, and there were soon rumors that the labor leader would eventually go to Rome for an audience with the Pope. Although the meeting with Wyszynski was ignored by Polish state television, Poles promptly learned of it through Radio Free Europe Polish-language broadcasts.

With the workers once again securely in the fold, the church was free to attend to its own unfinished business with the state. On the eve of the first live radio broadcast of Sunday mass in late September, the Polish bishops' conference renewed their long-standing demand to reach children and youth with special radio and television programs. "The holy church does not cease its appeal for suitable programs for everyone, especially for children," said the bishops in a statement that would be read in churches throughout the country. "It cannot renounce the right to spread the gospel by mass media." The bishops even offered a bit of theory about modern communications. Apparently not content with their own unusual revelatory methods of communication with higher powers, they pointed out that the "mass media are important instruments given to mankind by the Creator so that they could exert a positive influence on the development of the family." Whether or not the Marxist state agreed with this view of solid-state technology, mass from the Church of the Holy Cross in Warsaw was heard on the airwaves the next day for the first time since World War II.

A month later, Cardinal Wyszynski held his first face-to-face meeting with Polish communist party leader Kania. According to the official state news agency, church and party were in accord. "A unanimous view was expressed that constructive co-operation of the church with the state serves well the interests of the nation and, therefore, will be continued on behalf of the welfare and security of the Polish People's Republic," reported the state news agency PAP.

This relationship of "constructive co-operation" was extended into the councils of state in late November, when a member of the Catholic group in parliament was named a deputy premier. In one more unprecedented move by the Polish regime, Jerzy Ozdowski, a 55-year-old professor of economics and lecturer in theology at the Catholic University in Lublin, was elevated from the five-member Catholic parliamentary group Znak (in English, "Sign") into the ruling circle. It was

the first time in Poland or any of the Soviet-bloc countries of
Eastern Europe that a politician affiliated with the church had
achieved a position of such prominence in the state.

At the Lenin Shipyard, the workers had returned to their
traditional task of shipbuilding. But that fall they were also
building something else: a monument.

Although the story of its inception had an apocryphal ring to
it, it had achieved currency in the shipyard. On the first evening
of the strike, Bogdan Pietruszka, a designer at the Lenin Shipyard, lay on a makeshift bed in his department, and as if
working from the remnants of a dream, quickly sketched on a
scrap of paper an unusual soaring structure of a circle of tall
crosses, each bearing a ship's anchor where the crucified figure
might be expected to be found. He shoved the sketch partway
under his mattress and entered the strike-bound yard. Shortly
after, a friend from the designing department noticed the
drawing, took one look, and said, That's it.

The demand for a monument commemorating those who had
been killed during the 1970 strikes was a long-standing bone of
contention between shipyard workers and management.
Although promised as early as 1971, it had been shunted aside
repeatedly, and the shipyard workers had observed the occasion
each December 16 by taking flowers to the graves of the fallen.
In the late 1970s, ceremonials had begun to be held outside the
shipyard. In 1977, 800 people gathered for the observance; the
next year there were 3,000; and in 1979, despite official
harassment and detentions, 5,000 workers assembled to hear
Lech Walesa prophetically promise that a monument would be
erected the following year, even if it meant carrying stones to
the site themselves. When bargaining began during the August
strike, the demand for the monument was high on the list and
quickly acceded to by management. During the days of the
solidarity strike a model of Pietruszka's conception was on
display in the conference hall of the MKS.

The day after the strike ended, a monument committee was
formed. This time the idea would neither be dropped nor
delayed. Henryk Lenarciak, who had worked in the shipyard
since 1952, was chosen chairman of the committee. Though
most thought it unlikely that three 40-metre steel crosses and the
attendant sculpture could be put in place by December 16, 1980,
Lenarciak and his group worked away in a patient but persistent

style that seemed characteristic of the temperament of Walesa's old workmate.

By October 3, most of the arguments about placement, design and materials had been settled. The day that Solidarity was holding its first national warning strike, Lenarciak was in Katowice, dickering at the local steel mill. Three days later, the steel was in Gdansk. Bronze for the sculpture arrived. It was followed by sheet metal plating for the lower section of the crosses. Outside the yard, the men from the Budimor factory drove sixteen piles 20 metres into the ground.

Through the chill, wet months of October and November, work went on throughout the shipyard. One cross was given to each hull department—K-1, K-2 and K-3. The anchors were cast in W-3. In the metal shops, workmen pounded the bronze into figures of Polish workers. A few lines of the poetry of Czeslaw Milosz, the self-exiled Polish Nobel Prize-winning poet, were given permanent form.

Outside the shipyard gate, scaffolding went up on a gently sloping mound of reddish gravel, around which were scattered rough slabs of concrete. Through it all, the quiet Lenarciak worried over the details of the monument that, as he saw it, "would be a guarantee of our safety."

Everywhere, the country's institutions appeared to be in vigorous stages of construction or reconstruction, despite the gloomy figures of actual production periodically released by the government. The union was positively burgeoning. A month after its first national meeting, membership figures were estimated to have climbed to seven million. At the Lenin Shipyard, memorials to the dead were being raised. The church was busy with repairs and bridge-building of its own. The party was no exception to this process.

During the first three months of Kania's tenure, the party saw a series of dismissals, transfers, purges and shuffles as the first secretary reorganized the apparatus to his own liking. The squat grey-suited party leader, who gave no evidence whatsoever of possessing a sense of humor, carried out the changes in the same unobtrusive way that he had come to power. Sometimes party officials were dumped at the behest of angry local workers. Characteristic of the party's reluctance to be challenged, these demands were usually resisted to the last minute, and only acquiesced to after the situation had assumed mini-crisis proportions.

Others were removed to provide Kania with a central committee balance that more closely reflected his rather middle-of-the-road views. In early October, after the union's first demonstration of strength, six cabinet ministers were ousted along with eleven central committee members. In late November, after another spate of worker unrest, eighteen provincial secretaries in Poland's 49 provinces were dumped in what was seen as the biggest shakeup in the PUWP at the local level since the so-called "de-Stalinization" of 1956.

The upheaval in the party was not confined to the upper echelons. Among the places where party members led the strikes in August, one of the most significant was Torun. The MKS there was led by a party member named Zbigniew Iwanow, from the Towimor ship machinery plant.

When the August strike ended, Iwanow was elected first secretary of the party organization in his factory. As Iwanow subsequently explained, "Most party militants in Towimor were for the strike. Some were on the strike committee. After the strike, we soon realized that the union was a safeguard for the people. But we owed it to ourselves to seek safeguards within the party, because the party had already suffered too many crises and one more might be deadly." Seeing that the changes instigated in the factory party branch were insufficient, Iwanow and his comrades sought contact with like-minded members of other party organizations. The quickest response came from the party branch at Torun University.

An inter-factory party commission, modelled on the strikers' MKS, was established. "We had no confidence in anything the authorities said," charged Iwanow. "They were passive and did nothing. The people 'up there' were compromised." At the end of September there were eight party organizations in what they called a consultative commission. Instead of the exclusively vertical links from basic party organizations to ones higher up, the idea was to build horizontal links between rank-and-file organizations through the consultative commission. "The commission was not warmly received by the regional authorities," laughed Iwanow. "They sensed themselves to be in danger." Nonetheless, within a matter of months, 7,000 out of 17,000 party members in Torun were affiliated to the consultative commission. The body had become, in effect, an alternative leadership to the Torun city committee of the party.

The movement subsequently spread to seventeen provinces throughout the country, and was the force behind the call for an extraordinary party congress.

Eventually, the central committee agreed to such a gathering, but at the same time, First Secretary Kania, still grappling with his tenuous hold on the party mechanism, denounced the construction of horizontal links at the base of the party as a violation of "democratic centralism," the organization's basic method of top-down governance. It was over these matters of both style and substance that Iwanow came into conflict with the party leadership. "We are workers, not diplomats," explained the rebel communist. "We do not mince our words in the meetings. When we think someone is a thief or a gangster we say so. The people who do not want a regeneration of the party listen without pleasure because they are not used to it. They think we should always applaud the first secretary's speeches without questioning if it is right. They would not shout in the hall that he is an idiot or that he tells lies."

In late November, the Torun Party Control Commission expelled Iwanow "The Terrible" (as he had been dubbed by the press) on the grounds that he had challenged the Marxist-Leninist world outlook. "It was a bit like the Inquisition," he said. "One Sunday, I was told I must attend a meeting on Monday. On the Monday they expelled me. On the same day, the factory branch re-elected me. Hence, I am the only party secretary who is not in the party," chortled Iwanow, savoring the irony.

In addition to coping with hardliners at the helm and rebels in the ranks, Kania also had to convince his comrades in the Kremlin that he was doing a creditable job. This task apparently required periodic sudden flights to Moscow for consultation with Soviet leaders. In late October, during a particularly tense moment with the country's workers (detailed below), First Secretary Kania and Prime Minister Pinkowski zipped in and out of Moscow, staying just long enough for lunch and hasty talks with the Soviet brass. The Polish leaders arrived in the morning, were greeted at the airport by Soviet President Brezhnev, hustled off to a two-hour meeting in the Kremlin, and after a politburo-sponsored luncheon in their honor, flew back to Warsaw.

In early December, again at the tag-end of a dispute with Solidarity, the party issued a late-night statement that dramatically began, "Countrymen, the fate of the nation hangs in the balance." The next day Kania and fellow politburo member Stefan Olszowski were in Moscow for an unexpected Warsaw Pact conference on the Polish question.

Such unsettling journeys continued into the next year. That they took place was a fact; so were the persistent Soviet grumblings made through its official press agency, Tass, about Poland's boisterous unions and the endemic "antisocialist elements" in the country. Occasionally, leaders of other Eastern European countries provided unsolicited comments of a similar nature.

What all this meant, however, remained a matter of speculation. Various international intelligence agencies from time to time pronounced definitively on Soviet intentions, and various journalists, who apparently had access to sources even more extensive than the intelligence agencies, confided confidently on the meaning of the latest gesture of the great bear next door. Despite all this, it was clear that predicting Russian movements was not yet an exact science.

The most one could say was that the Soviets may have contemplated military intervention at various times, but had not so far intervened. The Polish party had certainly hinted at the possibility of Soviet intervention, but whether it did so for internal tactical reasons or out of sincere concern, it was impossible to tell. It was also true that Polish television appeared to assume that Poles had an inordinate fondness, during critical political moments, for seeing films of Warsaw Pact military manoeuvres—or else how could one account for their frequent showing? Finally, the Poles themselves, although willing to concede their worries about the Soviets in private conversations, went about their daily business during most of the storms of speculation as though nothing untoward was imminent.

Perhaps the most illuminating thing that could be said on the subject was a little story offered by Lech Walesa upon being asked about the danger of intervention. "There are these two rabbits at our border, one Polish and the other Russian," said the labor leader. "The Russian rabbit is running as fast as he can. The Polish rabbit asks him why, and the Russian rabbit replies, 'Because they're castrating all the bears.' 'But you're a rabbit,' the Polish friend says. 'Yes,' the Russian rabbit answers, 'but I'm not sure of that's a good enough explanation.'" The Polish rabbit with the mustache and pipe chuckled at his own joke.

Whether they had been egged on by the Soviets, or thought it up on their own, the Polish regime decided to make an issue of union registration.

Solidarity's leaders began to feel uneasy in mid-October. Three weeks had passed since the union requested legal recognition by filing its statutes with the Warsaw provincial court. A dozen other unions, which had pulled out of the withering central trade union council, had already received approval, but Solidarity's application was still being held up. The union leaders went to Warsaw for a meeting with a government commission to find out why.

Although the court had various technical concerns about a number of Solidarity's proposed statutes, the heart of the issue, apparently, was a sin of omission. Nowhere in the proposed rules and regulations did Solidarity explicitly acknowledge the "leading role" of the communist party. The union leaders emerged from their meeting with the government commission and issued a statement accusing the regime of unnecessary delay. "If the authorities do not register our union in the very near future, it will mean that they want to force us to the next strike," they said. The union's position was promptly bolstered by a statement of support from the church, which was obviously determined not to repeat the mistake it had made during the August strike. A communique from the conference of bishops urged the court to "normalize" the status of Solidarity.

While some Solidarity presidium members were left behind to wrangle with the government over the fine points of language, Lech Walesa headed south on October 18 for a campaign-style union-building swing through Silesia. The weekend trip quickly turned into a triumphant tour. In Cracow, 6,000 people jammed the marketplace on Sunday morning to offer a tumultuous welcome to the electrician from Gdansk. At the local sports stadium, Walesa told 12,000 workers that there was nothing to fear because Solidarity was now a mass movement. Whatever the courts did, the union would go ahead. "We do not care about bureaucracy," he said, before heading off in the direction of Katowice.

The state media ignored Walesa's tour, but they did find

room that day for a lengthy official news agency-produced interview with Judge Stanislaw Pawela in which the government's case was outlined. Pawela noted that the new unions were supposed to be based on the Gdansk Agreement. "It was stated in these agreements on which principles the new unions will be established. We do not find these principles in the Solidarity statutes," the judge argued. "In this respect, the statutes refer only to the constitution." That, apparently, was not good enough, even though the constitution specifically acknowledges the party's "leading role." The judge suggested that the two sides engage in further talks before the court hearing slated for next Friday, October 24.

Walesa was unmoved by Judge Pawela's reasoning. The next day he told a crowd of cheering Silesian miners in Jastrzebie that Solidarity would not rewrite its statutes to satisfy the Warsaw court on the matter of the party's leading role. "We will not include that formulation," he declared. Then, in one of those eloquent moments by which he wove his magic with fellow-workers, Walesa added: "Do not give in, for once you do give in, you will not rise back for a long time. Indeed, we cannot surrender, for those who will follow us will say, 'They were so close, and they failed.' History would not absolve us then."

The dispute simmered through the week. *Trybuna Ludu*'s Monday morning editorial argued that since the Gdansk Agreement recognized the party's primacy, there was no reason why the language should not be included in the statutes themselves. On Tuesday, Solidarity offered the government a compromise. The statutes would remain intact, but a protocol could be added to the charter—perhaps simply quoting the relevant sections of the August accord—that would satisfy the party's political demands. There were rumors that the deadlock had been broken.

Nonetheless, the next day, Solidarity adviser Tadeusz Mazowiecki complained about the pressure to include a pledge to recognize the party. "Nobody's cancelling the pledge out, but why must it be raised at every opportunity?" he asked. "There are some people who think we are going too far already in making concessions." If the union's reluctance stemmed from the realization that the "supremacy clause" would not find favor with a good portion of the rank and file, the party had its own reasons for stubbornly insisting on its inclusion, as

Trybuna Ludu suggested in its inimitable murky style the day before the court hearing. Not only would the recognition help the new unions in the factories, said the party paper, it would "simultaneously become for us a weighty argument in the discussions on the character of the developments in Poland." In other words, it would go over well in Moscow.

At week's end, the political litigants assembled in a Warsaw courtroom. Judge Zdzislaw Koscielniak presided over a three-man judicial panel. Outside the courthouse, which was festooned with banners proclaiming, "We demand registration," 3,000 Solidarity supporters awaited the outcome of the lengthy deliberations. Four hours into the proceedings, Walesa, bathed in television lights, rose to offer the bench verbal assurance that Solidarity had no intention of becoming a political organization and that it reaffirmed the pledges contained in the Gdansk Agreement concerning the role of the party. Judge Koscielniak carefully echoed the union leader's promise for the court record and then declared a brief recess.

In the interval, Solidarity's representatives, crowded by reporters, all but issued victory statements. Throughout the hearing the bench appeared to be pressing for the compromise in which allegiance to the party would be contained in a separate protocol. The union had clearly met the authorities more than halfway with its public statement honoring the political provisions of the Gdansk Agreement. All that remained was for Judge Koscielniak to come back from his chamber and make the historic ruling that would for the first time in a Soviet-bloc country give legal status to an independent trade union.

Koscielniak reappeared. Registration, he announced, was granted. The crowded courtroom erupted. The outburst of cheering was picked up in the streets below. The judge declared another short recess to restore order. When the participants were back in their places, Koscielniak resumed his ruling. Registration was granted, *but* the court found the union's statutes in conflict with existing law and was amending them. In stunned silence, the union officials and their lawyers listened as Koscielniak inserted into the statutes clauses that pledged the union to abjure from becoming a political party, to uphold Poland's system of international alliances and to respect the leading role of the Polish United Workers Party. In addition, the court struck out sections in the statutes that meticulously set down procedures for declaring a strike, ruling that such provisions must await the drafting of right-to-strike legislation by the parliament. The judge rose abruptly and swept off to his chambers.

As Walesa and the other union leaders strode through the marble corridors and down the stairs of the court building, the crowd surging around them chanted, "Strike! Strike!" From the courthouse steps, Walesa told the throng in the streets the good news first. The union had obtained legal status. But then, referring to the restrictions added by the court, he angrily shouted into the microphone: "This is not what we wanted! This is not what we wished. They can't do things to us we don't want done."

Later that evening, after the union leadership had retreated to the Rosa Luxemburg lamp factory to consider their next move, Walesa had cooled down enough to tell a press conference convened in the plant, "We do not want to act quickly and in anger." The union would decide what the next step would be at the national commission presidium meeting in Gdansk on Monday, October 27. However, he described the court's arbitrary decision as a violation of the union's independence. "We shall never agree to it. We have repeated many times that we want to decide alone on our problems." Walesa looked tired and glum.

Back in the bracing Baltic air, the spirits of Solidarity revived. Outside, a chill Monday morning drizzle was falling, but inside the union's newly-acquired enlarged headquarters on the top floors of the Hotel Morski in Wrzeszcz, the atmosphere was heated. The day-long meeting began with reports from 39 regional delegates, representing some seven million workers, who made it clear that the court's decision was unpopular with the rank and file. "The court acted on behalf of the party," said one angry delegate. "They think the law is their plaything."

As the day wore on, Solidarity's ruling body passed a series of successively more militant resolutions. First, they voted to tell Prime Minister Pinkowski to come to the Lenin Shipyard and negotiate with them by 8 p.m. the next evening or face the possibility of a strike. As was becoming strategically customary, the union avoided the danger of being hemmed in by a single demand. Although a reversal of the court's decision naturally headed the list of demands they wanted to present to Pinkowski, several other items were added, including greater access to the media, the right to start a union newspaper, resolution of outstanding wage grievances, an end to harassment of organizing activities, better food supplies, and the legal registration of a farmers' Solidarity organization.

The Gdansk delegates, who sat as a group on the podium facing the other representatives, pressed throughout the day for taking a strong stand. Finally, they proposed sitting in at the Lenin Shipyard, the site of August's strike. Initially only the Gdansk local was prepared to go there. But then a delegate in the audience yelled out, "Is there solidarity or not? If there is, we all go." The others joined in.

The next morning, in a symbolic challenge to the government, the union leaders moved their deliberations to the shipyard. Instead of Pinkowski, Deputy Premier Jagielski was sent to Gdansk to negotiate once more. He invited the Solidarity leadership to go to Warsaw and meet the prime minister on Friday, October 31. Throughout the day, the delegates in the big conference hall debated whether to back down from an insistence on immediate bargaining on their home ground. There were clear differences between militants and moderates in the organization.

Anna Walentynowicz, speaking for the Gdansk militants, argued that the government could not be trusted to abide by agreements and only responded to brute pressure. "Only when we are strong can we guarantee they will come to a decision," said the outspoken crane operator. "If we didn't press them to the wall before, we wouldn't have got anything." Others were fearful that a strike could lead to outside intervention.

In the end, a compromise between the two factions was reached. They voted that not just a small delegation, but all of the representatives would meet with Pinkowski. If the talks failed, then selective strikes would be employed. "The 12th of November is a day of strike alert," the final declaration said.

That week, pressure from outside was stepped up. The East Germans announced severe restrictions on travel between the two countries. The day before the meeting with Solidarity, party leader Kania and Prime Minister Pinkowski made a hasty trip to Moscow to consult with Brezhnev.

On Friday at 11 a.m. about 80 members of the union executive, led by chairman Walesa, trooped into the Council of Ministers building in the capital. The atmosphere was initially frosty as the union leaders told Pinkowski that unless the government was ready to listen, they would go on strike. The prime minister replied that the government would not negotiate under threat or give in to blackmail.

Almost fourteen hours of negotiations later, Walesa wearily emerged into the frigid air of nighttime Warsaw. It was nearly 3 a.m. The union's perseverence had begun to pay off. Pinkowski had promised that an appeal to the Supreme Court of the lower court's decision would be settled by November 10. In addition, the government promised that Solidarity could publish a weekly newspaper and that its access to state-owned television would be increased. Finally, the union would be permitted to retrieve printing presses, donated from abroad, that had been impounded at customs. "Even on our knees we shall go forward," said Walesa. "But for the time being we walk on our feet."

The war of nerves continued for the next ten days. In Gdansk, the Solidarity leadership made plans for rotating strikes throughout the country if the Supreme Court didn't provide satisfaction. National commission member Andrzej Gwiazda was in no mood for backing down. "The only thing they understand is this," said the engineer, flexing the muscles of his right arm. Nor was he willing to offer further lip-service to the notion of the independence of the courts. "If the prime minister calls a Supreme Court meeting within a week, there's undoubtedly a concession coming," said Gwiazda. The reason that the lower court had "pulled the dirty trick" of rewriting the union statutes, he contended, was because of the appearance of the softness on the part of some union leaders. Gwiazda wasn't apprehensive about division within Solidarity. "We are not worried about any split. If the other delegates try to break their region away from the national commission, we're confident the workers will dismiss them," asserted the militant.

The party, too, attempted to give the appearance of hanging tough. Central committee spokesman Josef Klasa said that the government and the party were determined to use every option at their disposal to prevent the threatened strikes, including "certain administrative measures." First Secretary Kania's tough-talking speech to party members at the Cracow steel mill was given wide coverage. "We must say it aloud: there are limits we must not transgress."

On Sunday, November 9, the day before the Supreme Court hearing, the government and a union delegation led by Bogdan

Lis failed to reach a compromise. A meeting of Solidarity's KKP, which began in the afternoon and lasted into the night, worked out the details of a strike plan. The regime, for its part, cancelled the visas of arriving foreign news crews and showed films of joint Soviet-Polish military exercises on television. Late that night the government called Bogdan Lis to resume talks with the union. They went on until 3 a.m.

Although the November 10 session of the Supreme Court, presided over by Judge Witold Formanski, moved at the same leisurely five-hour pace as that of the lower court two weeks earlier, the outcome would be quite different. The direction of the court's verdict seemed to be indicated halfway through the proceedings when the prosecutor denounced the lower court, saying it had "exceeded its prerogatives" in rewriting the union's statutes. His remark prompted one judge of the three-member panel to joke that the prosecutor appeared to be working for the union rather than the state.

At the conclusion of the formalities, Formanski, announcing the Supreme Court's decision, ruled that the charter legalizing Solidarity could stand without a reference to the leading role of the communist party. Instead, the court accepted a union proposal to attach the relevant part of the Gdansk Agreement to the statutes as an addendum. There was even a word of chastisement for the lower court. Formanski concluded that it "had no right" to change the union's charter.

The decision uncorked instant celebration. Court workers leaned out the windows to give a thumbs-up signal to the crowd of 5,000 waiting below. When Walesa appeared on the courthouse steps, many in the crowd threw bouquets of carnations and pressed forward to hug him. "We got the statutes the way we wanted them," the Solidarity leader shouted into an orange megaphone. "We've won what we set out for on August 31." He boarded a minibus and as it moved slowly through the jubilant crowd, Walesa led a rendition of the hymn, "God Who Has Protected Poland." The union leaders were taken to Cardinal Wyszynski's palace, and the primate, who had returned from consultations with the pope the day before, offered his congratulations and autographed copies of the New Testament.

For Solidarity, it was a major, but curious victory. Ostensibly, the debate had been over a bit of legalese in a document that, for the most part, had only formal significance.

In reality, it was a struggle over the redefinition of powers to be shared between civil society and the state, or more specifically, between two social groups: the state bureaucracy and the workers. It was a continuation of the process that had begun in the Lenin Shipyard, and in its way, was almost as important. That the conflict had occurred in the arena of the court was a fiction that fooled no one. It was an open secret that the orginal lower court decision had come from the party by way of the ministry of justice. If there was any puzzlement, it concerned the party's failure to accept the union's first offer of a compromise, and its subsequent miscalculations that led to a humiliating defeat. The Solidarity militants had been right: the party, despite its fulminations and brinksmanship tactics, understood only firmness. On that chill Monday in November 1980, an independent union, now representing ten million workers in 8,500 enterprises, had achieved formal recognition in a workers' state.

It might have been expected that tensions would abate after the exhaustive seven-week battle. At first, that seemed to be the case. With winter approaching and lines outside supermarkets growing longer daily, the government appeared ready to turn toward the problem of food supplies.

A few days after the Supreme Court decision, two outstanding local strikes were quickly settled. A sit-in of health workers at the municipal government offices in Gdansk was brought to a negotiated conclusion when the workers' representative, Alina Pienkowska, and the minister of health signed an accord. At the other end of the country, in Czestochowa, a provincial governor who, expecting a court decision against Solidarity, had prematurely declared a state of emergency to bring a local strike to heel, was removed from office. There were still sporadic disputes afoot involving railway workers, farmers and students. Nonetheless, a winter's calm seemed to be on the horizon when, on the night of November 19, a dozen secret policemen raided the Warsaw Solidarity offices.

They soon found what they were looking for: a pilfered thirteen-page secret document issued by the prosecutor general's office tracing the history of government policy toward dissidents since the August strikes and detailing methods to be used by authorities to combat "antisocialist elements." The police soon had in custody Solidarity printer Jan Narozniak and

Piotr Sapielo, an employee in the duplicating centre of the prosecutor's office.

The security forces, in recovering the document and apprehending the miscreants, had failed to take into account only one factor: Solidarity. Perhaps the word had not yet funnelled down to the offices out of which the police operated. In short order, the regime was once again embroiled with Polish workers. Within the week, the Ursus tractor factory and four other Warsaw plants were shut down in protest, and a list of demands had been drawn up.

At a rally in the Urusus community centre, Zbigniew Bujak, chairman of the Warsaw Solidarity branch, said, "It's no longer just a matter of Jan Narozniak." As if to underline his sentiment, a banner behind Bujak declared, "Today Narozniak, tomorrow Walesa." "We want to prevent any further acts of this kind of lawlessness," said Bujak. In addition to demanding the two arrested men be set free, the union called for the release of other political detainees, disclosure of the names of those responsible for the police document, release of an unpublished government report on the strikes of 1970, and finally, a public commission to investigate the methods used by the security police and prosecutors so that safeguards could be devised to protect people from arbitrary persecution. Bujak read out portions of the document, taking the position that the union was defending the public's right to know and that the document was only classified as secret because it disclosed embarrassing admissions that illegal searches had been made.

Two days later, on the eve of a threatened city-wide general strike, the government, in its now-familiar last-minute fashion, caved in to the union's main demand and released the two prisoners. The union agreed to call off the strike. Still, it was not quite over. On December 4, in an oddly timed delayed reaction to the incident, First Secretary Kania railed against "counter-revolutionary" elements in the union movement, likening them to the conductors of "a train rushing toward catastrophe." At the same time, the central committee issued an alarming statement that said, "We continue to find ourselves in a sharp political crisis. All Poles are overwhelmed by profound anxiety over the destiny of the homeland." The formulation was yet another lightly-coded reference to the Russians. Twenty-four hours later, Kania was in Moscow for a surprise

Warsaw Pact conclave on the Polish question.

For the next several days, the air was rife with rumors of a Soviet troop call-up. Various Western governments, believing they had heard a distinctly Russian growl, responded with bluster of their own. Around the world front-page headlines blared, "Invasion fear arises," but Western correspondents in Poland admitted they could find few signs of alarm among Poles. Then, as gently as the early December snowfall that covered Warsaw one morning, the impending crisis seemed to disappear under a round of assurances from state, church and union that there was no crisis. Perhaps the hibernating bear had merely turned in its sleep.

All through the afternoon of December 16, the crowd at the Lenin Shipyard swelled with new arrivals. There were miners from Silesia wearing traditional long black topcoats, railway workers from Lublin, and all the shipbuilders in Gdansk. Over half a million strong, they waited patiently in the early twilight. They had come to honor the memory of workers killed by police and army bullets ten years before.

Many had thought it impossible to construct a monument in the space of three months, but as electrician Stanislaw Bury had once said about the productive capabilities of the shipyard workers, "We have to know for what we're working, and for whom." This time, they had worked for themselves. It was done.

Three slender steel crosses, more than 40 metres high, each bearing anchors that gave the appearance of stylized Christ-figures, were bathed in floodlights outside the main gate of the Lenin Shipyard. At the base of each cross, bas-relief sculptures of workers were placed amid irregularly-cut pieces of ship's plating which rose about a third of the way up the monument.

Shortly before five o'clock, the representatives of government, party, church and union were introduced. Poland's president, Henryk Jablonski, a silver-haired figure in a dark overcoat, represented the state. First Secretary Fiszbach of Gdansk appeared on behalf of the party. The church had sent Franciszek Cardinal Macharski of Cracow. Then, greeted by a torrent of applause, and bundled in his winter duffel coat, Lech Walesa appeared.

After a minute of silence at 5 p.m., the city's church bells began to peal. Ships' sirens wailed from the port. After the singing of a nineteenth century hymn, the names of 28 workers known to have died in the 1970 uprising were read out one by one by Daniel Olbrychski, a young Polish film star. After he read each name, the crowd shouted back, "Yes, he is still among us!" Five relatives of the victims came forward to snip a ribbon and release a long red-and-white banner that fluttered in the mist-laden breeze.

Walesa lit a memorial flame, which at once burned brightly despite the light drizzle. "This monument was erected for those who were killed, as an admonition to those in power. It embodies the right of human beings to their dignity, to order and to justice," he said. "Our country needs internal peace. I call on you to be prudent and reasonable." Walesa's sentiments were echoed, almost identically, by the spokesmen of church and party. That the PUWP should be a participant in the unveiling of a monument that would stand as a permanent criticism of the party was an irony that the organizers of the ceremony had chosen to ignore in favor of proclaiming a moment of national unity. "Let the sun of justice rise above us," intoned the bishop of Gdansk into the evening drizzle during the mass that ended the memorial observation.

In Gdynia the next morning, Walesa and Deputy Premier Jagielski turned out for a pre-dawn mass and the unveiling of a plaque honoring the victims of the December 1970 violence in Gdansk's sister city. The Gdynia ceremony began at 5 a.m., the hour when tanks moved into position near the Paris Commune Shipyard a decade before. Further along the coast, in Szczecin, thousands attended the dedication of a plaque at the gates of the Warski Shipyard. "Many of our comrades lost their lives," recalled one speaker. "We had to wait ten years to be allowed to honor the memory of the dead and properly commemorate these painful events. Today's anniversary gives rise to many feelings. But pain and bitterness remain uppermost." As factory and ship sirens keened along the Baltic, there were hints that time had not healed all the grief, and that despite the fact these now-legal observances marked another victory for the workers against the state, not all scores were settled.

The "admonition to those in power" was not heeded for long. No sooner had the new year, 1981, arrived, than Solidarity and the government were at loggerheads. This time the issue was the classic trade union demand for a five-day work week.

The Gdansk Agreement was clear on the principle, but somewhat fuzzy on the implementation of the measure. "The principle that Saturday should be a free day should be put into effect," said the clause concerning point 21 of the workers' demands. "This should be worked out by December 31, 1980. The measures should include the increase in the number of free Saturdays from the start of 1981."

Prime Minister Pinkowski, in his inaugural address to the Sejm on September 5, was more precise. The question of the five-day week had been made more complex by the battered state of the Polish economy, "but we want to meet the demands of the working people half-way," said Pinkowski. "Hence the government proposes the introduction in 1981 of all free Saturdays for all employees." However, as the time for implementation approached, the government had a change of mind. Shortly before Christmas, Labor Minister Janusz Obodowski proposed that workers receive only alternate Saturdays off in 1981, and that a plan for full free Saturdays be phased in by 1985. While this was a slight improvement for Poles presently working three Saturdays a month on average, the proposition, replied Solidarity, "is not acceptable because it does not assure all workers two days off each week."

As the first working Saturday of the year, January 10, approached, the dispute heated up. The government declared that only three out of the five Saturdays in January would be free. The decree, announced while Walesa was meeting with Deputy Premier Jagielski in Warsaw on January 6, was seen by the union as a breach of the Gdansk Agreement as well as an attempt to impose rather than negotiate a decision. Solidarity's Warsaw branch immediately told its members to regard all Saturdays in January as days off unless an agreement was reached. At the union's national commission meeting in Gdansk the next day, the stand of the Warsaw branch was backed.

As the national commission debated, Jagielski went on television to plead the government's case. "In no socialist state were all Saturdays declared days off all at once," said the deputy premier. "In the Western countries, they were also not introduced all at once. We must stabilize our economy and consider whether we can afford to suffer the consequences of a rapid change of the length of work time.''

Assuming a tone of renewed militance, Walesa replied, ''They are trying to dismantle us quietly. We must realize that Solidarity is a mote in the eye of the authorities, and the authorities don't want us.'' Karol Modzelewski, Jacek Kuron's former colleague who had resurfaced as one of the leaders of the Wroclaw Solidarity branch and a national commission spokesman, added, ''The government is not our partner, but our opponent.''

The government stepped up the pressure toward the end of the week. *Trybuna Ludu* attacked ''noisy forces attempting to destroy a slowly created climate of calm and reason.'' On Friday, Labor Minister Obodowski threatened that unjustified ''no-shows tomorrow will mean a loss of the day's salary.'' In a lengthy television interview, the minister pounded his fist for emphasis as he argued that the government, too, was interested in shortening the workweek. ''For God's sake, the government wants the good of the country.'' Politburo member Stefan Olszowski also made a guest appearance on television that evening, urging a ''reasonable solution'' to the dispute. At the same time, he mixed his conciliatory language with criticism of ''counter-revolutionary forces'' and a warning that ''anarchy'' was spreading.

While the state monopolized the media, the workers met on the shop floor. At the Ursus tractor factory and the Fiat automobile plant in Warsaw, unwritten agreements were reached with management to miss work the next day, but to make it up later in the month. When the test came, most workers in Poland's heavy industries defied the government and heeded the call of Solidarity. Gdansk, Gdynia and Szczecin were off. So was Wroclaw. In Warsaw, the union reported that 80 per cent of 2,700 factories in the region were shut.

At the Huta Warszawa steel mill, Solidarity representative Seweryn Jaworski said that a small crew was keeping the blast furnaces going, but that management had accepted ''in principle'' the idea of a reduced work week. ''In the beginning, management was a little threatening,'' the furnace attendant grinned, ''but now they are very polite.'' At the darkened Rosa Luxemburg lamp factory, its 4,700 workers were off, and a half dozen union members kept watch at an office near the main gate. ''We're here to protect the property of the factory,'' joked

THE ROAD FROM GDANSK   171

one worker, "so that no antisocialist forces will try to remove anything while we are enjoying our free Saturday."

"Maybe it is necessary to work some Saturdays," conceded another union member wearing one of the ubiquitous red-and-white Solidarity lapel pins. "But our position is that this should be decided at the local factory level. We're the ones who know best what the factory needs."

During the next week, both sides retired, metaphorically speaking, to their respective corners. Marshal Victor Kulikov, the Soviet commander of the Warsaw Pact, arrived for "cordial" talks with Polish party boss Kania; union leader Walesa went to Rome to meet the pope. After the respite, the two unwilling "partners" held one more set of fruitless negotiations on Wednesday, January 21. Although Solidarity offered several compromises, including one in which workers would have three Saturdays off and work six hours on the fourth, the government's position, reported Andrzej Gwiazda, remained "hard as a rock." That night Walesa announced that selective warning strikes of up to four hours would take place throughout the country the next day.

At the same time, Solidarity attempted to make clear that the question of Saturdays was not a single issue campaign, but rather a rallying cry for a whole series of grievances stemming from the union's perception that the government was balking every step of the way on the road from the Gdansk Agreement. Other issues raised by the union included access to media, the question of political prisoners, farmers' rights, and the delays in drawing up promised laws to relax censorship and to formalize the existence of independent trade unions. That such a list was not simply a pretext was underscored by a variety of instances of national restiveness, including a student sit-in at the University of Lodz and attempts by farmers near Bydgoszcz to drive their tractors into town as part of a display of their grievances against the state.

If the regime wondered about Solidarity's ability to deliver on its instant warning strikes, their doubts were dispelled the next day. Hundreds of thousands of workers, from the seaport of Gdansk to the copper centre of Legnica, struck briefly in the largest co-ordinated nationwide protest since October 3. The next day, Friday, January 23, while Solidarity in Warsaw shut down the capital for four hours, Walesa issued a dramatic personal appeal.

"There must be an effective work boycott tomorrow, January 24, to preserve the unity of the movement," said the Solidarity leader. "One has to understand the problem: it's not only a question of work free Saturdays, but of many points of the agreement which are not being carried out. The government has made a clever move. It tries to convince society through the mass media that Solidarity doesn't understand the difficult economic situation and is irresponsible. It's a very comfortable position for the government to take. We have to remember, however, that it's not what this is all about.

"We understand the difficult position. We know that there are problems, but we also know that there are at least ten million of us, ten million members with whom the government should talk, whose views it should take into account, who it shouldn't attempt to split. The purpose of all this is to divide us, to divide us on a matter of free Saturdays. If we understand this, then we have to come to the conclusion that this time we cannot back down. If we are divided on this issue, then we'll become divided on other issues.

"That's why I, Lech Walesa, am asking you to understand. On the 24th of January we are not going to work. Nobody can be harmed. The union position is clear. Each case of repression will be reported to us. We'll defend everybody for not coming to work on Saturday."

Although not a word of this appeal appeared in the public media, within hours it had been telephoned, tape-recorded, and telexed to every corner of Poland. That it had been heard was clear the next day. This time, not hundreds of thousands, but rather millions of Polish workers took a "free Saturday" to back the demand for a five-day workweek, and much else.

On Tuesday, January 27, the government agreed at least to talk about the issue publicly, and for the first time, Polish television was enlived by an open debate between state and trade unions (both Solidarity and the old unions) on questions of the day. By then, however, a series of wildcat strikes had erupted throughout the country, giving the impression that even Solidarity might no longer be capable of controlling the situation. National commission member Andrzej Kolodziej appeared unruffled. "The national commission does not have to give authorization for any strikes. The union statutes fully authorize local chapters to declare strikes," he coolly reminded the authorities. Nonetheless, Walesa dashed to Rzeszow in southeastern Poland, the apparent centre of farmers' protests against the government, in an attempt to mediate. At the same time, he announced a one-hour warning strike for February 3, and said that the national commission would consider at its next meeting, February 18, the possibility of a one-day national general strike. The government could cry "creeping anarchy"— and indeed it did—but whether it could persuade public opinion that the deteriorating situation was solely the responsibility of others was another matter. In a less shrill voice, it announced the resumption of negotiations on Friday, January 30.

It wasn't until 4 a.m. on Saturday morning in Warsaw that the two sides emerged from a marathon thirteen-hour negotiating session. They had agreed on a formula for shortening the workweek. For the time being, three out of every four Saturdays would be nonworking days—almost exactly the compromise Solidarity had offered ten days previously. The exact allocation of the Saturdays to be taken off would be left to the discretion of individual enterprises. Workers who stayed off the job on January 10 and 24 would receive normal compensation.

In addition, the government agreed to turn over a one-hour weekly television program to the union. On a third sticking point, the question of farmers' rights, the government would send a commission in the next few days to Rzeszow to hold talks. Andrzej Gwiazda wasn't completely happy with the compromise. "We haven't achieved the formulations we wanted," said the militant engineer. He worried that the union had perhaps given up too much to achieve a settlement. The more moderate Walesa, however, was seen contentedly puffing on a new pipe.

In the five months since the Gdansk Agreement, the strikers who had occupied the Lenin Shipyard had built a national ten-million-member independent trade union. Solidarity had successfuly tested itself against the state in a series of battles (less of its making than as a result of the regime's outdated illusions). In the course of organizing, it had virtually decimated the old central trade union council (CRZZ). Above all, Solidarity had broken the Polish United Workers Party's monopoly on the claim to be the sole representative of the Polish working class. It was definitely an accomplishment that could be put in one's pipe and thought about.

7   Students, Media, Farmers

> *Why did the government stop a documen-*
> *tary film about the strikes in Gdansk?*
> *Because the people who couldn't stop the*
> *workers needed to feel they could still stop*
> *something.*
> —Jan Pietrzak

At the universities

Professor Robert Glebocki went back to school on September 1.

The Oliwa campus, one of the many branches of the University of Gdansk, consists of two modern three-story buildings housing the faculties of humanities and sciences. The Baltic coast post-secondary institution enjoys neither the architectural splendors of the University of Warsaw nor the ancient traditions of Cracow's Jagiellonian University, founded in 1364. Yet, in autumn 1980, it shared many preoccupations with its more prestigious counterparts.

It was a rainy Monday. The workers at the Lenin Shipyard had returned to their jobs after a regime-shaking eighteen-day strike. Glebocki, the bearded, fortyish astrophysicist who had travelled to Gdansk to convey the university's support to the strikers, returned to Oliwa, bringing with him lessons from the shipyard.

Inside the University of Gdansk's halls of learning that day, the topics of discussion were much the same as at similar institutions throughout the country. The ink on the truce between the working class and the workers' state was barely dry when Polish universities issued their own list of demands.

The first step at the University of Gdansk was to establish a new "independent, self-governing" union for teachers and staff. The outspoken Glebocki was promptly elected chairman of the school's Solidarity branch. The new organization immediately called on the government to grant university autonomy, in matters of both administration and curriculum.

Over the next several months, Polish and Western media would tend to concentrate on the changes taking place at the top (in party and government) and down on the shop floor among still-restive workers as they fought for legal recognition, a shortened work week and the right to commemorate their dead. The mid-level institutional changes, at universities and in the media, would go largely unreported, or at best, receive passing attention.

In the half-decade between 1975 and 1980, the student generation of 1968, and those that followed it, had forged a link between intellectuals and workers quite unlike anything to be found in most industrial countries. During the shipyard strike, intellectual institutions had demonstrated an especially strong solidarity with the workers. Now, within the climate of reform created by the workers, the universities and related institutions proposed to make structural changes in their own sector.

At the University of Gdansk, the rector (equivalent to the president of a North American university or college) had traditionally been chosen by a handful of members of the local communist party branch. The rector's post was one of those on the lengthy *nomenclatura* list that prescribed which public positions must be held by party members. "It was all games," sneered Glebocki, "and sometimes dirty games. It was terrible. Democratic elections were the only solution to this problem."

Perhaps just as important as the issue of democracy in university governance was the question of who controlled the curriculum. Before the August upheaval, the university curriculum was a gruelling, mind-numbing regimen set by the state. It attempted to cram the equivalent of a six-year Western program leading to a master's degree into a four-year package called a *magister* diploma. Students put in as many as 30-35 classroom hours weekly, leaving little time for study, and less for social activities. What they found particularly grating were obligatory courses in Russian language and Marxist-Leninist ideology, taught in an especially deadening style. Also protested were the compulsory hours of military training. "For students it was a waste of time," agreed Glebocki. "For the university, a waste of money." The academic branches of Solidarity proposed to change much of this.

While the union drafted proposals to shoot off to the ministry of education, Gdansk, during the first weeks of autumn, had something of the atmosphere of a festival of free speech. At the annual film festival, held in the Old City in mid-September, among other sights, there was a dramatic midnight showing of two hours of barely edited footage of the shipyard strike entitled *Workers '80*. Even the inadvertent star of the spectacle, Lech Walesa, was among the overflow audience. Eventually, the film would be temporarily suppressed by the state and turn into an issue in its own right.

Jacek Kuron, less than a week out of jail, arrived at the Oliwa campus in the first days of September to field questions. The session in the packed auditorium went on for four hours. In the lounge of the humanities faculty, two hand-lettered signs appeared on facing walls. One, attributed to Lenin, said: "The definition of a police state is one in which a policeman earns more than a teacher." On the other wall was a matching sentiment: "Democracy is a condition in which the place of the minority is found elsewhere than in prison." It bore the name of Kuron.

Everywhere, speakers talked openly about heretofore proscribed subjects. Forbidden topics were debated late into the night. In a country where conversation was still an art form, free speech was in the air.

A commission of educators, backed by legal counsel, began negotiations with ministry officials on new university legislation in November. Then, as with so much else of the machinery of "renewal," as it was called by the state, the process stalled.

It was only a question of where the protests would begin. One candidate was Cracow's Jagellonian University where the astronomer Copernicus had once studied. Earlier in the year, 700 Cracow students had written to the communist party congress asking for the right to set up their own organization separate from the government-decreed Socialist Students Union. The request had been rebuffed.

"Now they will try again," predicted art historian Jacek

Wozniakowski, a Catholic intellectual whose passport had been lifted because of his association with the KOR-related series of illegal lectures known as the "Flying University." "I hope that a strike is not necessary," he said, "but I wonder whether they will be satisfied with what they were seeking before. They will probably demand more, and they may be very stubborn about it."

At the University of Warsaw, where a brief sit-in of 200 students took place in late November, the protesters were placated with a plan for establishing an independent student association. A similar arrangement was achieved at the Catholic University of Lublin. Not everyone, however, would be satisfied with such partial solutions.

After two further months of government inaction, it happened at the University of Lodz on January 22, 1981. In the rather grim manufacturing city—the Polish Manchester, as it is called—with its red-brick textile mills and tenements, there were soon 4,000 students sitting in at the university.

"During the first week or ten days, nobody in Poland knew that there was a strike in Lodz," recalled Robert Glebocki. The news was suppressed to prevent contagion. In any case, the nation was taken up with other issues: the debate over the five-day work week; a farmers' sit-in in Rzeszow; and a wildcat walkout affecting 110 factories in Bielsko-Biala, near the Czechoslovakian border. Once the word got out, however, student delegations from Lublin, Wroclaw, Warsaw and Gdansk converged on Lodz to express solidarity.

What they saw was the paraphernalia of protest—sleeping bags in the corridor, sausages hanging from coat rack hooks, a cheap press to crank out a list of demands—and a determination to change the way education was run in Poland. A deputy minister of education was dispatched to the scene shortly after the student strike began. The demands, 47 in number and covering four single-spaced typewritten pages, were read out to him. Their scope precluded any thought the government might have had about a quick settlement. Talks broke off. By the end of the first week, nine of the twelve buildings at the 7,000-student university were occupied, and the campus at Lodz was soon joined by the nearby Polytechnic and the Medical Academy. The students received ample supplies of food from a sympathetic public. "We've started something and we're going to continue with it until the very end, until there's an agreement,'' said one student spokesman. They braced for a long sit-in.

As the Cracow art historian had predicted, the students *had* demanded more, and they were going to be stubborn about it. Education Minister Janusz Gorski arrived in due course, but several rounds of negotiations at the beginning of February produced little. The students stayed in their sleeping bags.

On February 9, with the government facing striking farmers in Rzeszow, workers in southwestern Jelenia Gora, and students in Lodz, the party dismissed Jozef Pinkowski and appointed the country's third prime minister in a year. The new man was four-star general and minister of defence, Wojciech Jaruzelski. The day of his appointment, students in Poznan began a sit-in at their university in solidarity with the University of Lodz strikers. Appealing for "90 strike-free days," Jaruzelski moved quickly to defuse the situation, perhaps with an eye to the forthcoming Soviet party congress in late February, where the Polish party would have to put in an appearance. The dispute in Jelenia Gora was immediately settled, and negotiators in Rzeszow and Lodz were ordered to come to terms.

Even so, the university strike dragged on until February 18, and there were hitches right up to the last minute. As in the case of the Gdansk Agreement, there was a row over recognition of the party's leading role, this time in return for registration of an independent student association. Minister Gorski stormed out of the negotiations; the students threatened to call a nation-wide university strike; the minister appeared on national television, vainly urging students not to strike; and by the eve of the settlement, the sit-in had spread to dozens of schools across the country, including Jagellonian University in Cracow. Many more students—among them, those at the University of Gdansk —were prepared to join the strike the next day, when the government made it unnecessary.

The result of the nearly month-long sit-in was a far-reaching accord between the Lodz strikers, speaking for the nation's universities, and the regime. It created as many precedents in the sphere of education as the Gdansk Agreement had in the area of trade union rights. In the sit-in headquarters at the University of Lodz, students—and Minister Gorski—crammed together as the 25-page accord was read out point by point.

When the provision for registration of an independent student association was reached, the occupiers jubilantly burst into applause. As was the case with the Gdansk Agreement, the requisite nod toward the party's primacy was relegated to an appendix of the registration document.

As emotionally satisfying as the achievement of a new student organization was, at the heart of the accord was an even broader victory for university autonomy. The government agreed that henceforth curriculum decisions could be made by individual university senates. This meant that the senate could replace compulsory courses in Marxism-Leninism with a variety of electives. Heretofore a rubber stamp body, the senate would itself be reconstituted on a "one-third" system, providing equal tripartite representation to professors, junior instructors and other campus workers, and students.

A program of language study options was substituted for mandatory Russian language training. As well, the government bowed to student wishes for an extension of studies to a fifth year, to slow down the previous harried pace. Finally, under the new arrangement universities would be self-governing in administrative matters, including election of the rector by the university community.

There were still other important points in the accord, ranging from the restriction of secret police on campus to an increase in the national educational budget. In a concluding section entitled "general social demands," the document touched on questions of free speech, passport regulations and the proposed new censorship law. As a finishing touch, the government even agreed to end the ban against the film, *Workers '80*.

"We have won," said one student leader. "But the government won, too," he added, observing the etiquette established by the labor movement for binding wounds after a triumphant protest. The regime was no doubt satisfied by the fact that the sit-in was over. But it could hardly have been comforted by the thought that prominent among the Inter-University Co-ordinating Commission—as the Lodz student organization was called—was Maciej Kuron, son of the prominent KOR leader. The authorities who had expelled the fathers from the universities of 1968 had been compelled to concede to their offspring at the universities of 1981.

Less than a month later, 3,000 students, professors and

Solidarity representatives gathered in the brisk spring air at the University of Warsaw to commemorate the suppression of student demonstrations in March 1968. Once again, Poles used their newly established right to hold public ceremonies that would have been unthinkable a year earlier. The gathering proposed to place a plaque along the university's main walkway, with a quotation from the nineteenth century poet, Cyprian Norwid: "We must not bow to circumstances and let truth stand behind closed doors."

Both workers and intellectuals were among the speakers recalling the violent crackdown of thirteen years before. Noting that workers had been enlisted as shock troops by the police, Solidarity leaders vowed that such a thing would never be repeated. "Never again splits and divisions, never again conflicts betwen workers and intelligentsia," declared Lech Sokolowski, a worker from the Huta Warszawa steel mill, on behalf of the new union.

Beginning at the university that day was a three-day university-sponsored symposium on the events of March 1968. The first address, delivered to an overflow crowd of students, was given by Jacek Kuron. Once again, his gravelly bass voice was heard, rasping away at the truth, or at least at the locks of the closed doors behind which it stood.

At the University of Gdansk, a board of 123 electors was specially created for the election of the rector in May. Students, professors and other groups working at the university, including everyone from junior lecturers to janitors, were all represented. Although a draft of the legislation legalizing the proceedings was still inching its way toward parliamentary ratification, the academics were sufficiently confident it would pass that they decided to hold the election before the school year ended.

Four candidates—only professors were eligible—were nominated for rector. When the ballots were counted, Robert Glebocki was named the first democratically chosen rector of the University of Gdansk.

Information, culture, censorship

"Why did the government stop a documentary film about the

strikes in Gdansk?'' asked the comedian, referring to the
suppression of the film, *Workers '80*. "Because the people who
couldn't stop the workers needed to feel they could still stop
something." The audience at the Pod Egida cabaret in Warsaw
roared.

Jan Pietrzak, the country's best-known political satirist,
quickly followed up with another gibe at the regime. "If we
applied some of our economic policies to the Sahara, soon there
would be no sand." The crowded cafe burst into cheers. Beer
flowed, spirits were high, and Pietrzak was back in business on
this icy December night, four months after the signing of the
Gdansk Agreement.

The cabaret had been shut down by the censors for a year.
After the enforced silence, Pietrzak began appearing on his own
in August. In November he formed a new company of writers,
actors and musicians, and three weeks later, with a fresh
collection of songs and skits, reopened the Pod Egida (its name
translates as "Under the Authority"; it's meant to be a play on
"offically allowed").

"What's the big deal about the Mafia?" shrugged Pietrzak.
"The Mafia runs only a few small towns in Italy, but our
Mafia—it runs the whole country."

The upheaval at the Lenin Shipyard had not only given birth
to a number of institutional changes, it had also unleashed a
flow of energies in the area of culture and communication,
ranging from Pietrzak to punk rock. "Ambition is your
damned religion," went the opening line of a current rock hit
that excoriated the regime. "I am sinless, because I have no
ambition," continued its plaintive cry.

Of all the challenges to censorship, the battle that was most
prominent, and that had the most practical significance for
workers, affected regulation of newspaper, radio and television
communications.

"My wife and I stopped listening to the evening news on
television years ago," explained Lenin Shipyard electrician
Stanislaw Bury after the strike. "The newspapers were filled
with nothing but the speeches of our leaders, and they didn't
sell. People were fed up with the bullshit," said Bury, who had
become a member of the shipyard Solidarity executive.

Since 1976, a KOR-inspired underground press had come into
existence, and during the strike, the shipyard workers had

published their own *Solidarity* strike bulletin, whose circulation at the height of the events of August reached 80,000 copies. Nonetheless, the version of the strike presented by the official mass media was infuriating to the strikers, as well as harmful to their cause. Daily, they engaged in heated debate with the somewhat shamefaced corps of Polish journalists covering the shipyard for the state-controlled media. Eventually a group of the journalists issued a protest statement.

Despite its prudence, it provided a glimpse of their discontent. "We, Polish journalists present at Gdansk during the strike," it began, "declare that much of the news published so far, and especially the manner in which it has been commented upon, does not correspond with what is happening here. This state of affairs leads to disinformation...the impossibility of publishing material which would show the facts in their true light is profoundly distressing to us and totally prevents us from honestly fulfilling our professional duties.

"We consider that it cannot but favor the solution of the conflict and contribute toward social development in the future to give the population the complete story of the events," the statement concluded.

Once the strikers had secured the right to their own publications and a government promise to produce a new, and presumably liberalized, censorship law within three months, the stage was set for an ongoing public debate on the matter. As soon as the Sejm reconvened on September 5 to ratify the terms of the Gdansk Agreement, the first salvo was fired. It came from Karol Malcuzynski, an avuncular 58-year-old television commentator whose popularity in Poland was similar to, say, Walter Cronkite's in the U.S. Malcuzynski, one of 33 "independents" sitting in the 460-member parliament, delivered a scorching attack—at least by Polish standards—on censorship.

The press, said the commentator, was not simply an amalgam of good and bad news articles. "Rather, it should serve as a seismograph of political opinion, as much for the people as for the authorities." Instead, he argued, it had been undermined by "the propaganda of success," which became a brake on honest discussion and reflection when the temporarily booming economy ran into trouble in the mid-seventies. The media had become a meaningless mouthing of slogans, Malcuzynski charged.

The veteran television journalist spoke from personal experience. Four years earlier, *Monitor*, his highly rated program of live interviews and commentary, had been abruptly scheduled out of existence. *Monitor* had been important because it was live and uncensored. "People knew that I couldn't say everything that I knew or thought, but still it was very different from the official propaganda," Malcuzynski said in a later interview. On the floor of the Sejm that day he ridiculed the type of program with which *Monitor* had been replaced. He chose, by way of example, a daily radio show called *Here's No. 1*, which mixed popular music with blaring anti-Western diatribes.

"In this manner, after returning from the lines in front of the stores, we could grieve over the problems of galloping inflation in England, or drugs in Scandinavia, or housing shortages in Austria," Malcuzynski said. "Half of Poland ridiculed it. The other half was angry about it. But in official circles, it was believed that the show was a clever strengthening of the ideological front. In a society like ours, which has access to many different sources of information, this type of propaganda is suicidal," said the commentator.

Such criticism was a novelty in itself. Further, the establishment of parliamentary committees to work on the new censorship law appeared to be a sign of progress. Still, there was a considerable discrepancy between intentions and deeds. Throughout the fall and into winter, as the government temporized to the point of crisis before acceding to Solidarity's demands for reform, the union repeatedly and bitterly complained about sparse and unfair coverage in the media.

Nonetheless, there were some observable changes. In November, journalists themselves moved to salvage their reputation by electing a blacklisted editor as chairman of the Association of Journalists. The scribe they brought in from the cold was 46-year-old Stefan Bratkowski. At the congress that elected him, attended by nearly 400 delegates from all over the country, the air was thick with demands, proposals, accusations and self-criticisms as the journalists lamented the fact that their profession had sunk to the level of pulp and propaganda.

Bratkowski looked a bit dazed at the press conference marking his election. He promised that his new position would not change him. He even pointed out that he was wearing the same old clothes—rumpled pants, a baggy green sweater and a black imitation leather jacket that matched the color of his luxuriant beard. Indeed, he was a marked contrast to the official sitting next to him. Jozef Klasa, the central committee's man in charge of press and television was nattily attired in a three-piece suit.

Because his articles became too critical of the regime, Bratkowski had been dismissed in 1973 from his post as editor of a weekly supplement of Warsaw's major daily, *Zycie Warszawy*. For seven years, his byline was rarely seen. During what he called his "years of silence" he wrote two historical volumes on Polish revolutionary traditions. Now, as well as a new professional position, he also had his old job back. "From now on, the authorities will be reading the newspapers," Bratkowski remarked dryly. "Until now, they didn't read them because they knew beforehand what would be in them...A revolution of common sense is now taking place in Poland," he added, "because common sense itself has become revolutionary in this country."

By late December the changes were conspicuous. Foreign observers noted that people were queuing up to buy newspapers they once laughed at. The deputy editor of *Polityka*, the pro-party but respected weekly intellectual newspaper, joked, "During the past few months, we've published all the articles that were confiscated by the censors over the past two years—well, maybe not all. Perhaps we've got two or three left." The same was true of movie theatres and television. Polish viewers were being presented with enough of the often grim news that some quipped it was "the propaganda of failure," thus registering the transition from the previously unrelenting paeans to success.

It was more a case of one-and-a-half steps forward, one step backward, however, than one of steady uninterrupted liberalization. In January 1981, as the political situation heated up with debates over the five-day work week, and sit-ins by farmers and students, the Polish press again fell under noticeably heavy censorship. The situation soon became objectionable enough that the printers of the censored newspapers decided to intervene.

They were in a good position to do so. Besides having literal control of the presses, they were able to see on the page proofs exactly what the censors had slashed with their heavy red-pencil markings and to read the information that was denied the rest of the country. Concerned by increasing evidence of the censor's deletions, the printers proposed to render this information public by printing blank spaces to denote omitted material—a practice that had been employed by their nineteenth century forefathers when the country was under foreign occupation.

Although negotiations with the government had already begun on the printers' complaints, the issue was forced on January 20 when the censor made several particularly large and objectionable cuts in copy prepared for *Zycie Warszawy*. The printers rebelled. The paper would be printed with blank spaces, they said, or not at all. "All we want is to print the truth," said Witold Slezak, head of the Solidarity pressroom local. "We feel that we have a moral responsibility for the information we provide to society through our work." A hasty set of negotiations was convened between the printers and the government and a compromise was reached. Instead of blank spaces, the paper would contain three dots set inside brackets to denote censored material. But when the paper appeared, the printers were dissatisfied. The three dots, they felt, hardly conveyed the breadth of material that had been cut.

Two days later, when an article outlining Solidarity's reasons for calling a strike over the question of free Saturdays was entirely suppressed, the printers refused to run the paper and *Zycie Warszawy* didn't appear that day. Negotiations between the workers and central committee member Jozef Klasa sputtered. The printers brought along texts printed during the nineteenth century occupation with the telltale blank spaces; as well they brought KOR's Adam Michnik as their adviser. Klasa refused to negotiate with Michnik in the same room and denounced the printers as "adventurists." Journalists' association chairman Bratkowski was rushed in to attempt mediation between the two sides.

The dispute was temporarily resolved in mid-February under the new, initially more conciliatory government of Jaruzelski, but not before the printers issued an ultimatum threatening to make Friday, February 13 a day of no newspapers in the entire country. Since 50,000 of the nation's 60,000 printers belonged to Solidarity, it was hardly an idle threat. The incident involving the printers was noteworthy more for what it said about the popular desire for a free press than for any agreement produced. In the end, both sides decided to cool off and await the appearance of the overdue new censorship law.

If the maintstream media made sporadic progress, the most tangible change in printed materials was a spectacular burgeoning of trade union publications that began immediately after the strike. In addition to the Gdansk *Solidarity Bulletin* and a similar newspaper put out in Szczecin called *Jednosc (Unity)*, Solidarity branches throughout the country, at the regional level and in factories, began regular publication of hundreds of uncensored newsletters and bulletins. Though printed on obviously cruder equipment than the official press, the union media were clearly more vigorous. Pages of verbatim transcripts of the internal debates of the Solidarity national leadership were made available to the readership, almost as if to underline the difference in democracy between the union press and the state's carefully-managed accounts of its high-level proceedings.

The union also made some advances above the counter. Various agreements were reached with local newspapers to provide space for Solidarity's viewpoint. In Gdansk, for example, three times a week the *Baltic Daily News* printed a half-page of articles written by Solidarity. Finally, after months of debate, a national *Solidarity Weekly*, edited by Tadeusz Mazowiecki, was authorized by the state in April. Its half-million copies were snapped up so fast that back issues quickly became collector's items.

Concurrent with these developments, there was a pervasive blossoming of information and culture throughout the society. Literary magazines, publications of various local groups, independent book publishing, photo exhibits, art gallery displays and film festivals appeared in such profusion that at times their relationship to the censorship, whether clandestine, semi-official, or merely tolerated, became irrelevant. In May, hundreds of Warsaw residents lined up day after day to enter a small gallery exhibiting stark black-and-white previously suppressed photos of workers' uprisings since 1956. Public ceremonies—recalling the crackdown on students in 1968, honoring the 1791 constitution, or commemorating the Poznan revolt—invariably drew large audiences. At times, there was the ironic sense that the entire society was a living admonition to the regime that ruled it. Poland, for the time being at least, had become a culturally open society the like of which had not existed in Eastern Europe since the war.

Jan Rulewski

Edward Gierek

Monument to those who died in the 1970 protests

Kania with Jaruzelski

*A photo exhibit
in Warsaw*

*An antisocialist
element*

Among the official media, television seemed to suffer least from rigid censorship. By mid-year, hardly an evening went by without Polish viewers saying in some amazement, "They'd never have had that on before." Although the evening news still featured the speeches of party bosses, people identified by small Solidarity badges became increasingly visible, and viewers could see Lech Walesa, just back from a visit to Japanese trade unionists, drolly complaining about the difficulty of using chopsticks. Among the surprising programs that summer were: an hour-long debate on unemployment, with Solidarity representatives lambasting a sweating official from the ministery of labor; live coverage of the assassination attempt against the Pope in mid-May; and television premieres of popular but politically controversial films.

At the Gdansk film festival in September 1980, just after the strike ended, film director Andrzej Wajda read a prepared statement to the 60 or so foreign critics present. "This is a time for truth," he declared. "We are in no way antisocialist. We wish to return to an earlier, more authentic meaning of socialism, as the working class envisions it and with which the intelligentsia agrees."

In late May 1981, Wajda's 1977 film, *Man of Marble*, which probes the unspoken and often-suppressed truth about the experiences of Poland's working class in the 1950s, received its first television showing. It came at an opportune moment. *Man of Marble* concludes with the hero's son, a worker at the Lenin Shipyard, beginning to learn the story of his father's life. Between September and May, Wajda had been attempting to answer the question, What happened to the son of *Man of Marble*? Within a week of the television broadcast, the director's answer to the question was shown at the Cannes film festival. The next day, the Polish press reported that Wajda's sequel, *Man of Iron*, had won the top award at Cannes.

From the farms

Outside Warsaw's Supreme Court building, about 250 farmers waited patiently under a steady end-of-December drizzle.

Like the Solidarity trade unionists, the farmers who had

joined the recently-formed Rural Solidarity went to Poland's Supreme Court seeking legal recognition of their union after it had been rejected by a lower court. Unlike the case of the workers, which involved relatively straightforward legal issues, that of the farmers posed a fundamental conceptual problem. The basic question, at least as the state conceived it, was: how could a group of self-employed private farmers claim the right to a form of organization designed to protect workers in relations with their employers?

That the farmers felt the need for such protection was perhaps a simpler matter to explain. As far back as 1956, with the return of Gomulka to power, private farmers had been assured of their rights. Unlike other East European countries, the pressures for collectivization of agriculture were successfully resisted in Poland, and the existence of a largely private farming sector became an axiom of the Polish model of socialism. A quarter-century later, there were 3.5 million private farmers in the country. They comprised about three-quarters of the agricultural workforce, and on their mostly small holdings produced about 80 per cent of the nation's food. Nonetheless, they had many complaints against the state. They felt insecure in terms of legal rights to their land, discriminated against in the allocation of farm machinery and other agricultural materials, and oppressed by the state, the sole formal purchaser of their production, which they regarded at least metaphorically as their employer.

By the late 1970s, farmers' self-defence committees had come into existence in the Lublin, Grojec and Rzeszow regions. Admittedly conservative in temperament and more closely tied to the church than were the trade unionists, the farmers nonetheless made common cause with the striking workers at the Lenin Shipyard in August 1980. "As peasants, we express our entire solidarity with you, the workers, and support your demands," said the joint appeal from the farmers' self-defence committee. At the same time, they reiterated their own grievances against the state and about the treatment they received at the hands of townspeople.

"We have to talk about a disagreeable thing," the farmers said to the workers. "For 35 years, the government and the party have been inciting the population to hatred of the peasants. No account is taken of our labor and our role as food providers. 'Yokels,' 'tramps,' and 'clods' are some of the epithets which we hear from the townspeople. We are received with disdain in the offices and we are detested when we come to queue in the shops of the town, although at home we've only got bread, salt, sugar and gruel...stories circulate about our incomes and our wealth, but you only have to visit any village, go into any house, to understand that these are only myths. The state tries to divide us and to provoke quarrels between us. We must do all we can to unite.

"The local authorities have an unlimited power over us," continued the poignant appeal. "At any moment they can take our land away, expropriate us, transfer our children to a distant school...You in the towns, the factories, you lack a proper trade union, your rights are not respected, but we in the country, we are treated as slaves."

Once the workers had won the right to a proper trade union, the farmers attempted to follow suit. Three weeks after the Gdansk Agreement was concluded, the farmers met and drew up statutes for a Rural Solidarity union, which were submitted to the Warsaw provincial court in late September. A month later the bid for registration was rejected. Although the farmers contended that their income was regulated by government-controlled prices and that their relationship to the state was therefore that of employees, the lower court took the position that private farmers couldn't be the subject of union statutes designed to lay down bargaining procedures between management and workers.

Two weeks before the slated December 30 Supreme Court hearing of their appeal against the lower court's verdict, the farmers held a rally in Warsaw. More than a thousand of them came from around the country to the domed meeting hall of Warsaw Polytechnic Institute. Some wore heavy black jackets, the traditional peasant garb for a church-going Sunday. Others were in jeans and had ridden to town from outlying areas in horse-drawn carts that were parked up and down the side streets. Inside the hall, speaker after speaker bitterly attacked the state's agricultural policies which, they said, channeled almost all investment, credits, tractors and fertilizer into state enterprises at the expense of the private farmer. Several speakers at the long and boisterous session warned of possible strikes if the government refused to grant them trade union rights. Andrzej Gwiazda, the Solidarity national commission member who spoke on behalf of several union leaders in attendance, encouraged the farmers to go ahead and organize. Although the meeting didn't end in the taking of a strike vote, the would-be farmers' union, which claimed the support of 500,000 of the 3.5 million private farmers, had put the government on notice.

Inside the courtroom on December 30, while the Rural Solidarity rally waited in the rainy streets below, the lawyers argued on technical grounds. In rejecting the farmers' original application, the lower court had cited an international ruling on agricultural workers that maintained self-employed farmers couldn't join together in trade unions. In the Supreme Court, Rural Solidarity's lawyer, Stanislaw Szczuka submitted a more recent document from the Geneva-based International Farm Workers' Organization which he claimed expanded the definition of agricultural workers to include private farmers and smallholders. Since most of the farmers' produce was sold to the state at state-regulated prices, said the lawyer, farmers were, for all practical purposes, in an employee-employer relationship. The argument was no more far-fetched than the state's frequent assertions that private farming in Poland is somehow consistent with socialism. In any case, said Szczuka, so many farmers had joined Rural Solidarity that "the new union has become a fact which the law should not ignore."

The farmers had gone to court to obtain satisfaction, but at the end of the two-and-a-half hour session what they got was delay. The three-member court decided to postpone, on technical grounds, a decision on the appeal. More time was needed, it said, to consider the international documents that had been submitted.

At a news conference afterwards, the farmers' organizers attempted to put the best face possible on the delay. "It's almost a victory," said one of the union leaders, Zdzislaw Ostatek, a orchardist from Grojec. The fact that the Supreme Court had "not recognized the verdict" of the lower court was termed a partial success.

Not all of the farmers who wanted a union were content to sit on their hands while the court made up its mind. The occupation of Rzeszow began on January 3. More than 200 farmers, accompanied by members of the local Solidarity branch, chose the three-story building on snow-swept Liberty Square as the site of their sit-in. Appropriately enough, the impromptu headquarters of Rural Solidarity had, until recently, housed the old trade unions of Rzeszow, which had virtually collapsed after Solidarity's legalization.

By the time the state officially got around to noticing the occupation—a near-total news blackout was imposed during the first weeks—the farmers were determinedly installed in their protest site. In the assembly hall an altar had been set up on the stage, and behind it were pictures of the pope and Our Lady of Czestochowa, a Polish flag and a two-metre cardboard copy of the Gdansk monument. A priest daily administered the sacrament. Security and discipline were strict, and alcohol was forbidden. Ample food—sausage, potatoes, homemade bread—was suppled by other farmers from the surrounding countryside. A public address system—the "strike radio station"—broadcast regular communiques from Solidarity branches all over Poland, news summaries, and even lectures on such topics as agricultural law in Sweden.

Although there were only a few sporadic sympathy strikes in the factories of Rzeszow, the chairman of the local Solidarity branch, 36-year old electrical engineer Jan Ogrodnik, was present to offer the union's support. "What the shipyards in Gdansk did for the workers of Poland, the workers and farmers here are going to do for the country's farmers," said Ogrodnik.

But not if PUWP First Secretary Kania had his way about it. In a mid-January speech to a joint gathering of the communist party and one of its appendages, the United Peasants' Party, Kania warned private farmers in no uncertain terms against trying to organize a Solidarity-type union. "We register our categorical opposition to all attempts at inciting the countryside, at sowing anarchy or creating a political opposition," thundered the party chief. Although a long table with microphones was neatly arranged in the Rzeszow meeting hall in anticipation of eventual negotiations, the state appeared determined to ignore the protest. Perhaps it hoped to wait out the farmers until March, when the spring weather would necessitate a return to their now frozen, unworked fields. In any case, the regime had enough to deal with as the debate on the five day work week became intense.

Solidarity, however, had no intention of ignoring the farmers in Rzeszow. In late January, as the union broadened its demands beyond work-free Saturdays, it took a stronger position in support of private farmers. Walesa spent most of the week before the end-of-January negotiations with the government conferring with the protesters in Rzeszow. When a compromise on the five-day work week was reached on January 31, the farmers' issue turned out to be the major sticking point in the marathon talks. Although no actual solution was reached, the government agreed to send a delegation headed by Deputy Agriculture Minister Andrzej Kacala to Rzeszow to open talks. As well, it was announced that the Supreme Court would issue a final ruling on the farmers' appeal on February 10.

While Solidarity's Bogdan Lis joined the farmers' talks, Walesa rushed to Bielsko-Biala and Jelenia Gora to mediate strikes. Party boss Kania contributed his bit with new denunciations of unnamed "instigators."

The weight of the various protests eventually toppled the government. The ineffective Pinkowski was replaced as prime minister by the military's General Jaruzelski the day before the scheduled Supreme Court decision on farmers. The Rzeszow talks were recessed, and in the pause before the court met on February 10, the church gave its formal backing to the farmers. The move was not unexpected, considering that the peasantry was perhaps the episcopate's staunchest constituency. Cardinal Wyszynski received a Rural Solidarity delegation, and his office issued a statement saying, "The Primate stressed that the farmers' right to free assembly, in line with their will and needs, independently from existing structures, is a natural right that does not originate from any state authority. This right requires protection by the state."

Despite this discourse on the difference between natural and legislated rights from the institution based on divine right, the Supreme Court seemed loathe to agree. The farmers carried Walesa on their shoulders to the Warsaw court in a pre-decision show of optimism and then spent several hours waiting in freezing temperatures, keeping up their spirits by singing religious and patriotic hymns.

At the conclusion of the proceedings, the court rejected the appeal that would allow farmers to form an independent trade union. It attempted to soften its ruling somewhat by issuing a complicated decision that said, in effect, that farmers had rights under international law to unionize but had no such right under Polish law because they were self-employed. Instead, proposed the court, the case should go back to the Warsaw provincial court which could register the farmers as an "association"—a grouping without collective bargaining rights.

Outside the courthouse, speaking to several thousand people who had gathered there, Walesa attempted to soften the blow. "The court did not reject us," he said. "It's really a draw."

In Rzeszow, far from the legal niceties of Warsaw, the sit-in continued into its seventh week. The farmers had yet to achieve a union or even a settlement on any of the other demands which were set out in a three-page document. They were prepared to wait. While the new Jaruzelski government dashed about the country putting out flare-ups in factories and schools, Solidarity was in no position to call for new support strikes on the farmers' behalf. Instead, they promised to continue to fight for farmers' rights in the current union-government negotiations then underway to shape a new trade union law, and to stand by the farmers while they waited.

On February 16, Jaruzelski sent Deputy Agriculture Minister Kacala back to Rzeszow to come to terms with the farmers. For two days, and much of the nights, the eight-member government team negotiated with fourteen farmers headed by Jan Kulaj (representing the National Founding Committee of the Trade Union of Private Farmers), two members of the Rzeszow Solidarity branch and Solidarity national commission members Walesa and Lis. On February 18, the government signed an accord with Rural Solidarity.

In the Rzeszow Agreement the authorities recognized in fact—but not yet in law—the independent Rural Solidarity union by signing an accord with its representatives. Although the agreement did not include the question of formally recognizing Rural Solidarity, it offered enough concessions to the farmers to get them back to their fields with something more than a victory in words alone. Under the agreement, private land ownership would be guaranteed by special parliamentary legislation that would incorporate the guarantee into the constitution. In addition, the government promised more capital investment in agriculture, improved prices, better pensions, democratic control of rural administration, and legal guarantees preventing reprisals against those who had participated in the occupation. In a country short of both democracy and food, it was at least half a loaf.

While workers and students had achieved their basic

demands, for the farmers, the fight wasn't over. Admittedly, the regime was moving toward legal recognition of Rural Solidarity at a pace that would have permitted snails to consume most of the forthcoming crop. Events would soon intervene to hasten a solution to the dilemma.

8   The Beatings at Bydgoszcz

*Internal democracy within the union is a
necessity. The condition in which it
flourishes is full openness... Its funeral
is when criticism is crushed.*
  —Andrzej Gwiazda, April 1981

It began as a "honeymoon." At least, that's the way some
observers characterized the two week period between the end of
February and early March. For the first time in months, Poland
was free of strikes, sit-ins or other strife. The media spoke of
"rebuilding" and of the country "settling down" to give Prime
Minister Jaruzelski's government breathing space to do something about the dismal economy.

But before the month ended, the nation would once again go
to the precipice. Andrzej Gwiazda's question, posed during the
August strikes—"Are we going to live in a democratic system or
a police state?"—would again be asked. Both Solidarity and the
party, in their different ways, would experience a crisis of
democracy. And the issue of farmers would once more appear
in bold relief.

As Poles contemplated the recently released details of a meat
rationing plan set to begin on April 1—a measure demanded by
the strikers in August to ensure more equitable distribution—
the country's leaders made another of their sudden journeys to
Moscow on March 4. Although Poland's internal situation
appeared relatively calm, party leaders Kania and Jaruzelski
issued a joint communique with Soviet boss Brezhnev on the
need for "urgent" action to counter the threat of "imperialist
and internal reactionary forces" against the country.

At 5:30 the next morning, while riding in a taxi on his way to take a train to Czestochowa, Jacek Kuron was arrested. Whether this represented a direct translation of the joint Polish-Soviet rumblings from Moscow, or was simply one of the state's periodic crackdowns on the opposition, was unknown. The fact that the police attempted to serve a prosecutor's summons on KOR's Adam Michnik the following day showed that it wasn't an isolated incident. Kuron was detained for seven hours and informed that he was under investigation for possible violation of Article 270 of the criminal code, slandering the Polish state. After his release, Kuron went about his customary business, which that week included opening the University of Warsaw's three-day seminar examining the state's repression of university students in 1968.

Within 48 hours, Solidarity's national commission convened in Warsaw and indicated that it wasn't amused by the arrest of one of its well-known advisers. "It looks like pressure is building up on all levels," said Solidarity spokesman Janusz Onyszkiewicz, "starting with harassment of our activists and ending with the detention of Jacek Kuron." He cited a number of recent incidents to back his contention. The union was also disquieted by indications of anti-Semitic activity. In the past few days, posters had appeared in Warsaw calling upon Poles to rise up against "Jewish chauvinists" and announcing a rally to coincide with the scheduled March 8 demonstration commemorating 1968. Although there were only a few thousand Jews in the entire country, the device of anti-Semitism had been frequently employed in the past under party sponsorship. Onyszkiewicz didn't believe the attempted campaign was likely to attract a following, but he made it clear that Solidarity was prepared to oppose it. On all these matters, the union was warning the government that forms of harassment weren't the best way to maintain the peace it claimed to want.

The Poznan opera house had never seen a show quite like this one. On March 8-9, nearly 500 farmers from around the nation used the elegant, pre-World War I hall for the first national congress of their still unrecognized union.

The speeches from the opera house stage were lengthy and sometimes meandering, and there were frequent humorous, earthy interjections from the audience. One of the objects of this democratic get-together seemed to be to make sure that everyone got his say. "It takes time to learn how to do these things," explained a Cracow farmer. "You have to expect a lot of noise at first. No one here has ever voted before, I mean really voted, with no one looking over his shoulder." As he spoke, ballots were being passed out and delegates moved forward in small groups to mark them and cast their votes in a large urn behind the blue opera house curtain.

The election was for an executive and a chairman of the nascent Rural Solidarity union. The choice was between two men, Henryk Gora, a journalist who had returned to the land, and Jan Kulaj, the 23-year-old activist who had led the Rzeszow sit-in.

Aside from electing a leadership, the congress had scores of items to deal with. The delegates seemed to attack each issue with the same enthusiasm, whether it was the large and complex one of uniting various segments of the farmers' movement, or the seemingly smaller matter of protecting beekeepers. When it turned out that one of the union's proposed statutes excluded those who owned less than half a hectare, a qualification that apparently eliminated beekeepers and mushroom growers, shouts resounded through the chamber. The statutes were amended to include them.

In their speeches, the delegates demanded registration of their union, supported the role of the church in the countryside, complained of police harassment, and criticized the authorities in general. "They're the ones creating the situation of opposition, not us," said a farmer from Jelenia Gora. Another speaker echoed his sentiments. "Why do they always tell us what to do? They pull us around like horses with their eyes blinkered." A third called for democratic elections to parliament and drew a standing ovation. Encouraged, he went on. "Why do you think I'm talking so bravely? Because the country's democratic renewal must take place. Walesa is right— workers and farmers are united."

At day's end, texts of messages to parliament were read, asking for a law to legalize the union, and condemning censorship. Then the results of the voting for the chairman of Rural Solidarity were announced. It was a landslide for young Jan Kulaj—by 452 votes out of 474.

The Rzeszow farmer was hoisted aloft, hugged, and handed flowers while the hall rose to sing "May he live a hundred years." Though the farmers had not yet formally accomplished

what the trade unionists had, perhaps they had found their own
equivalent of Solidarity's Walesa. Kulaj gave a brief acceptance
speech, thanking the delegates and God, a speech not unlike
those of Solidarity's chairman.

The calm continued through mid-March. There were a few
local disputes, but nothing of major proportions. In Lodz,
there was a one-hour warning strike over the dismissal of
several hospital workers. On the day the Lodz dispute was
settled, a small incident in Radom, site of the 1976
demonstrations, flared into a list of demands by the local
Solidarity chapter. The church's conference of bishops
appealed for calm. Walesa, Jacek Kuron and a priest went to
Radom and in the local soccer stadium filled with 15,000
workers, persuaded them to call off a threatened strike since
two civic officials they objected to had resigned. Meanwhile, a
few farmers began a sit-in at the headquarters of the PUWP-
affiliated Peasants Party in Bydgoszcz. On the whole, however,
the situation offered little cause for concern. The evening
television news turned its attention to the annual Warsaw Pact
military manoeuvres, "Soyuz '81," which were beginning in
and around Poland.

Jan Rulewski, the chairman of the Bydgoszcz Solidarity
chapter, noticed the police build-up. On Thursday morning,
March 19, when he looked out the windows of the union
offices, which overlook the Bryda River, he could see an
unusual number of militia trucks cruising the street below. The
state appeared to have developed an intense interest in his city.
Bydgoszcz, about 175 kilometres south of Gdansk, is the
largest of a cluster of industrial cities in north-central
Poland. The Bryda, a small tributary of the Wisla, meanders
through the town. It is known throughout the country for its
production of bicycles and mopeds. It also lies in the centre of
an extensive agricultural region, which is one of the reasons the
recently elected head of Rural Solidarity, Jan Kulaj, had chosen
it as the site of a farmers' sit-in a couple of days before. From
the perspective of Gdansk, Bydgoszcz is seen as a rather
provincial, architecturally ugly city, far less attractive than
nearby Torun with its elegant Gothic towers. But perhaps that's
merely a bit of typical coastal snobbishness. From the viewpoint
of Rulewski and the local Solidarity branch, it was considered a

good union town whose workers had been quick to support the Gdansk strikers the previous summer.

Rulewski, a bicycle industry technical worker in his early 30s, gathered up his notes outlining the union's support for the farmers. Just before 10 a.m., he entered the provincial council building at the head of a 30-person delegation of workers and farmers. Edward Berger, chairman of the provincial council presidium, had promised Rulewski that the farmers' case would get a hearing at the session. At the presiding table, Berger, the council presidium and various local dignitaries had taken their places.

The familiar items of provincial business were taken up. The local governor had recently resigned under a cloud of suspicion and the council went through the ritual of selecting a successor. At noon, the meeting took a break. Rulewski used the opportunity to check with Berger once more that Solidarity would definitely be allowed to speak. Of course, Berger reassured him, at the end, just as he had promised, during the last agenda item, "Questions and Opinions." When the session resumed, Deputy Governor Roman Bak delivered a long report on the plan for economic and social reforms in the Bydgoszcz region. Suddenly, the languid tempo of the proceedings started to pick up speed. A motion to postpone discussion of the reform plan was made and seconded by Berger on behalf of the council presidium. It quickly passed, the council delegates assuming that they would move on to the next item. Instead, the presidium and other local authorities were on their feet, leaving the hall.

Rulewski jumped up. He was bitter about what was now an obvious manipulation. He urged the delegates to remain in the hall and hear the representatives of the union and the striking farmers. At the podium microphone, he attempted to explain why they had come to the session. In mid-sentence, the sound system was cut off. Nonetheless, about 45 of the provincial councillors decided to remain in the hall, together with Rulewski's delegation. They, too, were unhappy with the back-stage manoeuvres.

Through the late afternoon, the remaining councillors and Solidarity deliberated over how to solve the situation that had been created by the provincial leadership. Finally, the rump group agreed to a joint communique in which an extraordinary session of the council would be proposed. As the two groups slowly haggled over the wording of the statement, out in the corridors of the assembly hall knots of unidentified men in civilian clothes had appeared. A few of them drifted into the hall itself.

It was after 6 p.m. A group of provincial authorities came back into the assembly hall. They demanded that the remaining councillors follow them to a different room for a discussion on the situation. Forty of them left. In the main hall, the workers and farmers waited. Instead of the councillors returning, Deputy Governor Bak and the provincial prosecutor came back. Bak called on everyone to clear the hall, while the prosecutor warned the delegation that their stay was illegal. At that moment, the plain-clothes men moved into the hall, followed by a squad of militia. At their head was Major Henryk Bednarek. While the police clicked off pictures of the Solidarity delegation, Bednarek gave them ten minutes to leave. Rulewski replied. He explained why the delegation had come and told Bednarek that the provincial commandant had given them a guarantee of safety. As Bednarek again demanded that the delegation get out, the missing councillors re-entered the hall. There were a few moments of confusion and haggling.

"What is it that you want?" Deputy Governor Bak angrily demanded. "Is it power? Tell me. Show me your real intentions."

"We only want to finish the communique," Rulewski answered.

Major Bednarek announced that the councillors and Solidarity had fifteen minutes to finish. His troops were withdrawn to the corridors. Soon they were back. Bednarek again issued an order to clear the hall. A Solidarity representative read out fragments of the statement. The councillors and Solidarity representatives moved forward to sign it. It was too late.

Bednarek gave the signal. "Major Bednarek, don't do that!" one of the councillors shouted. The plain-clothes men were already moving chairs out of the way to clear a path for the uniformed police. The union delegation formed into a group. The militia waded in. Solidarity began singing the national anthem. It was lost in the din, as the phalanx of troops, nearly 200 strong, slowly pressed the group against the wall. Michal Bartoszcze, a 68-year-old man, father of one of the local peasant activists, began to sing another patriotic hymn. The militia now led the unionists out of the building one by one.

Two plain-clothes men held on to the elderly Bartoszcze, who didn't resist. Outside, a third man came up to them. He hit Bartoszcze in the face. Then again. The old man's legs buckled under him.

In the courtyard of the building, the gate had been closed and a crowd of militia milled about. Suddenly, there were new shouts. It was the voice of Rulewski. He was surrounded by plain-clothes men. They beat him slowly and brutally. When he went down, they pulled him up, and began again. Next to Rulewski, another member of the Solidarity executive, Mariusz Labentowicz, fell, covered in blood. The two were hauled back into the meeting hall. They put Rulewski in a chair. He fell off onto the floor. One of the shocked councillors rushed up to him with a handkerchief. Rulewski, spitting blood through the gap where two teeth had been knocked out, refused it. "Let everyone see what they did, those who work in the name of People's Power."

It's two-and-a-half hours by road from Gdansk to Bydgoszcz. Lech Walesa arrived at the hospital just after 1 a.m. The streets of the darkened town were being patrolled by militia vehicles. Rulewski and Labentowicz were listed in serious condition, with concussion and other injuries. The elderly Bartoszcze was critical. He had a heart condition. Plans were being made to move him to Warsaw.

While there was some question as to who exactly had ordered the beatings in Bydgoszcz, it was instantly clear to all the major institutions of Polish society that their impact could not be confined to the medium-sized industrial city. Walesa was only the first of those to arrive in Bydgoszcz that night. He was soon joined at the hospital by Bishop Jan Michalski, representing Cardinal Wyszynski and the church. From Warsaw, Justice Minister Jerzy Bafia dispatched Jozef Zyta, of the prosecutor-general's office, to head an investigative team. It was an unfortunate choice. Zyta had been provincial prosecutor in Gdansk in 1970, a well-known fact that could only aggravate the sensitive memories of local residents.

Zyta's investigative work was also unfortunate. By morning—Friday, March 20—the government representative, rather than searching for clues, was issuing judgments. The brief item carried in local newspapers simply said that "a group of people" began to occupy the provincial council assembly hall and after refusing an order to leave, were "led out of the building." Zyta remembered to add that the militia "carried out their duties in a firm, but not brutal manner." While this sort of cover-up may have been standard operating procedure in the past, the Gdansk Agreement had made it obsolete.

Walesa and Solidarity had a distinctly different version of what had occurred. "What happened here was an attack upon the union," said Solidarity's leader after a sleepless night. "We shall respond resolutely, but calmly. We're not afraid. Our knees are not trembling. Someone's claws are getting too long, but we will trim them," he added. "Not all the authorities are pigs. We wish to trust some of them." The last remark was regarded as an olive branch to Jaruzelski, and was in line with the statement the union had drawn up in the night asserting that the police raid was "an obvious provocation directed against the government." It was reiterated by Solidarity spokesman Onyszkiewicz in Warsaw. "Certain forces are against the changes going on in the country," he said. While those responsible for Bydgoszcz might include some high up in the power structure, Jaruzelski himself was "being given the benefit of the doubt," Onyszkiewicz said.

Whether the beatings were a provocation designed to embarrass Jaruzelski, now in the midst of the Warsaw Pact manoeuvres, as Solidarity suggested, or simply the result of local authorities seeking vengeance against the union, it was clear they would produce a crisis of national proportions unless the government responded quickly. There had been removals of sit-in protesters before. In January, in southern Nowy Sacz, 45 farmers occupying the town hall had been moved out without violence by the state against workers. The Gdansk Agreement had, among other things, been intended as a guarantee against such arbitrary force. Both sides, the union and the regime, had gone to considerable lengths to emphasize the negotiated character of the settlement, of "Pole talking to Pole." Bydgoszcz could not be ignored.

Despite Solidarity's country-wide telexed appeal urging union branches to restrain themselves from immediate action while negotiations with Zyta were taking place, two-hour warning strikes were held in the region. Bydgoszcz, Torun, Grudziadz and Wloclawek shut down. Photos of the beaten men lying on the ground and spattered with blood were posted on walls and fences around the city, beneath red and white Polish flags.

Factory sirens and church bells announced the protest.

That afternoon, Solidarity met with the government investigators in Bydgoszcz and presented their immediate demands: dismissal of Deputy Governor Bak, police major Bednarek, the local party first secretary, publication of the photos of those attacked, and the names of policemen involved in the beatings.

The next day, Saturday, speaking to 4,000 people who had gathered outside the Solidarity headquarters along the Bryda, Walesa announced that the government had agreed to hold emergency talks in Warsaw the next day. The government delegation would be headed by Deputy Premier Rakowski. The Solidarity chairman urged restraint on the part of workers. "We want to settle the problem without further conflict," he said.

The state had also apparently received the message that the choice of prosecutor Zyta to head the fact-finding team was unsatisfactory. That day, Justice Minister Bafia arrived in Bydgoszcz to take charge of the investigation. However, the situation wasn't helped when local television that evening presented Deputy Governor Bak and provincial council chairman Berger, who proceeded to give their version of what happened.

In Warsaw on Sunday, the two sides met for several hours, but the talks ended inconclusively with no public statements to reassure the country that the crisis caused by the police attack had been surmounted. A one-line press release merely said the talks would be resumed on Wednesday. Other parties, however, were more forthcoming on the matter. During the weekly radio broadcast of Sunday mass, the union received measured support from the church. A message from Cardinal Wyszynski warned that the government must not abide "irresponsible acts by the security services." The authorities, said the cardinal, "must take into account the moral and physical inviolability of citizens," and then he added the church's usual cautionary note, reminding people that their demands required "time and patience" to be realized. Nonetheless, for the church it was a strong rebuke to the regime.

The party also had a message. While General Jaruzelski, attending Warsaw Pact exercises in southern Poland, conferred with Soviet field marshal Kulikov, the politburo held an emergency session. Its statement was featured on the evening news along with extensive footage of Soviet and Polish troops on manoeuvres. "The country faces serious danger," said the politburo, adding that it was "in the common interest of all Poles to urgently find a way out of the situation." However, the "way out" that the party hierarchy had in mind apparently involved the union accepting the party's version of what happened in Bydgoszcz as well as much of the blame for the ensuing crisis.

By the regime's account, Solidarity had attended the provincial council meeting for the purpose of staging a sit-in. Such an occupation, asserted the politburo, was "a visible violation of law" and could not be tolerated. Worse, the "tendency to develop activities of a political character" had gained the upper hand in the union, and included attempts to "illegally replace the constitutional representatives and executive organs." The last was a reference to the union's demand that those who called in the police should be dismissed. All strike activity in the country should cease, concluded the politburo.

Not all prominent party figures were prepared to accept this uncompromising position. "Our hardliners have no program other than confrontation and disinformation," wrote journalists' association leader Stefan Bratkowski in an open letter to party rank-and-file members the next day, March 23. "The present crisis is the last chance for those who want the party to abandon its policy of seeking agreement with the people, for those who are leading the state and society to catastrophe," claimed Bratkowski. "These are the people who don't want to come to agreement even with the party rank-and-file, are afraid of them and are attempting at all costs to delay the party congress," he added.

At the Solidarity national commission meeting, held in the Bydgoszcz railway workers' social centre, the debate raged all day. If some party members were disgusted by the politburo's attempt to exonerate the police, the union response ranged from anger to fury. The delegates to the KKP were unanimous on the first item on the agenda, the question of private farmers, and voted to demand that the government recognize the farmers' union. That was, of course, the basic issue underlying the Bydgoszcz incident, one that the party had chosen to ignore. By the time the national commission got to the issues of police brutality and deciding on a course of action, they were exhausted and tempers were frayed. This time Walesa's efforts to preach moderation were to little avail. He proposed a four-hour warning strike for Friday, March 27, to be followed by a general strike on Tuesday, March 31 if outstanding issues hadn't been settled. More militant KKP delegates were for an immediate nation-wide general strike. At three in the morning, with the commission in the midst of a confusing series of roll call votes, Walesa threw his hands in the air, announced that he was leaving, and stalked out of the hall. The session recessed until morning.

The KKP decision came on Tuesday. Walesa stayed away, in an implicit threat that he would resign if he didn't get his way; his supporters argued for his views, and the middle-of-the-night mood of militancy dissipated. When the vote was taken on the timing of the strikes, Walesa's proposal passed 33-2. Later, he was contrite. He apologized for leaving the hall and promised to use the resignation threat again only in a dire emergency. However, he continued to defend his position. "If something is on fire, I don't pour gasoline over it," he said. "I cannot endanger people who trust me. The only one I can put in danger is myself."

As was customary, the union had broadened its demands to more accurately reflect the scope of the current impasse. In addition to several points relating to the punishment of officials, Solidarity called for a farmers' union, guarantees of unobstructed operations for the labor movement, a right to respond to attacks in the controlled press and an end to prosecution of political prisoners. A ten-member crisis committee, headed by Walesa, was set up to run any future strikes from inside the Lenin Shipyard in Gdansk. It called on strike committees everywhere to move inside the factories for protection. If the government declared a state of emergency, the union would respond with an immediate full-scale general strike. A Solidarity declaration said that the struggle was to preserve "all the achievements of August 1980," and referring to Bydgoszcz, it said, "It was not we who broke the social peace."

Walesa may not have been the only one to threaten resignation. The union's reference to a government declaration of a state of emergency was based on rumors that a majority of the politburo had voted at their Sunday meeting, with Jaruzelski absent, to proclaim such a state as well as a ban on strikes. The move certainly would have triggered a general strike, and possibly bloodshed. Indeed, Bratkowski, who was closer to such discussions than most, may have been hinting at exactly such considerations when he penned his open letter. Reportedly, only the threatened resignation of Jaruzelski stopped the party leadership from taking such a step. Given the nature of party decision making, however, these various reports and rumors would remain in the realm of speculation.

On the face of it, the party maintained its tough front through mid-week. First Secretary Kania, upon hearing of the planned strikes, told an agricultural meeting that they "cannot be interpreted other than as an invitation to self-annihilation. Who has the courage to make out of a local incident a national cause threatening catastrophe?" Provincial council chairman Berger offered his resignation on Tuesday night, thus indicating some flexibility in the party's position. But when the two sides resumed talks in Warsaw on Wednesday, March 25, Deputy Premier Rakowski was unwavering.

Assailing the union's strike declaration, Rakowski said, "Without compromise, we shall plunge into chaos and may end in fraternal violence. Who will take the responsibility for all this?" He brushed aside the Bydgoszcz incident. Disregarding the direct victims of the attacks, he did concede that "the over-stepping of powers which may have taken place, whether it was done on purpose or resulted from emotion or incompetence, was harmful above all to state organs." Mainly he addressed himself to the union's motives. "What are you trying to prove by creating such tension in this country? Maybe you want to prove that independent trade unions cannot exist in a socialist country—since the state collapses as a result and social peace ends." He charged, "There are forces in Solidarity who want to declare a holy war against the authorities."

The meeting ended in an hour and a half. "There were no conclusions, so this time we finished quickly," explained Walesa. "They were not prepared. They did not have any solution or stand. The talks were postponed because Bafia had not prepared an answer. It is by the good will of Solidarity that the talks will be resumed," he said. The union leader didn't like being read a lecture.

Throughout the country, workers began bringing bedding into the factories. Solidarity posters splashed on walls said, "We will not be smashed in the face." Meetings were slated at schools and universities, in case Friday's warning strike didn't lead to a solution. The party announced a central committee meeting for Sunday. On Thursday, negotiations were put off until the next day, but Jaruzelski met with Cardinal Wyszynski, and the evening news also reported that the prime minister had received a report on Bydgoszcz from Justice Minister Jerzy Bafia, but had "found several matters lacking" and requested more information.

The shipyard cranes stopped moving in Gdansk at 8 a.m. when the ship sirens hooted. All streetcars and buses in Warsaw stopped at the stroke of eight, discharged their passengers and returned to their barns. A huge blue banner reading, "Bestial attack on Solidarity by police and special branch in Bydgoszcz" was strung across the closed gates of Huta Warszawa steel mill. Workers in yellow hardhats stood resolutely behind the bars of the gate. In southern Silesia, church bells pealed and the coal mines closed. Although the politburo had ordered party members who were also in Solidarity—nearly a million of them —not to take part in the strike, the order was defied. On national television, which normally displayed its logo as it began broadcasting at mid-day, there was instead a graphic that read, "The strike is on." At different times throughout the day the screens simply carried the logo of Solidarity. For four hours, millions of Poles held the largest organized protest in the 36-year history of the regime.

Like a field general, Walesa dashed from factory to factory in Warsaw, answering questions from the workers and checking on the progress of the strike. Everywhere he went, the message he delivered was the same. Solidarity hoped that a general strike could be avoided, that the union was not out to usurp power or undermine socialism, but only wanted to protect its members and its achievements. "It is very convenient to call us antisocial-ist," he added. "But the really antisocialist elements are those people in authority who bandy socialist-sounding slogans, but do nothing to implement them."

The strikers agreed. For Eugeniusz Garal, a Solidarity leader at the Nowotko diesel engine plant, the issue was "upholding the law and showing to this group of people that clings desper-ately to their chairs and the comforts they have achieved at the expense of society that people see what they are up to and are not willing to tolerate it anymore."

"There's no other way out," said Stanislaw Kania, a tool machine operator at the Ursus tractor factory who bore the same name as the first secretary of the party, a source of endless jokes for his co-workers. "We can't allow this kind of thing to go on, beating union members. Our rights are in question," said this very different Kania.

The bulletin issued by the Ursus strike committee said, "We are striking so that we might never again be beaten, jailed or slandered, so that the police will pursue criminals, not unionists.

"We are striking to make those in power realize that Solidarity is an inalienable part of Polish life and that any attempt to liquidate it would be the work of traitors or madmen."

Six hours after the show of strength by the union, Solidarity and government negotiators sat down for three hours of talks. The negotiations had been moved to the ornate Council of Ministers Palace near Warsaw's Old Town. Under an oil portrait of the sixteenth-century monarch, King Sigismund III, the meeting began with a reading of a thirteen-page report by Justice Minister Bafia. For the first time the government acknowledged that the demonstrators in Bydgoszcz had been beaten while in police custody, by officers in civilian clothes. "Now we want names," said Andrzej Gwiazda after the session, which had been devoted to a discussion of the government's revised account of the Bydgoszcz events.

The next day, March 28, the two sides reconvened for a second round of talks on Bafia's report. Sub-groups of the negotiating team discussed the union's other demands as well. Although no breakthrough was achieved, and the talks were recessed until Monday, expressions of guarded hope for a negotiated settlement began to be heard. "It's not an impasse," said Gwiazda. Chief government negotiator Rakowski said, "I think that Solidarity is also ready for compromise." For the most part, however, the session seemed to be marking time until tomorrow's emergency meeting of the party's central committee could be held. After the negotiations, Walesa and other Solidarity leaders met with Cardinal Wyszynski for an hour and a half. They were joined by the party's Stefan Bratkowski.

While most of the rest of the country was in church, the party's 140-member central committee was listening to a Sunday morning sermon by Kazimierz Barcikowski, last year's government negotiator at Szczecin. A good deal of the homily sounded as if it was being directly beamed to Moscow. Barcikowski charged that Solidarity was "penetrated" by people who were trying to push it into becoming a political organization. Anticommunist tendencies in the union had recently "been more visible, finding reflection in instigatory propaganda and political strikes," he said, echoing almost precisely an attack on the union published the day before by Tass, the Soviet press agency. The union's threatened general strike, he asserted, "is not a pressure on the authorities, but an open struggle against our party and state power, against socialism." Having mollified Poland's "fraternal neighbor" with a strong denunciation of Solidarity, Barcikowski then attempted to placate restive party members by coming out strongly in favor of democratic changes within the party, including free elections and limited terms of office for its leaders.

The politburo report presented by Barcikowski had repeated the now-standard accusations of shadowy enemies outside the party ranks engaged in open struggle against the PUWP. The danger, however, soon appeared much closer to home.

One central committee member after another rose to deliver scathing criticisms of the party hierarchy, charging that the leadership was cut off from lower echelons of the party and was moving far too slowly in carrying out the program of "democratic renewal." All that week, the politburo's original version of the Bydgoszcz events had come under internal fire. A growing number of local party organizations had sent resolutions to the central committee demanding that action be taken against the instigators of the incident. Now, the PUWP presidium heard the criticisms directly.

"Why do the comrades from the top avoid meeting the party organizations down in the provinces?" asked one delegate. "Why don't they want to listen to those on the front lines of the battle for the party? The feeling inside the party is that we shall not regain the people's trust if we do not oust those who discredited the party and abused power."

"We have to say it openly," declared another central committee member, a metal factory foreman from southern Kielce. "Many people holding top party posts want to keep them, without active commitment, at the expense of the working class, and they will use force." A committee member from Silesia added, "We cannot continue making personnel changes only after Solidarity has pointed to those who should be changed. We have to do it ourselves."

Nor was the Bydgoszcz affair entirely forgotten in the torrent of complaints. Janina Kostrzewska, a committee member who was a foreman in a computer plant in Wroclaw, said that her local party organization participated in last Friday's warning strike "even though we were aware we were violating party discipline. We read the events in Bydgoszcz as a clear violation of constitutional freedoms and civic rights. The guilt for the last strike is not carried by the determined workers who went on strike, but those who brought them to such determination."

It went on all day and far into the night. The nation's crisis over the issue of whether there was to be a relatively more democratic system or a police state seemed to be temporarily eclipsed as the party entered its own internal crisis over the same question. Although First Secretary Kania wasn't exempt from the stinging criticisms, much of the attack was directed at Stefan Olszowski and Tadeusz Grabski, politburo members seen as urging an uncompromising stance. At one point, according to reports that filtered out of the meeting, the two hardliners offered their resignations.

At four in the morning, eighteen hours after it began, the central committee ended its emergency deliberations. A final resolution was issued. It said, among other things, that a motion was offered and accepted "to withdraw resignations submitted at the plenum by some comrades." It was unclear whether the rejection of the proffered resignations indicated support for Olszowski and Grabski or reflected the pragmatic view that dumping the hardliners might bring in the Soviets. The resolution also called upon members of the politburo to meet immediately with party organizations in factories—a rebuke implying that the leadership had done so insufficiently to date.

It was clear that a significant portion of the party rank-and-file wanted increased party democracy. The calls for secret elections of delegates and unrestricted slates of candidates would have to be heeded at the next party congress, slated for summer. But these good intentions didn't address the issue at hand—the threat of a general strike. On the whole, the results of the meeting were inconclusive. The net effect of the turbulent session appeared to be a standoff between hardline and moderate factions over how far to go in seeking an accommodation with Solidarity.

When Andrzej Gwiazda arrived for last-ditch negotiations the next day, Monday, March 30, he didn't sound hopeful. "At the moment we are exactly where we have been before—nowhere." The party's apparent indecision was not encouraging. Walesa warned that the government must not stall for time if the union was to be able to rescind its strike call. While the two sides negotiated all day, throughout the country people grimly prepared for the worst. Meetings at factories and other institutions took up the details of what to do if the general strike was prolonged, or if the Warsaw Pact military exercises then underway turned into the real thing.

Both sides pulled back from the precipice. That night, after seven hours of bargaining, an accord was announced. Once again the government had been forced to conclude an agreement with the nation's workers. This time, however, the union made significant concessions of its own, and the gains were not as clear-cut as on previous occasions. A joint communique announcing the Warsaw Agreement was taken up largely with a carefully worded account of the Bydgoszcz incident.

The account didn't specifically accuse the police of having beaten the unionists, but it said that they should not have been called in and had been derelict in their duty for not protecting people in their custody. At the same time, the statement noted that the occupation by farm union activists of another Bydgoszcz building had contributed to tensions in the city.

In the agreement itself, the government promised to continue the inquiry and to punish those found guilty. Solidarity's demands for dismissal of government officials would receive further consideration. As well, special police units would be withdrawn from Bydgoszcz, the security of the union was again guaranteed, and workers who had participated in the warning strike would be paid. On the matter of farmers, the union appeared to have made some progress. While the issue of a farmers' union would have to await the drafting of the new trade union law, in the meantime the legal activities of Rural Solidarity "will not be questioned." The agreement pledged that farm union activists would not be harassed and that another commission would be sent to Bydgoszcz to attempt to settle the sit-in still in progress. On another major union demand, for a halt to proceedings against political dissidents, it was agreed that the union and the government would establish a joint commission to examine the question.

After the talks, Walesa and Gwiazda announced that the general strike call was temporarily in abeyance. The accord, they said, would be put before Solidarity's national commission, meeting in Gdansk the next morning. The commission could either accept it, or decide to go ahead with the strike. "We got all we could," said Walesa. "I don't think we could have gotten more." He said he was "70 per cent" satisfied with the pact.

At the Lenin Shipyard, Solidarity's national commission discovered during its meeting on Tuesday, March 31, that the union had a crisis of its own to face. The issue wasn't the just-concluded Warsaw Agreement, though many commission delegates were decidedly unhappy about it. Nor was it the decision to call off the general strike. There were those who would have preferred to go ahead with it, but the majority favored the decision. In any case, after Walesa and Gwiazda's appearance on the national news the night before announcing the postponement, everyone realized that there was no practical possibility of reversing the decision.

The issue was union democracy. Delegates were distressed by the manner in which negotiations had been conducted and the way decisions had been made. It took two days of debate for the KKP to begin to thrash out the various aspects of the question. The discussion ranged from minute details of how specific issues had been handled by union negotiators to far-reaching concerns about the future of Solidarity. Jan Kulaj and Roman Bartoszcze, the son of one of the men beaten in Bydgoszcz, complained bitterly on behalf of the farmers that little had been achieved in the Warsaw Agreement to further the cause of the farmers' union. From the still-hospitalized Jan Rulewski came a message condemning the settlement as a "sell-out." Others argued that the issues of political prisoners and harassment of union activists, although formally touched on in the accord, had in fact been glossed over.

Above all, there was concern about the process of decision making within the union. Some thought that a surfeit of union advisers was gradually usurping the authority of the KKP;

others felt that Walesa himself was becoming insensitive to the democratic procedures upon which the union was based. Whatever the specific grievances, overall there was a sense that the erosion of union democracy would lead to dire consequences.

"The openness of union activities is getting worse and worse," began one KKP member, in what would become a typical refrain. "This openness would have let us avoid many misfortunes. I think, Lech, that if you had presented the whole problem to us, all the difficulties of the situation, we would have understood it and there wouldn't have been any criticisms. We should always be treated seriously," he insisted.

Another member of the national commission offered a slightly different version that focussed on the danger of co-optation. Part of the problem was that "we think in the categories that the system has made us used to for 36 years. They can't fight against us openly, so they do it by tangling us up in legislation. They've got an entire mechanism which spits out hundreds and thousands of pieces of paper at us.

"Take the question of farmers," he continued. "The farmers are to have their union. Even a child knows that. And yet we go to hundreds of different talks, we get involved in those things, and we end up getting co-opted. It's like a chess game, and I ask: Who's given us the right to manipulate the feelings of millions of Poles?"

The most thorough and perhaps poignant assessment of the situation came on the second day of the discussion from Karol Modzelewski. The veteran of the struggle of the 1960s and of years of prison had been politically reactivated by the events of the previous August. A member of the Wroclaw Solidarity local executive, he had been elected to the KKP as the union's press spokesman.

What concerned Modzelewski most was the process by which the Warsaw Agreement had been reached, and the role of union advisers in shaping decisions. "From the point of view of internal union democracy, it is intolerable to allow advisers to manipulate the situation. Unfortunately, I have to call it manipulation. As a matter of fact," he said, "none of the negotiators except Lech felt that he was taking part in actual decision making. The final document, prepared by two advisers and I don't know who from the government side, was presented like a bombshell to the unprepared negotiators. All those elements indicate that the most important decision for both the union and Poland was made behind the union's back. And this is a terribly dangerous situation," Modzelewski stressed. "What I care for is the mechanism of decision making in the union. It will either be a self-governing union or it won't be independent. That's the alternative."

Modzelewski made clear that he wasn't attacking Walesa personally—"a weakening of his position as leader of the union would be suicidal"—but rather the structure that included the KKP chairman. "The mechanism of decision making is the key to everything. And ours is a monarchic mechanism," Modzelewski claimed. "This union has been shaped in the following way: there is a king and a court around him and there is also a parliament. And because it's not a 'painted' king, he himself governs, with his court, and not the parliament, not the KKP. Why do I think that this mechanism is a dangerous threat to the union? Because it'll rapidly develop. Any attempt at criticism will be considered a scheme, a plot against Walesa, against the union, a power grab by some clique. That's a totalitarian style of thought which may well turn out to be destructive for Solidarity," Modzelewski warned.

At the end of his lengthy and solemn remarks, as if to put the seal of authenticity on his concerns, Modzelewski announced his resignation as union press spokesman. The difference between his personal views and his union function was too great. Unlike the proferred resignations of party bosses, Modzewlewski concluded, "When I declare my resignation it doesn't mean that I want it put to the vote. Please accept it without any voting." His wishes were respected.

It had been a sobering debate. Issues had been raised which didn't admit of immediate solutions. Nonetheless, the dangers which various of the Solidarity leadership perceived within the union had been expressed openly; the debates themselves were published in the union bulletins for all to see. Many were moved by Modzelewski's warning and found themselves pondering his words. One of those who had been touched was Andrzej Gwiazda, who had participated directly in the Warsaw Agreement talks. A few days later, while party bosses were touring the country's factories as they had been ordered to do— First Secretary Kania was at the Lenin Shipyard hearing a barrage of criticism from party members—Gwiazda published an open letter addressed to Lech Walesa.

He, too, focussed on the issue of internal union democracy, just as Modzelewski had done. Despite the political circumstances that constantly created tendencies to walk away from democratic principles, Gwiazda warned that "if the union adopts the methods forced upon it by its enemies, it will be defeated." The decision to call off the strike, whether or not it was the right decision, was made without authority and without having consulted the union's national commission, said Gwiazda. "It was our fault, Lech, that union democracy was broken. I know that we both can think of thousands of explanations why it happened, but I also know that *internal democracy within the union is a necessity*. The condition in which it flourishes is full openness and a multidirectional flow of information. Its funeral is when criticism is crushed and union periodicals are censored. Each member of our union should have a right to criticize, even after a decision has been taken by the union.

"Otherwise, the union is governed in an autocratic way," Gwiazda continued. "The decisive influence is transferred to clerks and advisers who, uncontrolled, and without responsibility, have the full freedom of manipulation." Walesa's longtime colleague called on the Solidarity chairman to make a similar avowal of principles.

"You've written an open letter to me in which you remind me of our common struggle: free trade unions, the August strike, and Solidarity," Walesa replied. "I don't have to be reminded. I remember it well. I want the same now as then: that Poland will be Poland."

Walesa, characteristically, focussed on the pragmatic aspects of democracy. "I repeat all the time that union elections should be held within the time limits prescribed by our statutes," he said. "Then our union will be headed by people who have the trust of the factory work force and a feeling of responsibility before those who elected them. As you know, I'm not too strong on theory, but I think this is the most important thing in a democracy." By way of conclusion, Walesa added, "Let's leave off writing open letters until we retire. I think I can still do something for the union and the country. With courage and caution, I wish you that, too."

It was a typically terse Walesa reply. To observers there was something ironic in the spectacle of the nation's only democratic institution engaged in a microscopic self-examination of the quality of its democratic procedures. Nevertheless, for those who detected a messianic element in the personality of the union's leadership, the concern was not entirely groundless.

It had begun as a brutal incident in the heretofore obscure city of Bydgoszcz. Few could have foreseen its consequences. The crisis that it produced would not be the last time that the country would balance on a tightrope over a chasm. However, it would make the state more cautious about the undue use of force, at least for the time being.

For the party, it hastened the process of bringing a measure of democracy into the organization that ruled the state. In mid-April, a group of party members inspired by Zbigniew Iwanow held an extraordinary session in Torun. The group, known as "horizontalists," and consisting of delegates from local party organizations around the country, demanded changes in the politburo and a democratization of the party. Ultimately, the horizontalists would have little influence at the party congress in July. Nonetheless, their activities ensured that the mainstream of the party rigorously carried out its promises. A more genuinely democratic selection of national congress delegates was observable at local party congresses through the spring and into the summer. The impact of the liberalizing process would be felt when the PUWP gathered in mid-summer.

For the union, Bydgoszcz provided a new awareness of the dangers the union faced, not only from outside, but also internally. If the incident created hard feelings among some union members, it did not lead to a split. Walesa continued to lead. Rulewski recovered from the beating and returned to his union post, probably with an enhanced standing within Solidarity. The two men went to Japan together in May, as part of a union delegation invited by their Japanese counterparts, and their personal friendship appeared to be intact. Elections within Solidarity also began in late spring, and the appearance of an unrestricted number of union candidates, occasionally seen on television, probably pressured the party to do no less. The union's first congress was scheduled for fall 1981.

The most definite result, to which the Bydgoszcz affair had contributed, involved farmers. In late April, government and union negotiators finished drafting a trade union bill that codified the reforms won by Polish workers during the August strikes. In addition, it was agreed that a farm union law would simultaneously be introduced in the Polish parliament.

On May 12, Rural Solidarity received long-awaited legal sanction from the courts. Ironically, the decision which gave farmers the same labor rights as industrial workers was made by Judge Zdzislaw Koscielniak, the man who had handed down the original verdict rejecting Solidarity's legal status.

The Bydgoszcz incident itself was not fully resolved even several months later. Local officials resigned, the seemingly interminable negotiations continued, and in a mid-June mini-shakeup of the government by Prime Minister Jaruzelski, Justice Minister Bafia was dismissed, a move considered a nod toward union sensibilities.

The church, although not directly affected, played a part in mediating the crisis created by the events in Bydgoszcz. In the following months, it suffered shocks of its own, though not of a political nature. In mid-May, a terrorist in Rome attempted to assassinate Pope John Paul II. For a few days, until he was out of danger, the attention of Poles was taken up with the fate of their prominent compatriot. In due course, the pope recovered. Two weeks after the assassination attempt, the elderly Cardinal Wyszynski, who had been ill for some time, died of abdominal cancer at age 79. Hundreds of thousands of mourners followed his funeral cortege in Warsaw. A month later, Bishop Jozef Glemp was chosen to take his place as primate of the Polish church.

Final judgments on the Bydgoszcz crisis, naturally, have to be reserved. In the medium term, the massive movement for democracy, spearheaded by Solidarity, had moved forward, however haltingly.

9 Conversations with Comrade Fiszbach

In a regime of thought control, one has to multiply thoughts to the point where there aren't enough policemen to control them.
—S.J. Lec

During my stay in Poland I tried to see Tadeusz Fiszbach, first secretary of the Polish communist party in the Gdansk region.

Comrade Fiszbach was busy. It was understandable; it was the middle of May and provincial party organizations were in the midst of a flurry of local meetings to choose delegates and formulate positions for the upcoming special party congress. Gearing up a political machine, as one can well imagine, was a task requiring the undivided attention of the first secretary. Unfortunately, therefore, it was impossible to have a real conversation with him.

Instead, I had imaginary conversations with Comrade Fiszbach.

"Comrade Fiszbach," I'd say to the slight, balding man in his mid-fifties sitting behind the desk across the room, "how is it possible that your party has ruled Poland in the name of the working class, socialism and the highest ideals of mankind for 35 years, and you're not even able to produce a roll of toilet paper?" (The imaginary me, I must confess, is quite a bit more impudent than I should have been had we been engaged in a real conversation.)

While the conversations were imaginary, the questions I had were real enough. So, too, were the shortages of basic household commodities that sent exasperated Polish housewives into the endless queues that led into any store with something scarce to sell.

Even after leaving Poland, these imaginary conversations continued to stay in mind. I'll come to some of the reasons for my fascination with Comrade Fiszbach in due course.

For people who live "in a regime of thought control," the Polish satirist S.J. Lec suggests that it's necessary "to multiply thoughts to the point where there aren't enough policemen to control them." Good advice, but it's not quite as simple as it sounds. In a regime of thought control, the very activity of thinking faces considerable obstacles. Worse, the regime that is doing the controlling has appropriated many of the thoughts one might want to think, and turned them upside down.

This may seem like a roundabout way of beginning to assess Solidarity's accomplishments. In the long run, however, appreciating the difficulties that Poles have in enjoying the fundamental freedom of thought will prove to be a short cut in our understanding of recent events in Poland.

Poles themselves often reflect publicly on this problem. One of those to do so is KOR activist Adam Michnik, who gave a semi-legal lecture in November 1980, just days after the emotional scene in which the Supreme Court formally registered Solidarity. Michnik is one of the social thinkers in Poland who was most frequently attacked by the state-controlled media as an "antisocialist element." In thought-hungry Poland, more than 2,000 people arrived at the hall where he was speaking, and 2,000 more listened outside over loudspeakers.

"I would say that the debate over language is the debate concerning the entire intellectual life of these past 35 years," Michnik said. "This debate leads us to reflect on the technique that governs communication between people. During those years, most of our society lost its language. The reality was terrible, and we could not find appropriate terms to describe it."

As a recent example of the issue, Michnik cited the long, just-concluded court squabble over Solidarity's reluctance to recognize the "leading role" of the party. "The conflict surrounding the registration of the union was also fundamentally a conflict over language. Once again, the authorities sought to emasculate the Gdansk Agreement. The state seeks to impose elastic and interchangeable concepts that can serve an infinite variety of purposes," noted Michnik. "In this spirit, it demanded that the idea of the leading role of the party be inscribed everywhere. But what is the precise meaning of this phrase?'' he asked. It was not an idle question, considering that the argument over it had brought the country to the brink of a general strike.

"For me this has no other meaning than that, taking into consideration our geopolitical position and our place in Europe, our country must be governed by the communist party,'' Michnik explained. "But does this mean I am for or against socialism? To describe me as an enemy of socialism makes no sense as long as it has not been explained what it means to respect the leading role of the party. As far as I know, nobody has so far defined what this entails. A party journalist in *Zycie Warszawy* writes that the leading role of the party consists of *inspiring*.'' Michnik concluded sardonically: "To this I agree enthusiastically. I would hope for nothing better than for the party to inspire me!'' The audience burst into laughter and applause.

One Polish author, writing under the pseudonym Michael Szkolny in the American socialist magazine *Monthly Review*, sees the regime's takeover of classical socialist terminology in a darker light. "The very meaning of fundamental terms has been transformed beyond recognition,'' Szkolny writes. "Thus, for example, the words for 'socialism,' 'socialization,' and 'internationalism' today [in Poland] designate respectively the existing social order, state ownership, and subordination to the interests of the Soviet Union. The term 'antisocialist force' is used to denote any form of political opposition, while the word 'anarchist' is today reserved for those oppositionists who belong to some current of the European socialist tradition.

"These examples form part of a general phenomenon of *conceptual embezzlement* which reaches deep into the vernacular,'' Szkolny continues. "This Orwellian process fundamentally limits people's conceptual framework by rendering inexpressible a whole range of ideas.'' Anyone (and I include myself here) who's been the least bit attracted by Marx's vision of humanity freeing itself and making its own history must shudder at the thought of what's happened to that dream at the hands of Polish and other communist parties in the last half-century.

For someone attempting to understand contemporary Poland, the party's destruction of a normal political vocabulary creates special difficulties. In conversations with Polish friends, the attempt to establish the political identities of various groups along the familiar continuum of "left" to "right" was almost impossible. After several unsuccessful tries, someone in mock-didactic tones would say, "Now let's start with the party: the party is on the right," and the effort would collapse in laughter. Even attempting to determine whether a particular act is "political" in nature poses a problem in a situation where the main opposition force, Solidarity, has been compelled to pledge not to be political. Thus, one question which interests North Americans of both "left" and "right" political persuasions—"Are Polish workers in favor of socialism?"—encounters genuine difficulties. I'll return to that question later.

Despite these state-inspired obstacles, which Poles attempt to relieve with generous doses of humor, thoughts have been multiplying faster than policemen to control them. One method has been to reappropriate some of the party's own vacuous conceptions. Take the cumbersome phrase, "antisocialist element," with which the party frequently tars its opponents. The response of young Solidarity supporters to this repeated epithet was instructive, and perhaps characteristically Polish, in its irony. Fed up with denying such accusations, they made up T-shirts for themselves (the North American fad of inscribing T-shirts with slogans and phrases is also popular in Poland). Theirs carried the big block letters "AE," standing for "antisocialist element." Of course, wearing T-shirts which proclaimed that they were "antisocialist elements" didn't mean that they were opposed to socialism. Rather, they were opposed to the loaded linguistic usages of the regime.

A more pervasive method of trying to talk sense, utilized by Solidarity, has been to reach back into history for a language not thoroughly contaminated by the regime. This explains the Polish preoccupation with the era of the "rights of man" and the period of the French and American revolutions as sources of intellectual inspiration. During and after the August strike, Solidarity raised the slogan, "Man is born free." The basic concepts on which it built its world-view were those of dignity, truth, justice and democracy—ideas expressed with a sincerity that can only be fully appreciated under conditions created by regimes such as Poland's. Hence, too, the passion Poles display for ceremonies commemorating the Polish constitution of 1791, which I observed upon my arrival in Poland.

I should note, incidentally, that in commenting on the

distortions of thought in Poland, I do so with no sense of smugness. As a member of a very imperfect capitalist democracy, I'm painfully aware of the restrictions on thought in our society. Whereas the "workers' states" utilize censorship, state control of media and conceptual distortion, the repression of thought in our society is accomplished by the incessant drumbeat of a commercially-inspired culture of trivialization and monopoly ownership of the means of communication. While there are enough differences between the two systems to make preference for our own worthwhile, they are hardly cause for celebration.

The ideas of eighteenth-century revolutionary democracy, among others, have proved serviceable for the immediate tasks Solidarity has confronted: whether they will be adequate in the long run is more doubtful. In the "Western democracies," it is clear that freedom of thought doesn't eliminate poverty, exploitation or the economic uncertainties created by monopoly capitalism. And in the absence of economic democracy, political freedom is seriously undermined. It is here that the nineteenth century vision of Marx, with its concepts of class, mode of production and the exploitation of workers, comes into play. And it is here, too, that Polish thought is cut off by the mockery of this vision which Poles and others have endured in its name.

We are talking not only about thought turned on its head, but about reality itself. This is not meant as an abstract philosophical discussion about language, or about the relationship between thought and reality. When the rhetoric of "people's democracy" co-exists with citizens being jailed for promoting democratic behavior, and "workers' control" is the official truth in a country in which the manager controls and the state exploits—as has been the case in Poland—you don't merely have a problem with language and thought, you've got a problem with reality. It is in this realm of the real that Solidarity has made some remarkable accomplishments.

What Solidarity achieved

The major victory of the Polish working class in 1980 was the creation of permanent institutions of representation independent of the Polish "workers' state."

The existence of Solidarity stands as a daily refutation of the party's self-proclaimed reason for being: that it has a monopoly on representing the real interests of the working class. In fact, the establishment of "independent, self-governing" trade unions raises the heretical question: If the party doesn't really represent the interests of workers, then whose interests does it represent? Of course, in a society where "everybody knows, but nobody says," such questions are seldom heard. However, one can understand the PUWP's frantic efforts to get the workers officially to acknowledge in the Gdansk Agreement the "leading role" of the party. Not only did the regime have to satisfy the Soviet Union, it also had to justify itself. If the fiction could be maintained that the union represented the workers' interests at the level of the workplace, while the party represented their interests at the level of the state, then the party's continued existence was theoretically legitimated and unthreatened.

The permanent institutionalization of Solidarity is a marked advance over all previous levels of organization among Polish workers during the past three decades. When workers revolted in Poznan in 1956, the nation heard the cry of an inchoate mass. In 1970, workers along the Baltic brought into temporary existence strike committees and even, in places such as Szczecin, rudimentary forms of an inter-factory strike committee. Similarly, in 1976, when workers established the de facto right to veto certain impositions by the state, the mechanism of resistance was the local strike committee. Although each of these previous upheavals was paid for in blood and resulted in a form of defeat—the promised concessions of "consultation" and improved representation were soon forgotten—it's fair to say that Solidarity was built upon these experiences. This is true not only in terms of the "lessons" learned from failure, but also with respect to the growing self-consciousness and confidence developed by workers in the course of such actions.

In the period after the 1976 strikes a new element appeared. Aided by intellectuals who formed the Workers Defence Committee (KOR), a conscious ideology of independent representation was developed by workers, many of whom were veterans of previous struggles. These ideas were communicated by the illegal, but not clandestine, workers' groups established under the banner of Free Trade Unions. When workers struck at the Lenin Shipyard in August 1980, the demand for independent unions soon headed their list. The depth to which the idea of independent unions had permeated the consciousness of workers could be seen in the rapidity with which Solidarity was organized.

One of the things that "everybody knows" in Poland is that Solidarity is not simply a trade union, but a mass political movement. It is locked into an uneasy relationship of dual power (I use the term metaphorically, rather than its semi-technical Marxist sense) with Comrade Fiszbach's party. What "everyone says," however—in fact, insists upon—is that Solidarity is simply a trade union negotiating trade union questions and, well...perhaps a few other matters with the Polish government (which is, as everyone also knows but doesn't say, largely a fiction).

Solidarity's second major achievement is that it has evolved into a broad-based democratic front or coalition. Drawing together all the major forces in the country seeking to transform the totalitarian character of the present regime, it then spawns a network of independent organizational forms. The proliferation of independent organizations among farmers, students and other social groups is a clear product of Solidarity's efforts. All of this—from independent trade unions to what some Polish intellectuals call "the reconstruction of civil society"—is unprecedented in Soviet-style states, both theoretically and in practice. Hence, the events in Poland have generated a worldwide interest that goes far beyond the pragmatic concerns of the Soviet Union's international opponents.

But why did this happen in Poland and not in some other Eastern European country in the Soviet bloc? I don't propose to provide any detailed answer to that frequently asked question. It is quite beyond the scope of my intentions and is so obviously complex that I will permit myself only an obvious over-simplification in order to emphasize a lesser point.

Either there is something special about the Polish regime, which agreed to this "liberalization" out of conviction or because of strategic considerations, or else there is something special about Polish workers and their various allies which allowed them to win this victory. I suspect there is nothing "special" about either, though a plausible case can be made for the courage and tenacity of Polish workers. But other workers have also been courageous and tenacious without achieving similar results. The point to be emphasized, though, is that in the particular historical circumstances which permitted the creation of Solidarity in Poland, the workers and others *acted* to maximize the possibilities for freedom. The small bit of moralizing contained in that observation, insofar as it applies to the rest of us, need not be spelled out.

Finally, the one other significant achievement of Solidarity, which is easily observable and was invariably commented upon by all Poles I talked to, is the present atmosphere of freedom, which marks such a change from what Andrzej Gwiazda called "the barrier of fear." Although one can't live on the air of freedom, as commodity-short Poles know all too well, Polish friends repeatedly remarked on how differently they feel since August 1980 in terms of being able to express themselves. This isn't only a feeling, but a reality, as Solidarity recurrently demonstrated in defending its militants as well as farmers and intellectuals. The fact is, the regime today can't arbitrarily throw its opponents in jail, a significant change that Poles greet with a deep sigh of relief.

The strategy of reconstructing "civil society"

In explaining the process unfolding in Poland, the participants themselves have frequently described it as the struggle of *civil society against the state*. This strategic conception has been usefully examined in an essay of that title by social researcher Andrew Arato. In speculating on future developments in Poland, it is useful to consider what meaning this debate has to the Poles and where they think it might lead them.

For North Americans, the notion of civil society takes some getting used to, not because it's unfamiliar to us, but because we take it for granted. Between the private realm and the state, there's a large social sphere which takes in everything from trade unions to movements designed to improve our morals to lobbyists for private enterprise. Although the latter organizations are invariably more effective than we want them to be, it's one of our basic assumptions that they are independent of the state and have a right to make some impact upon public policy.

In Poland, this situation has not prevailed since World War II. Between the intensely felt private loyalties of the family and the totalitarian regime, there has been, with the exception of the church, a yawning social gap effectively patrolled by the forces of the state and various intermediary organizations in which the leading role of the party was fully inscribed. The idea developed in the last decade, as Jacek Kuron puts it, is that "society organizes itself as a democratic movement and becomes active outside the limits of the institutions of the totalitarian state." In short, the strategic scheme is to rebuild the sphere of civil society.

It's easy to see why Poles opposed to the regime have chosen this route. The overriding factor in their considerations is the possibility of intervention by the Soviet Union. Two of the main roads that might lead to the reconstitution of civil society have been closed—both the overthrow of the authoritarian regime from below (attempted in Hungary in 1956) and the attempt to reform the state from above through the party (tried in Czechoslovakia in 1968) have proved impossible.

In the wake of several working class eruptions in Poland, a third possibility opened up: structural *reforms* of authoritarian socialism *from below*, different both from reformist attempts inside the party and revolutionary challenges from outside it. What was proposed by the theoreticians of this strategy—primarily Kuron, Adam Michnik and exiled philosopher Leszek Kolakowski—was that a society more in harmony with the people's needs could be wrested from the state. Contrary to classical revolutionary theory, they suggested that partial structural reforms that would weaken the existing system were attainable. The basis for this strategy (and what would save it from doom) was the development of a labor movement and the powerful Catholic church's defence of civil rights.

For the successful reconstruction of civil society, the regime would have to be weakened to the point of having no option but to tolerate these new forces. In fact, the Polish regime's dismal economic performance, particularly the failure of Gierek's policy to build a viable industrial infrastructure based on borrowing from the West, did provide such weakness. Thereby the conditions were created in which the dynamic of civil society could develop. The period 1976-80 saw several partial victories for the democratic civil sector—the creation of KOR, winning an amnesty from the regime for the 1976 strikers, the development of an underground publishing network, and the establishment of labor organizations. When the economic crisis and burgeoning opposition movement converged in 1980, workers were able to win victories unheard of in Soviet-type systems: the institutionalization of independent representation and a set of promises amounting to the legalization of an autonomous civil sphere.

The question then became: What kind of society can emerge which is based on structural reforms from below and which leaves intact the old system's institutional core (i.e., the party's continued control of the state and the economy)? Further, how will the various factions of the regime respond to such a situation?

Sections of the party apparatus, but not the whole leadership, opt for a strategy of suppressing the gains won in 1980, even at the cost of Soviet intervention. This, presumably, is the view of party "hardliners." A second possibility, represented perhaps by the "moderate" Kania-Jaruzelski leadership, is that the most the ruling party can yield, without inviting outside intervention, is a compromise in which other major social institutions such as the church, Solidarity and the military would be allowed to participate more visibly in the affairs of government. The advantage to the party of this "state corporatist" solution, as it is sometimes dubbed, is that the institutions of opposition in the society would be integrated into the regime, and made responsible for its decisions, rather than be permitted to operate at large where their oppositional character is more apparent and where every disagreement between party and opposition tends to generate conflicts of crisis proportions. It should be noted that in this model the party, naturally, would continue to play its "leading role." The exact dimensions of the "state corporatist" model provides the subject of debate between party "moderates" and "liberals." A third model, emanating from rank-and-file party "radicals" and some "progressives" such as Gdansk first secretary Fiszbach, envisions a more fundamental restructuring of relations both within the party and between the party and other institutions. Although circumstances hardly permit this notion to be spelled out in a programmatic way, at the very least its proponents envision investing the party's rhetorical offers of "partnership" between the regime and Solidarity with a measure of actual substance. This "radical" alternative, mild though in fact it is, is given little chance of success.

There is also a variety of proposals from within the ranks of the democratic opposition. Some Catholic intellectuals powerful in Solidarity favor the "depoliticization" of society as a diametrical opposite to the total political tutelege of the party in the social sphere. This would mean restricting the independent union movement to narrow trade union concerns and limiting other efforts to expand democracy to the areas of culture and religion (e.g., more diversified access to the media, less censorship restriction in the artistic field, increased opportunities for religious teaching, etc.). The model is based on the church's role during the last decade and might be described as a "societal corporatist" alternative. It differs from state corporatism, in Arato's view, "because of its insistence on the independence of institutions and in particular, on a public sphere guaranteeing not only the population's cultural autonomy, but also a structure of compromise involving genuine controls on state activities."

Adam Michnik, on the other hand, interprets the Gdansk Agreement as a potentially new social contract between two organized agents: state and society. The knowledge of limits by both sides (i.e., the threat of Soviet intervention) makes possible an institutional solution in which a variety of social sectors could participate in decision-making, Michnik argues. The stability of such a partnership depends on the party-state becoming a credible partner (Solidarity already enjoys public confidence). Only a new respect on the part of the regime for legality and for the actual plurality of public opinion, suggests Michnik, could relegitimate the state. He describes this general framework as "the crossing of the totalitarian structure of power with the democratic mechanism of corporate representation," and believes that it can be the basis of a stable, but flexible, equilibrium. This model is sometimes known as "societal pluralism" and is distinguished from "societal corporatism" by the maintenance of independent political activity on the party of society.

Finally, another alternative, sometimes identified as the view of Kuron and dubbed "syndicalism" by Arato, differs from Michnik's model in that it de-emphasizes the role of the party in actual policy making (although it leaves its "leading role" formally intact) and stresses a self-democratizing society on a plurality of levels—all of which actively participate in policy making. Such an arrangement would reduce the existing party-state to executing the will of society in internal affairs, and obeying the will of the Soviet Union in external affairs (to create a situation not unlike that of Finland).

Church, economics, party

One frequent question about Solidarity concerns its relationship to the Catholic church. Simultaneously, there is the question of the role of the church in the Polish state. Clearly, the church has an influence upon Solidarity. The evidence is plentiful—the visibility of religious symbolism within the union, the demands on behalf of the church advanced by the strikers in August 1980, Lech Walesa's much-publicized audience with the pope, his frequent meetings with Polish religious leaders, etc.

The political visitor to Poland, at least in my experience, quickly comes to accept the mixture of religion, nationalism and working class militancy that characterize the scene—perhaps in part because the Poles themselves seem to take it so much for granted. Certainly, too much can be made of the church-union connection. There are some diehard defenders of the regime who argue that Solidarity is an instrument of the church, and even go on to blame that venerable institution, rather illogically, for most of the failures of the regime, as though the party they support hadn't been in power for over 35 years. Most party officials I talked to, however, were willing to recognize Solidarity as an authentic expression of the working class and not a creature of the church.

One can agree easily enough, I think, with Michael Szkolny's view that, owing to the church's relative independence from the state in Poland, "the symbolism of religion became the unique language capable of expressing ideas of social emancipation." Or at least, if not the "unique language," certainly one of the strongest vehicles of expression. One can even revive, as Szkolny does, the forgotten half of Marx's famous aphorism in order to note that if religion is the opiate of the people, it also has been, at times in Poland, the "heart of a heartless world."

Nonetheless, it would be simplistic to ignore the organizational character of the church and the dangers it poses for Solidarity. Although many see the church as an ally in Solidarity's defence of democracy against the party's totalitarianism, it must be remembered that nobody votes for the revered primate of Poland. In many ways, the church—with its special language, rituals and authoritarian structure—resembles nothing so much as the party.

The same difficulties emerge at an ideological level. Many of us philosophical sinners who support Solidarity advocate a rationalistic explanation of natural phenomena, a system of ethics based on humanist ideals, and a method of social organization rooted in democratic procedures as the best framework in which to achieve the goals of Poland's democratic opposition. It is sometimes forgotten that the church, for all its virtues, offers a phantasmagorical account of creation, an ethical system based on obedience to "divine" authority and a rigidly hierarchical model of social organization.

The practical danger posed by the church concerns its role in the state. The ruling party can have a "state corporatist" solution, Arato argues, only with the help of allies. In this respect, the church is crucial. Although it is part of the anti-state movement, the church's emphasis on social order and its internal hierarchical organization may well predispose it toward corporatism. This is often disregarded by the democratic opposition because of its desire to preserve its new alliance with the church. But neither the church's past nor its present provide unambiguous clues to its future. Is the church an "unyielding repository of traditional libertarian values" or is it interested primarily in defending its own particular interests? Does it condemn militance from below and preach restraint only because of its fear of Soviet intervention, or also because of its own conception of social order?

This is not the place for a detailed examination of the Polish economy. Even tentative explanations of the economic failure of the Polish regime must be left to others. However, there is something to be learned about the regime by examining one or two economic questions.

The factors that brought the Polish economy to its present plight seem straightforward enough; they are regularly cited in journalistic accounts. The cause most commonly referred to is Gierek's disastrous plan to modernize industry rapidly with credit-financed imports from Western industrial countries, and then to pay off the investment credits by exporting the products so produced. The policy neglected several matters, including the fact that capitalism, too, undergoes crises and might be unable to purchase the goods intended for export.

As it turned out, the increase in production in the export sectors was insufficient and the growth strategy of the 1970s failed. As a result, the traditional sectors (e.g., agriculture) have to provide the necessary exports, which results in shortages of basic foods (e.g., meat) for domestic consumption. Because of the developing credit bind, less raw materials and fuels could be imported, leading to production stoppages. Worse, the terms of trade (the ratio of export and import prices) deteriorated. The income from energy exports (e.g., coal) was no longer able to cover the cost of energy imports (e.g., oil). Finally, there was the problem of credit-financed industrial imports. The consequence of all this by the late 1970s was Polish indebtedness to the West in excess of $20 billion, and few prospects of repayment. In fact, the interest burden to service the debt was absorbing an increasing proportion of the money generated by Poland's faltering exports. According to some estimates, as much as 80 cents of every dollar produced by exports goes to debt servicing.

Economists can spell out the details of this disaster. The relationship between the failure to invest in agriculture or consumer goods while pouring funds into an inefficient industrial sector is indeed a matter of interest. The mystery that remains, however, is: Why did the government fail so badly? Clearly, it wasn't in the political interests of the regime to fail, as can be seen from the social upheavals that accompanied each admission of failure.

Looking at the shambles of Polish industrial investments, one sees obvious incompetence at various levels of authority. But why should the planners of the Polish economy be incompetent? Is there something in the character of the regime that prevents it from competently organizing the economy? Is there something in the theory of central planning and its implementation, upon which the regime relies, that leads to botched production plans? Does the absence of democracy within the regime make it impossible for those who see the errors to take corrective action? Does the absence of democracy in the society and the lack of decentralized management, or workers' control, reduce incentives and productivity? Obviously these are questions not only for interested observers, but ones that must be answered by Poland itself.

The Polish communist party deserves a study unto itself. The only intention of these brief observations is to suggest that its realities are as complex as those of other aspects of Polish society.

It might be convenient for hardline anticommunists to portray the three-million-member Polish party as an undifferentiated monolith, but that view, however comforting, is simplistic and misleading. Some of the Poles I spoke to assured me that the overwhelming proportion of party members joined for reasons of purely personal opportunism. Some Marxist observers, such as Michael Szkolny, insist that "the rulers of Poland, as of other Eastern European countries, do not for the most part believe in the ideals of socialism or in Marxist theory; there is no evidence that they are even aware of Marx's methodology."

My own encounters, as well as some of the public evidence, suggest that the situation is less black and white. The first person I interviewed about the events of August 1980, Jerzy Borowczak, one of the organizers of the Lenin Shipyard strike, told me how, as a child of twelve in 1970, he had been bullied at school because he was the son of a party member. That his father's attachment to the party was based on principle seemed to be confirmed by the fact that he turned in his membership card after the regime's murderous assault on the workers in 1970.

Another friend whom I sought out in my Diogenes-like quest for an honest party member offered, after some sceptical remarks, the example of her father. She described him as a sincere communist whose ideals pre-dated World War II. When I asked how he felt about the party now, she said, "Well, he's very disappointed, but of course, he tries to hide it, even from himself."

A student in Warsaw who worked as a volunteer translator for Solidarity seemed typical. Both his parents were party members, had worked in minor government posts for over 20 years, and his mother was now facing the shock of being laid off as a result of the present reorganization and paring down of the bureaucracy. "Would you ever think of joining the party yourself?" I asked him, naturally expecting a negative reply from this member of the Solidarity-identified generation. Yes, he said, and then went on to explain that the party, as the most powerful force in the country, was, in his view, still the best place to work for change. Being within the party would allow him to fight for its democratization. His words had a familiar ring, not unlike those of Western youth who want to work "inside the system" in order to change it. Whether such aspirations are realistic (in either case), encounters like this do much to undermine one's stereotypes.

Apart from the usefulness of these anecdotal exchanges, there is also public evidence to suggest diversity within the party. The membership of such disparate figures as Comrade Fiszbach, journalist Stefan Bratkowski and the rebellious Zbigniew Iwanow tend to confirm this notion. More important, the obvious existence of contending factions within the party points to something more than simply a pragmatic argument over the best means of controlling the population. I talked with several ranking party members who appeared to hold all the criticisms of the party advanced by Solidarity members; nonetheless they were prepared to offer a defence of the party in terms of its record. Despite the obvious current economic failures, it had organized the reconstruction of the country after the war, presided over the nation's industrial modernization, and attempted to reverse the inequities of social class.

Similarly, the movement for party democracy, whose presence was felt at the party's special congress in July 1981, clearly represented authentic concern, not merely the aspirations of various individuals for a fairer route to advancement. Nonetheless, despite a perhaps naive desire to give the party as much of the benefit of the doubt as possible, after all the evidence is weighed the doubt itself remains. Although the Western press exhibited considerable enthusiasm about the democracy evident at the July congress (replete with secret ballots, unlimited candidacies and sweeping changes of personnel), the result of the week-long self-examination was a party hierarchy whose views were quite in accord with the present centrist leadership of Kania and Jaruzelski. The process may have changed, but the policies are likely to remain the same.

As with the intentions of the church or the prospects for the economy, the character of the party remains a question mark.

Frequently asked questions

A relevant section of the Gdansk Agreement might provide a useful point of departure for answering some of the questions North Americans most frequently ask about Poland. In return for government concessions, the workers pledged to accept the "socialist system...the leading role of the PUWP in the state ...and the existing system of international alliances." To what extent do workers, and other Poles, actually believe the things to which they are willing to pay lip-service?

Despite the formal acceptance of certain points in the Gdansk Agreement by Polish workers, there is no escaping their thorough condemnation of the present regime.

In truth, the Polish people do not willingly accept "the existing system of international alliances"—the euphemism for domination of Poland by the Soviet Union. Rather, they want national independence. In fact, much of the nationalistic fervor evident in Poland is explained by the Poles' resistance to the Soviet Union. Since that resistance can't be openly expressed, it takes the forms of an intense interest in Polish history, the public celebration of historic national events, and a generalized patriotism. Being realistic, the Poles would be willing to settle for what exists in Soviet-bordering Finland—limited sovereignty in foreign affairs in return for genuine control of domestic matters.

Nor do the Poles willingly accept the "leading role" of the communist party. On the contrary, the PUWP enjoys little popular support in Poland. Although there was a goodly amount of self-congratulation among party members about the "democratic" party congress in July, the fact remains that parliamentary democracy is non-existent in Poland, despite the formal accoutrements of such a system.

Left to their own devices and democratic elections (an unlikely possibility in the immediate future), the Poles would undoubtedly create a recognizably pluralistic political system, one that would likely find some form of social democracy in the majority—possibly along Scandinavian lines.*

As for whether the majority of Poles support socialism—the question that makes North Americans both of leftist and rightist political views equally uneasy—the answer doesn't come in a single word.

For many Poles, "socialism" means the deteriorating, state-

* Solidarity's first congress, held in September 1981, which, among other things, passed a resolution calling for democratic elections in Poland, seems to bear out the speculations above. A complete account and analysis of the PUWP congress in July 1981, Solidarity's congress, and the subsequent crisis inspired by Soviet insistence that the Polish party crack down on Solidarity—as well as other developments occurring while this manuscript went to press—must be left to others.

owned economy and a totalitarian absence of democracy that the party has bestowed upon the nation for three-and-a-half decades, and they're against that. However, the absence of support for the regime should not be confused with opposition to socialism, since there is considerable question as to how to characterize the regime.

Some political analysts on the left refuse to recognize any of the Soviet-type regimes as socialist, and prefer to describe them as "state capitalist," despite their Marxist trappings. Michael Szkolny views such regimes, which he calls "state collectivist," as neither capitalist nor socialist. Understandably, those of us who are socialists want to insist, with respect to the Polish regime, "But that's not really socialism." Such special pleading, I fear, begs the question. For those on the left, it's probably better to face up to the fact that, however distorted, Poland has experienced some form of socialism. For myself, I prefer the term "state socialism"—as employed by that bastion of capitalist thought, the *Economist*—as the phrase which best encapsulates both the excesses and absences of the form of socialism experienced in the Soviet Union and the Eastern European countries.

When you ask Poles in factories, schools and every other workplace what they want, the response most frequently heard is "self-government." Even in the safety of private conversations, they do not generally propose the installation of a capitalist system, though they would no doubt be happy to have access to some capitalist consumer goods. Amidst all its other failures, perhaps the one ideological success that the party has had is to persuade the majority of Poles of the virtues of public ownership of the major means of production. Of course, this is not solely due to the party, since Poland has an indigenous socialist tradition, apart from the party, to which Poles can and do historically refer. When pressed to explain the recurrent phrase "self-government," my respondents regularly described situations in which the workers of a particular enterprise collectively "owned" and democratically ran the institution in question.

Whether political scientists would describe such a system as "syndicalism," "producers' co-ops," "workers' councils" or "democratic socialism," everyone appeared to agree that the real issue was to replace the present monopoly of power with genuine democracy.

I return to Comrade Fiszbach for a last imaginary conversation.

My choice of him is not so mysterious. He represents the mystery of power. The questions I have can only be addressed to the party. The ideas and aspirations of Solidarity, after all, are readily understandable to us.

Why Fiszbach, rather than some other notable? Well, for one thing, First Secretary Kania, at least by the evidence, promises to be a bit dull. And because Gdansk is the region of Poland I know best, Fiszbach is rather handy to the imagination.

However, his political fortunes have declined somewhat since I last imagined him. At the party congress in July he was swept from the central committee; the party's new spirit of democracy proved too cautious to encompass Fiszbach's reputedly radical temperament. Nonetheless, he remains in his post of first secretary of the Gdansk region, and is, no doubt, as busy as ever. He does, though, have time for one rather abstract question.

In my imaginary conversation with him, I finally ask, "Comrade Fiszbach, after three-and-a-half decades in office, on what basis does the party justify its continued exercise of power?"

In that imaginary conversation, Comrade Fiszbach remains silent.

A Rough Guide to Pronunciation

Without attempting to provide an instant course in Polish pronunciation, here is a rough guide that will make some of the names in the text appear less formidable. None of the Polish diacritical marking have been reproduced in this book (e.g., the diagonal slash through some "l's" that renders the sound "w," or the mark above some "o's" that makes for the sound "oo"); readers will simply have to take it on faith, for example, that the city of Lodz is approximately pronounced "Woodge." In the guide below, accented syllables are in italics.

Persons and Places	*Approximate Pronunciation*
Jerzy Andrzejewski	*Yer*-zha And-jay-*ev*-ski
Edward Babiuch	Ed-*vard Bob*-i-ookh
Lech Badkowski	Leck Bond-*kov*-ski
Kazimierz Barcikowski	*Kaz*-i-meerzh Bar-che-*kov*-ski
Jerzy Borowczak	*Yer*-zha Bo-*rov*-chak
Bogdan Borusewicz	*Bog*-dan Bo-roo-*say*-vich
Stefan Bratkowski	*Ste*-fan Brat-*kov*-ski
Stanislaw Bury	*Stan*-i-swav *Boor*-ya
Bydgoszcz	*Bid*-gosh-ch
Miroslaw Chojecki	*Mi*-ro-swav Kho-*yet*-ski
Czestochowa	Ches-to-*ho*-va
Piotr Dyk	Pee-*oat*-r Dick
Tadeusz Fiszbach	*Tad*-e-oosh *Fish*-bok
Gdansk	Ga-*dansk*
Gdynia	Ga-*din*-ya
Edward Gierek	Ed-*vard Geer*-ek
Robert Glebocki	*Rob*-ert Gwem-*bot*-ski
Klemens Gniech	*Kle*-mens Ga-*nyeck*
Wladyslaw Gomulka	*Vwad*-i-swav Go-*mool*-ka
Wojciech Gruszecki	*Voy*-chek Gru-*shet*-ski
Andrzej Gwiazda	*And*-jay Gvee-*azh*-da
Zbigniew Iwanow	Za-*big*-nee-ev *Ee*-van-ov
Mieczyslaw Jagielski	Mee-*ech*-i-swav Yog-i-*el*-ski
Piotr Jaroszewicz	Pee-*oat*-r Yar-o-*she*-vich
Wojciech Jaruzelski	*Voy*-chek Yar-u-*zel*-ski
Jastrzebie	Yast-*zheb*-ie
Leszek Kolakowski	*Le*-shek Kol-a-*kov*-ski
Andrzej Kolodziej	*And*-jay Ko-*wodj*-iay
Jerzy Kolodziejski	*Yer*-zha Ko-wodj-*iay*-ski
Zdzislaw Koscielniak	*Zhees*-wav Kos-*chel*-ni-ak
Jacek Kuron	*Yat*-sek *Koor*-on

239

Jan Kulaj	Yon *Ku*-way
Henryk Lenarciak	*Hen*-rik Le-*nar*-chak
Bogdan Lis	*Bog*-dan Leese
Lodz	Woodge
Karol Malcyzynski	*Kar*-ol Mal-tsu-*shin*-ski
Tadeusz Mazowiecki	*Tad*-e-oosh Ma-*zo*-vi-et-ski
Adam Michnik	*Ah*-dam *Meekh*-nik
Adam Mickiewicz	*Ah*-dam *Mits*-key-e-vich
Karol Modzelewski	*Kar*-ol Mod-zhe-*lev*-ski
Stefan Olszowski	*Ste*-fan Ol-*shov*-ski
Janusz Onyszkiewic	*Yon*-oosh O-nish-*ke*-vich
Alina Pienkowska	Ah-*leen*-a Pee-en-*kov*-ska
Jan Pietrzak	Yon Pi-*et*-shak
Jozef Pinkowski	*Yo*-zef Peen-*kov*-ski
Tadeusz Pyka	*Tad*-e-oosh *Pee*-ka
Jan Rulewski	Yon Ru-*lev*-ski
Rzeszow	*Zhesh*-ov
Solidarnosc	Sole-i-*dar*-nosh
Jadwiga Staniszkis	Yad-*vi*-ga Stan-*eesh*-kis
Szczecin	Sh-*chets*-in
Maciej Szczepanski	Ma-*chay* Sh-che-*pan*-ski
Anna Walentynowicz	*An*-na Va-len-ti-*no*-vich
Lech Walesa	Leck Va-*wen*-sa
Andrzej Wajda	*And*-jay *Vie*-da
Florian Wisniewski	*Flor*-i-an Vis-nee-*ev*-ski
Cardinal Wojtyla	Voy-*tee*-la
Wroclaw	*Vrots*-wav
Wrzeszcz	Ve-*zhesh*-ch
Cardinal Wyszynski	Vi-*shin*-ski

Notes, Sources, Criticisms

Part One: Eighteen Days That Shook the Communist World

The account of the strike at the Lenin Shipyard in August 1980 is primarily based upon interviews with participants conducted in May 1981. Major secondary sources are Adam Orchowski's "Chronology" and the *Solidarity Strike Bulletin* (see bibliography for complete citation). In addition, I made use of Daniel Singer's *The Road to Gdansk* and the daily and weekly reportage in the New York *Times*, *The Times* (London), the Washington *Post*, *Time* magazine and the *Guardian* (New York). Given the narrative style adopted for the purposes of a popular account, there are, naturally enough, ambiguities, lacunae and conflicting versions of events which have been smoothed over in the text. It may be useful for those doing further scholarly work in the area to be aware of some of the problematic moments in the foregoing account. They are noted below from time to time.

One general, but minor, terminological difficulty pertains to whether "shipyard" should be used in the singular or plural in English. I've opted for the singular when referring to an individual enterprise (e.g., the Paris Commune Shipyard), although my usage varies in generic references (e.g., "yards," "the yard," etc.). Further, there is a question concerning the name of the principal shipyard in Gdansk. Above the main gate there is a large metal sign bearing the name "*Stocznia Gdanska im Lenina.*" Local usage in the region is the "Gdansk Shipyard," and the use of that phrase was recognized and preferred by most respondents I interviewed. Nonetheless, I have retained the "Lenin Shipyard" as my primary designation in accordance with the preferred usage of the international press, as well as to avoid confusion with other shipyards in Gdansk.

Ch. 1 Strike

As is evident from the text, the account of the first moments of the strike relies heavily on the testimony of Jerzy Borowczak, whom I found to be a particularly coherent and helpful respondent. Nonetheless, it would be useful to gather the testimonies of other direct participants, such as Bogdan Felski and Ludwig Pradzynski, which I was unable to do.

The description of the activities of Jerzy Borowczak, Bogdan Borusewicz, Klemens Gniech, Anna Walentynowicz, Alina Pienkowska and Jacek Kuron on the morning of August 14, 1980, is based on interviews with each of the above named people. The account of the meeting at Piotr Dyk's apartment on August 7, 1980, is compiled from interviews with various of those present, including Piotr Dyk and Andrzej Kolodziej.

The leaflet about Anna Walentynowicz's case distributed by strikers on the morning of August 14, 1980, is contained in Orchowski's account. The background material on these events is taken from Singer, *Time*, the New York *Times* and *The Times* (London). The description of Walesa's speech on that morning comes from interviews with Borowczak, Stanislaw Bury, Henryk Lenarciak and the account by Orchowski.

241

Ch. 2   Long Memories

The account of the Poznan uprising is based on Flora Lewis, *A Case History of Hope*. The brief overview of Polish history is derived from Lewis and M.K. Dziewanowski, *Poland in the 20th Century*. The account of Kuron and Modzelewski's open letter is based upon the text of the letter itself and Peter Raina's version of the events in *Political Opposition in Poland 1954-1977*. Documentation for the events of March 1968 comes from Raina. The events of December 1970 are taken from George Blazynski, *Flashpoint Poland*, Singer, and Raina, as well as the personal reminiscences and second-hand accounts provided by several of my respondents. The account of the events of 1976 is primarily from Blazynski. The documentation on the development of KOR is contained in Raina. The discussion of the views of Kuron and Michnik in 1976 is based on their essays referred to in the text. The declaration of the Baltic Free Trade Unions is to be found in *Survey*, and the story of its inception was related to me by several respondents.

Ch. 3   Three Minutes at the Gate

The discussion of management strategy in response to the strike is based on an interview with shipyard director Klemens Gniech. It should be mentioned that once the strike assumed general proportions, and negotiations were underway, Gniech, according to the testimony of various strikers, was quite co-operative. He subsequently continued in his position as director of the shipyard.

The stories of Anna Walentynowicz and Andrzej Kolodziej are based on interviews with them. The description of the strike at Elmor is based on an interview with Bogdan Lis. The role of Andrzej Gwiazda, whose centrality throughout the strike was pointed out to me by numerous participants, is no doubt underplayed in this account. Gwiazda was ill during the period I conducted the interviews and to my regret I was unable to talk to him. As well, I failed to interview Joanna Duda-Gwiazda, who was also a member of the MKS presidium, and later, of the Gdansk regional presidium.

The strike of the transportation workers, who have been characteristically militant throughout Poland, was of importance in the Tri-Cities strike and is only mentioned in passing in this account. Unfortunately, I was unable to interview Henryka Krzywonos, a driver for WKP (the initials by which the Gdansk area transit system is known) and a member of the MKS presidium representing the transportation workers.

The account of Alina Pienkowska's speech on August 16, 1980, is based on an interview with her. Quotes from the local Gdansk press are contained in Orchowski's account.

There is some dispute over the organization of religious services in the Lenin and Paris Commune shipyards, which were, by all accounts, of political importance. Bogdan Borusewicz reports having visited several different priests in Gdynia before securing someone to perform a field mass. The point at issue, however, concerns the authorization of the Lenin Shipyard mass on August 17. Although it might be supposed that permission of the local bishop would be required, one account I heard has it that before such permission was granted, clearance was sought by church officials from the Gdansk PUWP apparatus. Since the relations between church, party and union are of consequence, further investigation of such matters would be useful.

It should also be noted, by the way, that various "performances" of mass are vigorously subjected to aesthetic judgment by participants. The political implications of this are alluded to in my account, based on the evaluation provided by Andrzej Kolodziej.

Ch. 4   Sticking Together

Walesa's speech to the workers outside the gate on Monday, August 18, was decisive, according to both Orchowski and Bogdan Borusewicz. Jerzy Borowczak, however, remembers a speech, spontaneously delivered by a young unidentified shipyard worker, as having performed the function of bringing undecided workers into the yard to strike.

The account of events in Szczecin is taken from the invaluable *Labor Focus on Eastern Europe*, Vol. 4, Nos. 4-6.

The exact day-to-day count of enterprises belonging to the Gdansk MKS is reported variously in different accounts. What everyone agrees on, however, is that the MKS grew dramatically from 20 or so factories at the beginning of the strike to at least 350 by the middle of the first week. By strike's end, the MKS had reached 700 enterprises. Because of lack of space in the meeting hall, at a certain point the MKS ceased accepting additional delegates and merely registered the latest enterprises to join.

As indicated in the text, there was a significant split between the Lenin Shipyard workers and those of the Remontow, Northern and Northern Harbor enterprises that lasted throughout the period of negotiations with Pyka. It was an oversight on my part not to interview the participants from those workplaces in order to obtain their accounts of the events; as a result, my report of the unsuccessful negotiations with Pyka correspondingly suffers.

Documentary information recounted in this chapter is based on the *Solidarity Strike Bulletin*, Orchowski's account, and the reportage of the international press. The vignettes describing how individual participants became involved in the strike is based on interviews with Leslaw Ludwig, Anna Maksymiuk, Piotr Dyk, Wojciech Gruszecki, Robert Glebocki and Mariusz Wilk. The description of the MKS delegation's first meeting with Deputy Minister Jagielski is based on an interview with Wojciech Gruszecki.

A word on the portrayal of Lech Walesa in these pages might be appropriate. My own strategy in constructing the narrative was to try to somewhat counter the understandably over-emphasized portrait of Walesa presented in the mass media. I've instead opted for a more "balanced" version of events, emphasizing both the organizing group and the class character of the organization of the strike. There has yet to appear in English an extensive first-hand account of the events as Walesa saw them. A series of interviews with Walesa by journalist Oriana Fallaci (which appeared in various newspapers in March 1981) succeeds in presenting aspects of his personality which are confirmed in numerous other instances, but her resurrection of the "Great Man (as interviewed by the Great Woman) Theory of History" is, on the whole, not particularly helpful in getting at the sequence of events.

Ch. 5   A Dialogue Heard 'Round the World

The account of the negotiations on August 23, 1980, is taken from a lengthy report by Murrey Marder in the Washington *Post*, August 31, 1980, which contains verbatim passages from the talks. Fiszbach's speech at the central committee meeting of August 24 was subsequently reprinted in the Polish press and translated for me by Zbigniew Jakowczyk. The description of the talks of August 26 are collaged from various sources, including Orchowski, the *Solidarity Strike Bulletin*, and the international press. The text of Cardinal Wyszynski's sermon on August 26 is available through the Polish Interpress Agency. The account of the meeting of the "experts" is largely taken from Staniszkis (see bibliography for citation). The account of talks on August 28, 30 and 31 comes mainly from Orchowski.

Part Two: Solidarity

The account of events from September 1980 through May 1981 is unapologetically intended as a stopgap measure, awaiting a thorough study of the organization of Solidarity and the crises it encountered. Although I was able to make use of some interview material in this part, especially Robert Glebocki's account of changes in the university system in chapter 7 and Jan Rulewski's description of the Bydgoszcz events, my major source is the reportage of the international press, particularly that of John Darnton in the New York *Times*. Nonetheless, for the moment, this is probably as extended an overview of the period as exists in English.

Ch. 6   The Road from Gdansk

The return to work at the Lenin Shipyard, the opening of the first union office, settlement of the coal miners' strike, and the Szczepanski scandal are reported by John Darnton and John Vinocur, New York *Times*, September 2, 4, and 5, 1980, and in *Time* magazine, September 15, 1980.

The speeches of Prime Minister Pinkowski and First Secretary Kania on September 5, 1980, are available through the Polish Interpress Agency. The information service for new unionists is reported by Vinocur, New York *Times*, September 9, 1980; the Lublin founding committee appeal is found in *Labor Focus on Eastern Europe*, Vol. 4, Nos. 1-3; the account of the Odra election is from Oliver MacDonald, "Building Solidarity in Szczecin," *Labor Focus on Eastern Europe*, Vol 4, Nos. 4-6. The account of Solidarity's lengthy battle with the courts over registration from September to November 1980 is based on the reportage of Darnton in the New York *Times* and Dessa Trevisan in *The Times* (London), and on an interview with Bogdan Lis. The story of building the monument outside the Lenin Shipyard was provided in an interview with Henryk Lenarciak. The interview with Zbigniew Iwanow, upon which my account of his activities is based, is found in *Labor Focus on Eastern Europe*, Vol. 4, Nos. 4-6. The description of the debate over the five-day work week is based on reportage in the international press.

Ch. 7   Students, Media, Farmers

The section on changes in the universities is primarily based on an interview with University of Gdansk rector Robert Glebocki. Speculation on student activities in Cracow is taken from R.W. Apple, New York *Times*, September 17, 1980. The Lodz strike is reported by John Darnton, New York *Times*, January 29, 1981, and following. The text of the Lodz Agreement is available through the Polish Interpress Agency.

Pietrzak's performance is reported by Nina Darnton, New York *Times*, December 19, 1980. Malcuzynski's speech is reported by John Darnton, New York *Times*, September 14, 1980. The election of Stefan Bratkowski is described in the New York *Times*, November 10, 1980. The account of the printers' dispute is from John Darnton, New York *Times*, February 6, 1981. More on the views of Andrzej Wajda can be found in *Cineaste*, Vol. 11, No. 1.

The statement of support for the striking shipyard workers by Polish farmers is from the *Solidarity Strike Bulletin*. The farmers' meeting in Warsaw is reported by John Darnton, New York *Times*, December 15, 1980; the court ruling of December 30 is reported by Dessa Trevisan, *The Times* (London), December 31, 1980; a description of the Rzeszow sit-in and an account of Kania's speech opposing the farmers' union is provided by James Markham, the New York *Times*, January 11 and 15, 1981. The Rzeszow Agreement is available through the Polish Interpress Agency.

Ch. 8   The Beatings at Bydgoszcz

The characterization of the brief "honeymoon" period is by John Darnton, New York *Times*, March 2, 1981, and various Associated Press dispatches. Details of the arrest of Kuron on March 5, Solidarity's response to it, and the farmers's convention in Poznan are found in reports by John Darnton, New York *Times*, March 6, 8 and 10, 1981.

The account of the Bydgoszcz incident is primarily based on the pamphlet produced by the Bydgoszcz Solidarity chapter, "Farsa..." and an interview with Jan Rulewski. For details of the subsequent negotiations, I also used Darnton's reportage in the New York *Times*, March 20-30, 1981, as well as Rakowski's speech, published in the *Guardian* (London), April 5, 1981, and William Ryan's analyses in the *Guardian* (New York), April 8 and 15, 1981.

The version of the KKP meeting of March 31-April 1, 1981, as well as the Gwiazda-Walesa exchange of letters is from BIPS, Nos. 1 and 2, April 1981, published by the Press Information Bureau of Solidarity (Gdansk). English translations are by Kasia Kietlinska and Leslaw Ludwig.

Ch. 9   Conversations with Comrade Fiszbach
The epigraph by S.J. Lec is cited in Dziewanowski, *Poland in the 20th Century*. Michnik's lecture is contained in *Telos*, No. 47. Szkolny's essay is found in *Monthly Review*, June 1981. The section on civil society is based on Arato's essay in *Telos*, No. 47. For more on the Polish economy, see Renate Dumas, "The 1980 Polish Strike and the Strike Cycles in the 1970s," *Telos*, No. 47. The general claims made about the attitudes of Polish people is based on impressions acquired during my visit and on Nowak's findings, reported in *Scientific American*, July 1981.

Bibliography

Jerzy Andrzejewski, *Ashes and Diamonds* (Weidenfeld and Nicolson, London, 1962, [1957]). Set in the period just after World War II, Andrzejewski's novel offers, apart from its literary qualities, a useful sociological portrait of Poland at the time of the transition to communist rule.

Andrew Arato, "Civil Society Against the State," *Telos*, No. 47, 1981; a survey of theories of social reform under totalitarian rule.

Rudolf Bahro, *The Alternative in Eastern Europe* (New Left Books, London, 1978). A provocative critique of "actually existing socialism" from a Marxist perspective.

Nicholas Bethell, *Gomulka, His Poland and His Communism* (Longmans, London, 1969). The standard biography of the first secretary of the PUWP from 1956-70.

Daniel Bickley, "The Cinema of Moral Dissent," *Cineaste*, Vol. 11, No. 1, 1980-81; provides, in addition to a survey of current Polish cinema, an account of the Gdansk film festival held in September 1980.

——and Lenny Rubenstein, "Interview with Andrzej Wajda," *Cineaste*, Vol. II, No. 1, 1980-1981.

George Blazynski, *Flashpoint Poland* (Pergamon, New York, 1979). Contains chronological accounts of workers' uprisings in Poland since 1956, and a lengthy review of the Gierek regime.

Bydgoszcz Solidarity, "Farsa...," May, 1981. A mimeographed pamphlet providing an account of the Bydgoszcz incident of March 1981; tr. for the author by Iza Laponce.

Adam Bromke and John W. Strong (eds.), *Gierek's Poland* (Praeger, New York, 1973).

Kazimiera Janina Cottam, *Boleslaw Limanowski (1835-1935)* (East European Quarterly, Boulder, Colorado, 1978). Biographical study of an early Polish socialist thinker and founder of the Polish Socialist Party.

M.K. Dziewanowski, *Poland in the 20th Century* (Columbia U., New York, 1977). A useful general introduction to contemporary Poland.

Alvin Fountain, *Roman Dmowski, 1895-1907* (East European Monographs, Boulder, Colorado, 1980).

Peter Green, "The Third Round in Poland," *New Left Review*, Nos. 101-102, February 1977.

Chris Harman, *Bureaucracy and Revolution in Eastern Europe* (Pluto, London, 1974). An account of Eastern European workers' uprisings from 1953-1970 that takes the position that the regimes in those countries represent "bureaucratic state capitalism," not socialism.

Leszek Kolakowski, *Main Currents of Marxism*, Vol. 3, *The Breakdown* (Oxford U., Oxford, 1978).

Jacek Kuron, "Reflections on a Program of Action," *The Polish Review*, Vol. 23, No. 3, 1977; provides a strategy for Poland's "democratic opposition."

——and Karol Modzelewski, "Open Letter to the Party," in George Weissman (ed.), *Revolutionary Marxist Students in Poland Speak Out (1964-68)* (Merit, New York,

1968). Contains the text of the most important Marxist analysis of Poland under the PUWP.

Labor Focus on Eastern Europe, "Polish Free Trade Unions," Vol. 4, Nos. 1-3, 1980; contains the text of the *Solidarity Strike Bulletin* and the Gdansk Agreement, as well as other valuable source material and analysis.

——"Poland: Solidarnosc in Action," Vol. 4, Nos. 4-6, 1981.

David Lane and George Kolankiewicz, *Social Groups in Polish Society* (Columbia U., New York, 1973).

Mika Larsson, *Det borjade i Gdansk* (ForfattarForlaget, Malmo, Sweden, 1981). A journalistic account in Swedish of events in the Lenin Shipyard during the August 1980 strike.

Flora Lewis, *A Case History of Hope* (Doubleday, New York, 1958). A readable account of the events of 1956 in Poland.

Robert Littell (ed.), *The Czech Black Book* (Avon, New York, 1969).

Adam Michnik, "The New Evolutionism," *Survey* 100/101, 1976; provides analysis and strategy for the Polish "democratic opposition."

——"What We Want to Do," *Telos*, No. 47, 1981; a public lecture delivered in November 1980.

Ralph Miliband, *Marxism and Politics* (Oxford U., Oxford, 1977). An excellent examination of how Marxist theory applies to politics.

Stefan Nowak, "Values and Attitudes of the Polish People," *Scientific American*, July 1981.

Adam Orchowski, "Chronology of the Occupational Strike at the Lenin Shipyard, 14-31 August 1980," *Punkt*, No. 12, December 1980 (Gdansk), tr. for the author by Leslaw Ludwig.

Peter Raina, *Political Opposition in Poland, 1954-1977* (Poets and Painters Press, London, 1978). Particularly useful for its thorough presentation of first-hand documents.

John Reed, *Ten Days That Shook The World* (International, New York, 1919).

S.L. Shneiderman, *The Warsaw Heresy* (Horizon, New York, 1959).

Daniel Singer, *The Road to Gdansk* (Monthly Review Press, New York, 1981). Primarily a series of essays about developments in the Soviet Union and Poland. The manuscript, which speculates on the possibility of an uprising by Polish workers, was completed shortly before the August 1980 strike. Singer subsequently went to Poland, conducted interviews, and appended a succinct and useful account of the August events to his text.

Jadwiga Staniszkis, "The Evolution of Forms of Working Class Protest in Poland," *Soviet Studies*, April 1981; provides, in addition to analysis of working class organizing, a first-hand account of the meetings of "experts" during the August strike.

Survey, "Poland from Inside," No. 109, 1979; provides documentary materials and analysis by and about the "democratic opposition" and other groups in Polish society.

Tadeusz Szafar, "Resolving the Polish dilemma," *Encounter*, May 1981.

Jan Szczepanski, *Polish Society* (Random House, New York, 1970).

Michael Szkolny, "Revolution in Poland," *Monthly Review*, June 1981.

Telos, "Poland and the Future of Socialism," No. 47, 1981.

Appendix: The Gdansk Agreement

Here is the text of the agreement between the MKS and the Polish government ending the Gdansk strike on August 31, 1980.

(*This protocol was signed on behalf of the strikers by Lech Walesa [president of the MKS], Andrzej Kolodziej and Bogdan Lis [vice-presidents], Mr. and Mrs. L. Badkowski, W. Gruszewski, A. Gwiazda, S. Izdebski, J. Kmiecik, Z. Kobylinksi, H. Krzywonos, S. Lewandowski, A. Pienkowska, Z. Psybylski, J. Sikorski, L. Sobieszek, T. Stanny, A. Walentynowicz and F. Wisniewski.*
(*It was signed for the Governmental commission by President Mieczeslaw Jagielski [vice-prime minister], M. Zielinski, member of the secretariat of the Central Committee of the PUWP, T. Fiszbach, president of the party committee of Gdansk Voivod, and the mayor of Gdansk, J. Kolodzieski.*)

The government commission and the Inter-factory Strike Committee (MKS), after studying the 21 demands of the workers of the coast who are on strike, have reached the following conclusions:

On Point No. 1, which reads: "To accept trade unions as free and independent of the party, as laid down in Convention No. 87 of the ILO and ratified by Poland, which refers to the matter of trade union rights," the following decision has been reached:
1) The activity of the trade unions of People's Poland has not lived up to the hopes and aspirations of the workers. We thus consider that it will be beneficial to create new organizations, which will run themselves, and which will be authentic expressions of the working class. Workers will continue to have the right to join the old trade unions and we are looking at the possibility of the two union structures co-operating.
2) The MKS declares that it will respect the principles laid down in the Polish constitution while creating the new independent and self-governing unions. These new unions are intended to defend the social and material interests of the workers, and not to play the role of a political party. They will be established on the basis of the socialization of the means of production and of the socialist system which exists in Poland today. They will recognize the leading role of the PUWP in the state, and will not oppose the existing system of international alliances. Their aim is to ensure for the workers the necessary means for the determination, expression and defence of their interests. The governmental commission will guarantee full respect for the independence and self-governing character of the new unions in their organizational structures and their functioning at all levels. The government will ensure that the new unions have every possibility of carrying out their function of defending the interests of the workers and of seeking the satisfaction of their material, social and cultural needs. Equally it will guarantee that the new unions are not the objects of any discrimination.
3) The creation and the functioning of free and self-governing trade unions is in line with Convention 87 of the ILO relating to trade union rights and Convention 97,

relating to the rights of free association and collective negotiation, both of which conventions have been ratified by Poland. The coming into being of more than one trade union organization requires changes in the law. The government, therefore, will make the necessary legal changes as regards trade unions, workers' councils and labor code.

4) The strike committees must be able to turn themselves into institutions representing the workers at the level of the enterprise, whether in the fashion of workers' councils or as preparatory committees of the new trade unions. As a preparatory committee, the MKS is free to adopt the form of a trade union, or of an association of the coastal region. The preparatory committees will remain in existence until the new trade unions are able to organize proper elections to leading bodies. The government undertakes to create the conditions necessary for the recognition of unions outside of the existing Central Council of Trade Unions.

5) The new trade unions should be able to participate in decisions affecting the conditions of the workers in such matters as the division of the national assets between consumption and accumulation, the division of the social consumption fund (health, education, culture), the wages policy, in particular with regard to an automatic increase of wages in line with inflation, the economic plan, the direction of investment and prices policy. The government undertakes to ensure the conditions necessary for the carrying out of these functions.

6) The enterprise committee will set up a research centre whose aim will be to engage in an objective analysis of the situation of the workers and employees, and will attempt to determine the correct ways in which their interests can be represented. This centre will also provide the information and expertise necessary for dealing with such questions as the prices index and wage index and the forms of compensation required to deal with price rises. The new unions should have their own publications.

7) The government will enforce respect for Article I, paragraph 1 of the trade union law of 1949, which guarantees the workers the right to freely come together to form trade unions. The new trade union will not join the Central Council of Trade Unions (CRZZ). It is agreed that the new trade union law will respect these principles. The participation of members of the MKS and of the preparatory committees for the new trade unions in the elaboration of the new legislation is also guaranteed.

The Right to Strike
On Point No. 2, which reads: *"To guarantee the right to strike, and the security of strikers and those who help them,"* it has been agreed that:
The right to strike will be guaranteed by the new trade union law. The law will have to define the circumstances in which strikes can be called and organized, the ways in which conflicts can be resolved, and the penalties for infringements of the law. Articles 52, 64 and 65 of the labor code (which outlaw strikes) will cease to have effect from now until the new law comes into practice. The government undertakes to protect the personal security of strikers and those who have helped them and to ensure against any deterioration in their conditions of work.

Freedom of Expression
With regard to Point No. 3, which reads: *"To respect freedom of expression and publication, as upheld by the Constitution of People's Poland, and to take no measures against independent publications, as well as to grant access to the mass media to representatives of all religions,"* it has been added that:
1) The government will bring before the Sejm (Parliament) within three months a proposal for a law on control of the press, of publications, and of other public manifestations, which will be based on the following principles of state secrets, and of economic secrets in the sense that these will be defined in the new legislation, the protection of state interests and its international interests, the protection of religious convictions, as well as the rights of non-believers, as well as the suppression of

publications which offend against morality.

The proposals will include the right to make a complaint against the press-control and similar institutions to a higher administrative tribunal. This law will be incorporated in an amendment to the administrative code.

2) The access to the mass media by religious organizations in the course of their religious activities will be worked out through an agreement between the state institutions and the religious associations on matters of content and of organization. The government will ensure the transmission by radio of the Sunday mass through a specific agreement with the Church hierarchy.

3) The radio and television as well as the press and publishing houses must offer expression to different points of views. They must be under the control of society.

4) The press as well as citizens and their organizations must have access to public documents, and above all to administrative instructions and socio-economic plans, in the form in which they are published by the government and by the administrative bodies which draw them up. Exceptions to the principle of open administration will be legally defined in agreement with Point No. 3, paragraph 1.

With regard to Point No. 4, which reads: "To re-establish the rights of people who were sacked after the strikes in 1970 and 1976 and of students who have been excluded from institutions of higher education because of their opinions, (b) to free all political prisoners, including Edmund Zadrozynski, Jan Kozlowski and Marek Kozlowski; (c) to cease repression against people for their opinions," it has been agreed:

(a) to immediately investigate the reasons given for the sackings after the strikes of 1970 and 1976. In every case where injustice is revealed, the person involved must be reinstated, taking into account any new qualifications that person may have acquired. The same principle will be applied in the case of students.

(b) the cases of persons mentioned under point (b) should be put to the Ministry of Justice, which within two weeks will study their dossiers. In cases where those mentioned are already imprisoned, they must be released pending this investigation, and until a new decision on their case is reached.

(c) to launch an immediate investigation into the reasons for the arrests of those mentioned (the three named individuals).

(d) to institute full liberty of expression in public and professional life.

On Point No. 5, which reads: "To inform the public about the creation of the MKS and its demands, through the mass media," it has been decided that:

This demand shall be met through the publication in all the national mass media of the full text of this agreement.

On Point No. 6, which reads: "To implement the measures necessary for resolving the crisis, starting with the publication of all the relevant information on the socio-economic situation, and to allow all groups to participate in a discussion on a program of economic reform," the following has been agreed:

We consider it essential to speed up the preparation of an economic reform. The authorities will work out and publish the basic principles of such a reform in the next few months. It is necessary to allow for wide participation in a public discussion of the reform. In particular the trade unions must take part in the working out of laws relating to the enterprises and to workers' self-management. The economic reform must be based on the strengthening, autonomous operation and participation of the workers' councils in management. Specific regulations will be drawn up in order to guarantee that the trade unions will be able to carry out their functions as set out in Point No. 1 of this agreement.

Only a society which has a firm grasp of reality can take the initiative in reforming the economy. The government will significantly increase the areas of socio-economic information to which society, the trade unions and other social and economic organizations have access.

The MKS also suggests, in order that a proper perspective be provided for the development of the family agricultural units, which are the basis of Polish agriculture, that the individual and collective sectors of agriculture should have equal access to the means of production, including the land itself, and that the conditions should be created for the recreation of self-governing co-operatives.

On Point No. 7, which reads: "To pay all the workers who have taken part in the strike for the period of the strike as if they were on paid holiday throughout this period, with payment to be made from the funds of the CRZZ," the following decision has been reached:

Workers and employees participating in the strike will receive, on their return to work, 40 per cent of their wages. The rest, which will add up to a full 100 per cent of the normal basic wage, will be calculated as would holiday pay, on the basis of an 8-hour working day. The MKS calls on workers who are members to work towards the increase of output, to improve the use of raw materials and energy, and to show greater work discipline, when the strike is over, and to do this in co-operation with the management of the factories and enterprises.

On Point No. 8, which reads: "To increase the minimum wage for every workers by 2,000 zlotys a month to compensate for the increase in prices," the following has been decided:

These wage increases will be introduced gradually, and will apply to all types of workers and employees and in particular to those who receive the lowest wages. The increases will be worked out through agreements in individual factories and branches. The implementation of the increases will take into account the specific character of particular professions and sectors. The intention will be to increase wages through revising the wage scales or through increasing other elements of the wage.

White collar workers in the enterprises will receive salary increases on an individual basis. These increases will be put into effect between now and the end of September 1980, on the basis of the agreements reached in each branch.

After reviewing the situation in all the branches, the government will present, by October 31, 1980, in agreement with the trade unions, a program of pay increases to come into effect from January 1, 1981, for those who get the least at the moment, paying particular attention to large families.

On Point No. 9, which reads: "To guarantee the sliding scale," the following decision has been reached:

It is necessary to slow down the rate of inflation through stricter control over both the public and private sectors, and in particular through the suppression of hidden price increases.

Following on from a government decision, investigations will be carried out into the cost of living. These studies will be carried out both by the trade unions and by scientific institutions. By the end of 1980, the government will set out the principles of a system of compensation for inflation, and these principles will be open to discussion by the people. When they have been accepted, they will come into effect. It will be necessary to deal with the question of the social minimum in elaborating these principles.

On Point No. 10, which reads: "To ensure the supply of products on the internal market, and to export only the surplus," and Point No. 11, which reads: "To suppress commercial prices and the use of foreign currency in sales on the internal market," and Point No. 12, which reads: "To introduce ration cards for meat and meat-based products, until the market situation can be brought under control," the following agreement has been reached:

The supply of meat will be improved between now and December 31, 1980, through an increase in the profitability of agricultural production and the limitation of the export of meat to what is absolutely indispensable, as well as through the import of extra meat supplies. At the same time, during this period a program for the improvement of the meat supply will be drawn up, which will take into account the possibility of the introduction of a rationing system through the issue of cards.

Products which are scarce on the national market for current consumption will not be sold in the "Pewex" shops; and between now and the end of the year, the population will be informed of all decisions which are taken concerning the problems of supply. The MKS has called for the abolition of the special shops and the levelling out of the price of meat and related products.

On Point No. 13, which reads: "To introduce the principle of cadre selection on the basis of qualifications, not on the basis of membership of the party, and to abolish the privileges of the police (MO) and the security services (SB), and of the party apparatus, through the abolition of special sources of supply, through the equalization of family allowances, etc.," we have reached the following agreement:
The demand for cadres to be selected on the basis of qualifications and ability has been accepted. Cadres can be members of the PUWP, of the SD (the Democratic Party, which draws its membership from small private enterprises), of the ZSL (the Peasant Party—these three parties make up the National Front) or of no party. A program for the equalization of the family allowances of all the professional groups will be presented by the government before December 31, 1980. The governmental commission states that only employees' restaurants and canteens, such as those in other work establishments and offices, are operated.

On Point No. 14, which reads: "To allow workers to retire at 50 years for women and 55 for men, or after 30 years of work for women, and 35 years for men, regardless of age," it has been agreed that:
The governmental commission declares pensions will be increased each year taking into account the real economic possibilities and the rise in the lowest wages. Between now and December 1, 1981, the government will work out and present a program on these questions. The government will work out plans for the increase of old age and other pensions up to the social minimum as established through studies carried out by scientific institutions; these will be presented to the public and submitted to the control of the trade unions.
The MKS stresses the great urgency of these matters and will continue to raise the demands for the increase of old age and other pensions taking into account the increase of the cost of living.

On Point No. 15, which reads: "To increase the old-style pensions to the level paid under the new system," it has been agreed:
The governmental commission states that the lowest pensions will be increased every year as a function of rises in the lowest wages. The government will present a program to this effect between now and December 1, 1981. The government will draft proposals for a rise in the lowest pensions to the level of the social minimum as defined in studies made by scientific institutes. These proposals will be presented to the public and subject to control by the unions.

On Point No. 16, which reads: "To improve working conditions and the health services so as to ensure better medical protection for the workers," it has been agreed that:
It is necessary to immediately increase the resources put into the sphere of the health services, to improve medical supplies through the import of basic materials where these are lacking, to increase the salaries of all health workers, and with the utmost urgency on the part of the government and the ministries, to prepare programs for improving the health of the population. Other measures to be taken in this area are put forward in the appendix.

On Point No. 17, which reads: "To ensure sufficient places in creches and play schools for the children of all working women," it has been agreed that:
The government commission is fully in agreement with this demand. The provincial authorities will present proposals on this question before November 30, 1980.

On Point No. 18, which reads: "To increase the length of maternity leave to three years to allow a mother to bring up her child," it has been decided that:
Before December 31, 1980, an analysis of the possibilities open to the national economy will be made in consultation with the trade unions, on the basis of which an increase in the monthly allowance for women who are on unpaid maternity leave will be worked out.
The MKS asks that this analysis should include an allowance which will provide 100 per cent of pay for the first year after birth, and 50 per cent for the second year, with a fixed minimum of 2,000 zlotys a month. This goal should be gradually reached from the first half of 1981 onwards.

On Point No. 19, which reads: "To reduce the waiting period for the allocation of housing," the following agreement has been reached:
The district authorities will present a program of measures for improving the accomodation situation and for reducing the waiting list for receipt of accommodation, before December 31, 1980. These proposals will be put forward for a wide-ranging discussion in the district, and competent organizations such as the Polish town-planners association, the Central Association of Technicians, etc., will be consulted. The proposals should refer both to ways of using the present building enterprises and prefabricated housing factories, and to a thoroughgoing development of the industry's productive base. Similar action will be taken throughout the country.

On Point No. 20, which reads: "To increase the travelling allowance from 40 to 100 zlotys, and to introduce a cost-of-living bonus," it has been agreed that:
An agreement will be reached on the question of raising the travelling allowance and compensation, to take effect from January 1, 1981. The proposals for this to be ready by October 31, 1980.

On Point No. 21, which reads: "To make Saturday a holiday. In factories where there is continuous production, where there is a four-shift system, Saturday working must be compensated for by a commensurate increase in the number of holidays, or through the establishment of another free day in the week," it has been agreed that:
The principle that Saturday should be a free day should be put into effect, or another method of providing free time should be devised. This should be worked out by December 31, 1980. The measures should include the increase in the number of free Saturdays from the start of 1981. Other possibilities relating to this point are mentioned in the appendix or appear in the submissions of the MKS.

After reaching the above agreements, it has also been decided that:
The Government undertakes:
—to ensure personal security and to allow both those who have taken part in the strike and those who have supported it to return to their previous work under the previous conditions;
—to take up at the ministerial level the specific demands raised by the workers of all the enterprises represented in the MKS;
—to immediately publish the complete text of this agreement in the press, the radio, the television, and in the national mass media.

The strike committee undertakes to propose the ending of the strike from 5 p.m. on August 31, 1980.